Winning in Asia

Winning
in Asia

Strategies for Competing
in the New Millennium

Peter J. Williamson

HARVARD BUSINESS SCHOOL PRESS
Boston, Massachusetts

Library of Congress Cataloging-in-Publication Data

Williamson, Peter J.
    Winning in Asia : strategies for competing in the new millennium / Peter J. Williamson.
        p. cm.
    ISBN 0-87584-620-3
    1. Business enterprises—East Asia.   2. International business enterprises—East Asia.
3. Business enterprises—Asia, Southeastern.   4. International business enterprises—
Asia, Southeastern.   5. Competition, International.   6. Industrial management.   I. Title.
    HD2906.W55 2004
    658'.0095—dc22

                                                                        2003019436

Contents

Preface

In one sense, this book has been almost twenty-five years in the making, because it is over that time that I have had the good fortune to be involved in research and consulting with Asian companies, governments, and multinationals operating in the Asian region. Whatever insights *Winning in Asia* is able to offer have been made possible by the many people that I have met and worked with in the course of this immersion in Asia—a journey that has taken me from Asia's bustling cities through to remote corners of the continent such as a trading post on the upper reaches of the Kinabatangan River in Borneo or the open-air market at Kashi in western China, and where I have been honored to be the guest of generous individuals spanning the gamut from government ministers and corporate czars through to Buddhist monks in northwest Thailand and nomads in the Altai mountains of Outer Mongolia.

Part of this experience was the excitement of being amid the economic boom that in 1994 Jim Abegglen described in his influential book, *Sea Change*, as the rise of "Pacific Asia as the new world industrial center."[1] It also included working in the trenches with companies and individuals being buffeted by the 1997 Asian financial crisis. Much has been written about both the boom years and the Asian crisis and its immediate aftermath, its implications for the future of Asia's economies, and the need for reform of her institutions. But the implications for the kinds of business strategies required for success in Asia going forward have been less well addressed. A prime motivation for this book was to begin to fill that gap by examining how companies should be changing their strategies and organizations in response to the new realities of Asia as we enter this new millennium.

Having now researched that question intensively for more than five years since the crisis erupted, I have come to believe that the Asian competitive environment is undergoing another "sea change" of no less significance than the one Abegglen identified and that this changed competitive environment, in turn, demands the creation of a new breed of Asian company with a new set of strategic priorities and a new set of organizational capabilities and processes.

If that assessment is correct—something the reader can judge in the pages that follow—the challenge becomes to outline the blueprints for what that new breed of successful Asian companies might look like. Given my "classic" training in strategy at Harvard Business School and The Boston Consulting Group, it was tempting to jump to the conclusion that the successful Asian company of the future might look much the same as today's leading firms in North America and Europe. But experience in Asia told me this was not the case because to use these Western models as the core would be to negate much of the potential competitive advantage that can come from harnessing Asia's unique business heritage and culture. At the same time, I was able to identify a considerable quantity of "baggage" from past ways of doing business in Asia that would need to be jettisoned by the successful Asian companies of the future. The trick, I concluded, would be to fashion a new Asian hybrid that would combine those elements of Asian business heritage that would remain strengths in the new competitive environment with some of the best practice available globally. The challenge was then to define as precisely as possible what that new hybrid might look like and the ways to build it. Most of *Winning in Asia* is devoted to how this challenge can be met.

In the quest to make that task manageable, I have focused the analysis on "East Asia"—primarily countries in the Association of South East Asian Nations (ASEAN), China, Taiwan, and Korea. Japan, as a major economy but at a different stage of development, receives less emphasis, while India (a major but distinctive subregion of its own) is largely outside the scope of this book.

Winning in Asia is aimed at two main groups of readers. First are senior managers in Asian-owned companies who, I argue, will need to reinvent their businesses to succeed in the next round of Asian competition. For these managers, the book aims to help in shaping strategic priorities and in building the successful Asian multinational of tomorrow. The second primary audience is the management of Western multinationals operating in Asia (or planning to enter the Asian market). The book aims to assist Western multinationals both to better understand the powerful competitive threat that is starting to emerge from local Asian companies and to restructure their existing presence in Asia or to reshape their entry strategies accordingly. I hope *Winning in Asia* will also be of interest to researchers and students of Asian business.

I have already alluded to the fact that Asian managers and others living and working in Asia too numerous to mention by name have contributed directly or indirectly to this book. To each and every one, my sincere thanks. I would particularly like to acknowledge a special debt to Keeley Wilson, Research Fellow at INSEAD and my partner in the research on which much of this book is based, who assembled much of the data underpinning the arguments as well as contributing many invaluable insights from her own knowledge and experience in Asia. Other critical case examples were expertly researched, largely through face-to-face interviews with executives in Asia, by Charlotte Butler, Chua Chei Hwee, Deborah Clyde-Smith, and Sarah Meegan. The material has benefited greatly from discussions with my colleagues at INSEAD's Euro-Asia Centre, particularly Professors Ben Bensaou, Henri-Claude de Bettignies, Arnoud De Meyer, Philippe Lasserre, Gordon Redding, Helmut Schutte, and Ming Zeng. Likewise, the project has benefited from the insights of many old friends in Asia including Lo Chi Ko, Dr. Tan Chin Nam, and Professor Michael Y. Yoshino. I would like to thank the anonymous reviewers who made important comments on an earlier draft. I also gratefully acknowledge the financial support of INSEAD Euro-Asia Centre for what was an ambitious, multiyear research project.

Finally, my thanks to editor Hollis Heimbouch, who worked tirelessly to improve the exposition and clarity of the argument and through her sustained efforts and gentle prodding saw this project to completion.

Despite the excellent help I enjoyed from these many quarters, misinterpretations and deficiencies, of course, remain fully my own.

London, England
July 2003

Chapter 1

Asian Competition: The Next Round

It will take a different kind of company to succeed in Asia's next round of competition. This book is about what that company will need to look like and how it can be built. It is about grasping the challenges and exploiting the opportunities that the changing face of Asian competition is bringing in its wake.

Winning in Asia tomorrow will require Asian companies to combine their traditional strengths with the best business practices from around the world to create new and distinctive Asian multinational companies. Faced with these new-style Asian competitors, Western companies operating in Asia will need to reassess and refuel their own sources of competitive advantage—complacency and lack of real understanding about the local competition risks becoming their Achilles' heel.

Some Asian companies are already well on the road to creating the kind of company well positioned to win in the next round of competition. Consider Thailand's Charoen Pokphand (CP) in agribusiness. By the time the Asian financial crisis hit in 1997, CP's agribusinesses were part of a far-flung business empire with group sales estimated to exceed $5 billion. Starting from a single seed shop in Bangkok's Chinatown in 1921, its success had been nothing short of stunning. But its early 80 percent productivity advantage over competitors had been narrowing; despite moving from seeds through animal feed into production of chicken, pork, and tiger prawns, it still captured only a limited proportion of the potential value-added between farm and final consumer; the majority of sales were unbranded; its significant operations spread across twenty countries, including Thailand, India, Indonesia, Malaysia, Taiwan, Turkey, Vietnam, and 110 operations across China, ran as "a group of SMEs (small and medium-sized enterprises)" rather than a tightly integrated network; and despite its size and reach, its profitability was still hampered by industry fragmentation (in China's animal feed sector, for example, it faced competition from twelve thousand independent feedmills).[1]

Today however, CP has transformed itself for a new round of competition, building on its traditional strengths and combining them with new ones. Disposing of interests in satellite and cable television, motorcycle manufacturing, petrochemicals, and brewing, it has refocused its investment on agribusiness. Building on its intimate understanding of the Asian agribusiness supply chain, CP is pushing for another step-change in productivity by going beyond farming and processing productivity to attack inventory costs and sales and administration expenses—driving for productivity improvement in "overhead" activities where output is more difficult to measure and automation is more challenging. It is moving into higher value-added, processed foods like shrimp packaged in attractive layouts that can be placed directly onto a hotel buffet in the United States, skewers of chicken, pork, and vegetables ready-prepared for the grills of Japanese yakitori bars, and ready-made chilled meals for European supermarkets like Tesco, Britain's largest retailer, now with extensive operations overseas. Working in partnership with key customers, CP is building new sources of advantage and opening up new opportunities in a quest to become the "kitchen of the world." But these new initiatives are firmly built on an existing knowledge base and set of capabilities that, literally, go down to the grass roots of agribusiness on farms, feedmills, and local markets across Asia. In parallel, CP is beginning to put resources behind building its international brands, such as Costa Seafoods, to capture more of the extra value it creates for customers.

Rather than simply borrowing technology from overseas, CP is also leveraging its unique knowledge of Asian climatic and environmental conditions with an investment of between 3 percent and 5 percent of sales in R&D to generate a broad range of innovations. These span its development of a unique breed of fish, "Tabtim," engineered for high productivity in Asian ponds, but without the "muddy" taste that reduced the appeal of farmed fish; seeds optimized for local soils and rainfall patterns; the application of high technology to shrimp breeding and pond toxicology; and the development of genetically modified orchids.

Meanwhile, CP is steadily moving to turn its former fragmented structure from a "group of SME's dotted around Asia" into a unified network capable of reaping cross-border synergies and feeding the consistent, stable supply chain demanded by the world's supermarkets and catering suppliers, while maintaining traditional adaptability to differences in the local conditions (down to the variations in the mentality and experience of farmers in different regions). Finally, where possible, CP is seeking to reshape its competitive playing field. Along with major competitors like Hope Group (a pioneering $1 billion private company in China that has acquired thirty former state-owned feed and flour milling operations), for example, it is driving consolidation among the twelve thousand feedmills in China toward a cost-effective industry structure of approximately two thousand scale-efficient mills that will be viable in the long term.

None of these strategies represents a silver bullet, nor do they offer a surefire guarantee of success. But they do point the way to the kinds of changes that Asia's companies will need to make to win in the next round of competition. To develop and implement these kinds of strategies requires much more than the absorption of new technologies and skills. It demands fundamental changes in yesterday's mind-sets, organization structures, and management processes. Yet these changes do not amount to mimicking the ways of multinationals from the United States and Europe. Instead, this transformation requires Asian companies to combine their traditional strengths with the ability to cherry-pick and integrate the best technologies and ideas they can cull from around the world. Such efforts will not only create a new and distinctive breed of Asian corporation but, ultimately, reshape the Asian competitive playing field.

Today the key questions managers in Asian companies should be asking themselves, therefore, are these:

- Do I know what my company will need to look like to win in the next round of competition?

- Do I have the strategies to get there by leveraging and extending my distinctive Asian heritage and capabilities in new ways?

Much of the rest of this book is devoted to marshaling the concepts and evidence that will help managers of Asian companies develop a robust strategy that enables them to answer "yes" to these questions with confidence.

If you are the manager of a Western multinational operating in Asia (or of one planning to enter the region), you are probably asking yourself whether you should read on. Consider the following data. In 1995, just a few years after China opened its personal computer (PC) market to international competition, multinational companies including IBM, HP, and the (now merged) Compaq, had won more than a 50 percent share of the market. At that time *The Economist* predicted that the multinationals' share would rise to 80 percent by the year 2000, with the local Asian players being forced back to a 20 percent share. In fact the opposite happened. By 2000 the number one desktop PC brand was the Chinese company Legend with a 29 percent share; followed by two other local firms, Founder with 9 percent and Great Wall with 5 percent. The next largest slice of the PC market had been captured by other Asian companies like Taiwan's Acer and Japan's Toshiba. Western multinationals had retreated back to a combined market share of just 20 percent.

The implications are clear: As we enter the next round of competition in Asia, it is time for Western multinationals to understand the local Asian competitors, and how they will evolve in the future, with a new seriousness. As they face ever-stiffer competition from a new breed of Asian companies that combine "home-team" advantages with tomorrow's world-class capabilities, Western multinationals will need to fundamentally challenge the strategies that have been successful in winning them a share of Asia's rapid growth over the last two decades. Managers in Western multinationals will need new approaches to the market that allow them to more accurately pinpoint, and then to fully exploit, their potentially unique strengths in the next round of Asian competition. This book aims to provide both an understanding of how the best Asian competitors are likely to evolve and some insights into where the potential strengths and weaknesses of multinationals in the future Asian market might lie.

Pressures for Change

These new strategies are required because Asia's competitive environment is undergoing a sea change. Repeating what worked in the past is unlikely to succeed in the face of these new realities. These changes are being driven by the rapid development of China, the cumulative impact of gradual but sustained deregulation and trade liberalization across Asia, and the implications of a new generation of demographic and social forces that is beginning to reshape Asia's economic future. These are all long-term trends, but their immediate impact on Asian competition has been arrested because many Asian companies have been shackled by the aftereffects of the 1997 financial crisis for much of the last five years. Only now are these shackles being removed as debt has been restructured or finally repaid, giving these Asian corporations the elbow room to respond to the pent-up pressures for change.

Understanding the drivers of change in the Asian environment and what they mean for the way Asian competition will work in the next round is the first step toward creating the new kinds of strategies and companies that will succeed in the future.

Reverberations of the 1997 Crisis

The remarkable period of growth and prosperity in Asia for nearly two decades up to 1997 was, in many ways, "a miracle." The growth rates for East Asia averaged 8 percent between 1980 and 1990 and 8.1 percent between 1990 and 1998. In addition to the much-publicized fortunes accumulated by Asia's business elite, many individual investors shared in the rising wealth and a wide range of consumer goods and services came within the reach of millions of Asians for the first time, while poverty and illiteracy declined dramatically, and nutrition, health, and life expectancy advanced markedly.[2] But like the reality behind many so-called miracles, it wasn't quite everything it seemed.

Along with the many achievements came a number of unsustainable imbalances. Foremost among them was the distortion created by massive amounts of capital chasing productive investment opportunities faster than they could be created. For evidence, look no further than the fact that the average ratio of bank debt to gross domestic product (GDP) across the East Asian economies rose from 46 percent in 1980 to 105 percent in 1997.

When eager investors run out of high-quality investment opportunities, they start to look at less solid ones. Because they don't want to miss out on the boom, they convince themselves that it's fine to build new production lines, office buildings, or hotels even when potential customers haven't been identified. They further convince themselves that companies with no experience in a new industry will magically learn to run a new business smoothly overnight; that new products and services are sure to take off even when their value to users remains unproven; that massively inflated asset prices represent good value. The rising tide of growth, they surmise, will wash away all these shortcomings.

Even for starry-eyed investors, however, there comes a time when investments are supposed to generate profits and cash. Of course the many marginal, unproductive investments made during the latter part of Asia's boom times couldn't deliver. Their supporting foundations— their customer base, the associated infrastructure and services, and the skills and capabilities required to run them successfully—were simply too weak. When the returns failed to materialize, investors lost confidence. Those who had advanced debt began to ask for their money back. Equity investors tried to sell their shares. The financial crisis of 1997 was born.

At the macroeconomic level, these problems are now well understood. But what is less widely acknowledged is that the long boom left companies in Asia with a dangerous addiction: a dependence on "rent collection" (returns from ownership of assets), rather than creation of new value for customers, as their primary way to make money. Those sources of rents have now largely dried up.

The End of Rent Collection

Creating new value means finding ways to provide customers with goods and services that either better fit their needs or do so more efficiently than competitors. That was not the way a lot of companies in Asia made money during the boom. Instead, most grew rich by collecting "rents" on the assets over which they had gained control. Consider some examples of these rents:

Speculative gains. Many companies amassed large portfolios of physical assets, ranging from real estate to large chemical plants, and shareholdings in other companies. As capital poured into Asia, the prices of these assets were inflated. So never mind if you are really creating value as, say, a property developer by efficiently putting up buildings on viable sites that the tenants will find helps their businesses thrive. Instead, bet big and build assets as fast as possible borrowing other people's money. Then sit back and watch the value of your asset soar. Capital gains became a more important source of surplus for many companies in Asia than profits from supplying goods and services.

National preference and local monopolies. The profits of many companies in Asia were underpinned by preferred access to restricted permits and licenses that created virtual monopolies in many local markets across Asia. It wasn't world-class competitiveness that allowed these companies to thrive. Instead, it was the fact that they controlled the bottlenecks in the chain, such as market access and distribution, which allowed them to benefit from the economic boom. Put your efforts into maintaining control of the neck of the bottle and sit back and collect the rents from those who need to pass through.

Resource arbitrage. Successful companies in competitive markets are those that find out how to add more value at lower cost than their rivals. But even companies that deliver a less attractive offering or poorer service and squander resources through inefficiency can succeed if they have access to resources at an artificially low cost. Tie up monopoly rights to a fast-growing equatorial rain forest, or subsidized capital from a state bank, and you get access to quality resources at below-market value. Even if you turn these resources into shoddy, low-value products, offer poor service, and waste a high proportion of the inputs you use in the process, you can still benefit form the rents you collect by exploiting the resources you obtained on the cheap.

A supplier's market. In Asian economies growing between 7 percent and 8 percent per annum over decades, companies got used to the pleasure of demand constantly outstripping supply. Despite a few bumps created by the business cycle, it was basically a supplier's market. In this supply-constrained environment, those who can pull together the resources to expand capacity rapidly do well. The ability to supply in volume is key. Whether the quality is excellent, whether the product or service is customized to the user's exact requirements, or whether operational efficiency is world-class, are all secondary considerations. Corporate performance is largely driven by those who have the assets, resources, and capacity in an environment of frequent scarcity. Again, if you control the assets in the face of rising demand, you can enjoy the rents.

Even as they continued to benefit from these kinds of rent collection, too many senior managers in Asian companies were happy to bask in the illusion that they were creating new value through world-beating competitiveness and thriving in a dynamic, open market. The same was true for many of their multinational counterparts operating in the region, whose management was more inclined to attribute their success to brilliant strategy and execution than to favorable market conditions.

The Asian financial crisis shattered that illusion because, almost at a stroke, it removed most of those same sources of economic rent that had been the unspoken secret of success for many Asian companies. Instead of capital gains as asset prices rose year after year, Asian management was faced with a sustained period of asset price deflation. Those with cozy local monopolies faced a collapse in domestic demand, yet their attempts to switch to export markets demonstrated that they had never been competitive outside their protected cocoon. Resources were now in excess, so the rents from arbitraging resources turned to losses. Meanwhile, Asia became a "buyer's market" where the customer with cash was king. What mattered now was having attractive products and services suited to choosy customers' needs and a superefficient supply chain; high-volume, undifferentiated capacity became a liability rather than an asset.

Reinvention Post Crisis

It may seem surprising that despite the disappearance of rents from company profits and massive deflation in asset prices, most firms made so little change to the fundamentals of their competitive strategies in the immediate aftermath of the crisis. In a survey of managers in 127 Asian corporates and multinationals operating in Asia that I conducted in 1998, for example, almost 50 percent of respondents indicated that they were planning to "sit it out" and "weather the storm" until better times came; only 13 percent were initiating a program of aggressive restructuring (involving selling some businesses, paying down debt, and strengthening other businesses through changes in strategy or bolt-on acquisitions).[3]

An important reason why much of the predicted restructuring and changes in strategy by Asian businesses never materialized is to be found in the predicament faced by creditors after the crisis hit. An old adage among lenders runs like this: "If you owe the bank a small amount of money and can't repay, then it's your problem. But if you owe the bank a large amount of money and you can't repay, then it's the bank's problem." Those two sentences sum up the reason why many Asian companies managed to avoid dramatic restructuring of their businesses in the wake of the 1997 crisis. The banks had little choice but to reschedule or restructure their debt: Repossessing assets was of little use because assets could only be liquidated at fire-sale prices, if at all; and the banks generally weren't in a position to take over the running of the companies, while competent administrators were scarce. Some banks, meanwhile, wanted to avoid recognizing the reality of their loan portfolios; as Min Haeng Cho of Korea's Hansol Paper wryly observed: "Ironically companies with bad credit and which had bank loans had them extended because the banks could not afford to declare them in default."[4]

The process of adjusting to the cracks revealed by the 1997 crisis has taken more than five years to work through the system. Governments set up asset management companies, like IBRA in Indonesia and Danaharta in Malaysia, that embarked on the grindingly slow process of dealing with the nonperforming loans on banks books; creditors ultimately took "haircuts" or reluctantly converted debt to equity; companies like First Pacific sold non-Asian assets to clear their balance sheets and began making acquisitions again; and family groups like Eastern Sugar controlled by the Wattanavekin clan in Thailand set about restructuring their debts—a task they eventually completed in 2003, after which they were able to begin launching new initiatives. While these processes inched forward, the hands of many management teams, whether the old guard or managers newly parachuted in, had their hands tied when it came to renewing their strategies.

A prime example is Daewoo, once Korea's second largest corporate group. Despite defaulting on more than $80 billion of debt and an early announcement of aggressive restructuring plans after the crisis hit, Daewoo descended into limbo. Instead of restructuring, the company claimed it would be able to cut its debt-equity ratio to below 200 percent by the year 2000 by raising new equity on the stock market. It abandoned plans to sell Daewoo Heavy Industries (its shipbuilding and machinery operation) and Orion Electric (a producer of computer monitors) to foreign buyers. Meanwhile, it was resisting the plan to cede its consumer electronics business, Daewoo Electronics, to Samsung in a swap for Samsung's automotive business.

It took more than two years before Daewoo eventually collapsed, shortly after which Kim Woo-choong, the company's then chairman and founder, disappeared. In his absence twenty Daewoo executives were jailed for accounting fraud that had inflated the company's assets by $30 billion.[5] The restructuring, which split Daewoo into a series of smaller companies including Daewoo Shipbuilding and Daewoo Heavy Industries and saw assets of the former Daewoo Motor sold to General Motors, was not completed until 2003.

But when the changes in strategy eventually came, they were dramatic. What has ultimately emerged from the original Daewoo, however, is a set of much more focused companies that are much less reliant on "rent collection" and access to preferential capital from state banks. These new, independent companies like Daewoo Shipbuilding have embarked on policies to dramatically improve their productivity in order to restore profitability and lay the foundation for future competitiveness.

Other Korean *chaebol* (literally "big money"), such as Samsung, are also starting to make big changes in strategy. Shortly after his appointment to head Samsung Electronics, Yun Jong-yong faced the crisis. At first, change was limited. But more recently, Yun has shed one third of the former workforce, sold loss-making businesses, and hired three hundred U.S.–educated M.B.A graduates and seven hundred Ph.D.–level engineers. He describes himself as the "chaos-maker."[6] In late 2002 Samsung announced a step-change in its efforts to build a leading global brand for its products, signing a new $400 million per annum advertising contract with Madison Avenue's Foote, Cone & Belding agency.

Obviously not every Asian company is making these kinds of dramatic changes. But the fact that companies are now, at last, throwing off the bonds imposed by the 1997 crisis portends a different competitive environment in the next round. At the same time, increased pressure to change the way they competed in the past is coming from the failure of the "good old times" to return in Asia despite improved growth rates, combined with a profound recognition that the days of rent collection are over. The nature of competition will change as a result, shifting competition toward those companies that can add the most value to the resources they use and away from those that simply add new capacity. The next round will reward those that can do more, and differently, with less, not those who have built the largest corporate empires or assembled the biggest caches of assets and resources from which they collect rents.

Asian Markets as the Engine of Future Growth

The end of rent collection as a profit generator, therefore, is the first force that is driving change in the Asian competitive environment. A second major force for change is growing Asian market demand: Demand from within Asia is now replacing exports to the United States as the primary engine of growth. This shift has been gaining momentum over time, but now the pendulum is swinging decisively. It used to be said that when the United States sneezes, Asia catches influenza. But after the U.S. economy slumped in 2001, growth rates in Asia fell much less than expected. Certainly, Japan remained stuck in its deflationary trap, while some sectors and economies, like Singapore, that were linked most directly to U.S. demand for electronics suffered setbacks. Yet while U.S. imports from Asia fell 14 percent between 2000 and 2001, growth throughout most of Asia continued at between double and triple the rate achieved in the United States.

An important reason for this break with the pattern of the past was that Asian economies have now begun to develop their own, self-sustaining growth dynamic. To see evidence of this dynamic at work, consider Acer, Taiwan's largest supplier of branded computer goods. Between 2000 and 2001 the share of Acer's total sales revenue coming from China increased from 10 percent to 18 percent, while North America's share fell from 30 percent to 20 percent. The pattern is repeated in industries from agriculture to natural resources and services. And in rapidly growing industries like tourism, almost 70 percent of tourists to Asian countries now come from their other Asian neighbors. This trend will only strengthen in the future, not least because a more open China is now becoming an important engine of Asian internal growth through its rising imports of Asian-produced goods and services. Chinese tourists to Thailand alone accounted for 8 percent of the total in 2000, up from 1 percent in 1990.[7]

There are a number of other reasons why Asian market demand will become increasingly more important than exports. First, over the next fifteen years, Asia's workforce will grow at an average rate of more than 1 percent per year. That compares with a European workforce whose numbers will stagnate or decline, and a U.S. workforce that will grow at no more that 0.7 percent per annum.

These statistics are not speculation. Workforce growth over the next fifteen years is one of the few trends we can forecast with a pretty high degree of accuracy because those future workers have already been born. Provided there are neither mass migrations of people around the world, so large that they materially shift the size of the populations in any one region, nor mass unemployment, the numbers of children alive today will be equal to the growth in the workforce tomorrow.

In the fog of short-term forecasting, this simple equation is often forgotten. But it shouldn't be ignored because the implication is that through increased workforce alone, Asia starts with a baseline growth dynamic that is significantly higher than that of either Europe or the United States. In practice this growth differential in favor of Asia will be even more marked because in addition to today's children, more Asian women will enter the workforce outside the home or family farm—a shift that has already taken place in Europe and the United States.

The second reason why Asian markets will be key is the scope for rapid growth in Asian income levels through the productivity improvements brought about by implementing technologies and processes that have already been mastered elsewhere in the world. If the Southeast Asian countries, including Thailand and Malaysia, were even to move up to the productivity levels reached by Korea today, average income levels would double. If they reach the productivity levels already achieved by

Europe or the United States, average incomes would be triple or quadruple compared with today. The potential for China to grow based on improved productivity alone is even more striking. If the average Chinese worker could be as productive as her Korean cousin is today, China's market would be thirteen times as large as it is today; if it reached today's European average, China's economy would be more than twenty-five times its current size. If China could reach the productivity levels that the United States had achieved by the year 2000, it would have a market a staggering forty times as large as the current one.

These dramatic improvements in productivity won't be easy to achieve. But the point is this: They are achievable because the technologies, processes, and systems required to underpin this kind of increase already exist. In the United States, by contrast, much of the productivity growth will have to come from technologies that haven't yet been invented or at least not yet widely commercialized. Asia's ability to grow its markets by closing the productivity gap will also be helped by rising education levels: In the coming decades, those entering the Asian workforce will be much better educated than ever before. An impressive 68 percent of young Koreans newly entering the workforce today, for example, have a tertiary-level (college) qualification. And these students frequently are among the top ranked in international comparisons of their capabilities in disciplines such as mathematics and science. Throughout the more developed Southeast Asian countries like Thailand and Malaysia, between 20 percent and 30 percent of those starting their first full-time job have completed tertiary studies. Even in China and Indonesia, with their large rural populations, the figure is 11 percent and 6 percent, respectively, and rising rapidly. Adding a high proportion of well-qualified people to its workforce (in contrast to the situation a generation ago) gives Asia a strong chance of rapidly improving productivity levels and growing rapidly without being unduly constrained by skill shortages.

A third reason that Asian demand is likely to drive growth in the future lies in the history of high savings rates in Asia. Over the past decade, on average, East Asians have saved more than 20 percent of their incomes. China has sustained a net saving rate of more than 30 percent of income for over a decade. Comparative rates of saving in Europe average around 10 percent, and U.S. consumers have been saving only 5 percent to 6 percent of their incomes.

This accumulated pool of Asian savings provides hidden potential for Asia to grow faster than other parts of the world over the next decade or so without taking on dangerous levels of debt.

Since the 1997 Asian financial crisis, Asians have tended to channel their savings into bank deposits. The result was that by 2002, bank deposits in Asia had reached an all-time high. Chinese households alone have over $1 trillion in local banks and an estimated additional $250 billion under proverbial mattresses. Being leery of backing all but the most cast-iron investment proposals, banks saw a dramatic rise in their ratio of deposits to lending. Together, these developments have created an Asia that, far from being starved of cash, was awash with liquidity.

But eventually Asian savers will start to move their money out of bank deposits and into bonds and equities as the memory of the 1997 crisis fades and confidence strengthens. Banks with newly improved risk-management and loan approval systems will begin to lend more to solid investment projects. Asia's sea of liquidity will therefore start to fuel tomorrow's investment and growth.

High savings rates also provide headroom for increased consumer spending to stimulate demand in the future. Once better economic times arrive, some of those venerable Asian savers (including a new generation of income earners who have known only relative prosperity rather than the crippling poverty of the distant past) might start to loosen their purse strings. The fact that they have the scope to spend more without taking on the burden of high levels of consumer debt (unlike many consumers in the United States and some parts of Europe who are already close to their borrowing limits) offers yet another source of potential for Asia to grow faster than the West without taking reckless risks. By 2002 this had already started to happen in Korea, the country where restructuring following the crisis has been more aggressive and where, therefore, a new foundation for future growth was first to be put in place. Other countries have now begun to follow.

The combination of these two forces—the switch out of bank deposits into bonds and shares, and the gradual shift away from an environment where wary consumers are hoarding cash toward one where they are prepared to spend—will contribute to the growing importance of strategies for penetrating Asian markets in the next round of competition. Undoubtedly the United States and Europe will remain important markets for Asian companies, but the reliance on export demand as the primary driver of Asian growth has come to an end. Asia is now becoming a growth engine in its own right. Some have gone so far as to predict that internal demand within Asia will be the prime driver of global economic growth for the next ten to twenty years.[8]

This shift also has important implications for the strategies Asian companies will need to adopt in the future because it means that instead of competing to displace goods and services locally produced in the United States and Europe, the focus will shift to competing with other Asian players for a share of Asia's markets. The consequences of this shift are profound.

The cost advantages that allowed Asian companies to take market share from high-cost suppliers in the United States and Europe will be of little help in winning the battle for Asian markets. The primary competitors, whether they be other Asian firms or multinationals operating in Asia, will all enjoy the same Asian cost advantages. Low costs will be an entry ticket into the game. New sources of advantage will be necessary to win in the next round of competition for Asian markets.

Yesterday's quest to understand the U.S. and European markets will shift toward developing a deeper understanding of the diverse consumers and business buyers across Asia and responding accordingly. But don't Asian companies already understand Asian markets? No. This idea is a dangerous myth. Look no further than the litany of failures when companies with a subtle knowledge of one Asian market have ventured into neighboring countries including Singaporean banks that hemorrhaged cash in Thailand and Filipino conglomerates that notched up heavy losses in China. The shift in focus to Asian markets will require new and different approaches to everything from market research and customer relationship management to brand building and meeting the Asian definition of good service.

Building effective and efficient distribution channels across Asia will be key. In the last round of competition, gaining access to distribution in the United States and Europe was a high priority. This was often difficult, time-consuming, and costly. But compared with Asia, the United States and Europe had an efficient and sophisticated network of distribution, wholesaling, and retailing already in place. U.S. and European channels were already capable not only of getting good and services into the hands of users but also of moving information to and from customers and providing back-up support services. The situation differs in Asia where, in many markets, the distribution network, and the wholesale and retail channels within it, is often a "black hole." Efficiency is generally much lower. But even more important, much of the Asian distribution system is ill-equipped to understand customer needs, deliver marketing information, and provide responsive service. To be successful in winning share in Asia's future growth markets, companies will have to proactively strengthen their distribution networks, not just gain access.

The shift from U.S. and European markets toward Asian markets as the primary source of growth presents new and different challenges and opportunities for how to compete.

China Scatters the Flying Geese

Asia's traditional model of economic development was often described as "flying geese" in formation. Each country began by manufacturing and exporting simple, labor-intensive goods like garments and shoes. As it accumulated more capital and know-how, it moved on through intermediate industries like basic chemicals and plastic molding, and then to high-value-added products like semiconductors and pharmaceuticals. As one country moved on to the next level of value-added industries, consistent with supporting a higher living standard and increased labor costs, another developing country would take its place at the lower-value end. Japan led the flock, followed by Hong Kong, Singapore, South Korea, and Taiwan. Then came Malaysia, Thailand, the Philippines, Indonesia, and Vietnam in the tail. Albeit somewhat simplistic, this concept of national geese flying in formation underlay many a government policy and corporate strategy. It shaped the pattern of what diversified Asian-owned companies invested in next and where multinationals located their activities in Asia.

Then along came China. *The Economist* magazine aptly summed up the result with a cartoon. It depicted a jet aircraft, piloted by a panda, zooming straight through the flock of Asian geese.[9] China wasn't flying in the cozy formation; by the new millennium it was producing everything from simple manufactures to high-technology components and equipment, from rag dolls and plastics to semiconductors and specialized machinery. And China is doing this on a scale large enough to redraw the competitive map.

Now that the flying geese model of where to invest to leverage your country-based advantage has been exploded and the neat formation is in disarray, companies will have to reevaluate in which products, services, and activities they can be competitive in the future. And it is time for both companies and governments to forget about trying to pair up countries with industries. In the next round of Asian competition, it will matter much more *who* you are (and the quality of your capabilities) than *where* you are from or *what* industry you are in.

With China now a key part of the Asian game, the winners will be those who can offer a distinctive part of a more integrated Asian jigsaw where successful firms supply specialized components, products, or services or focus on particular activities within the overall supply chain. Yesterday's world, where companies in one country made textiles while those in another country made laptop computers, will give way to a new environment: Companies in every industry and in different locations will exchange differentiated products and services. For instance, China will sell specialized container-handling equipment to Korea at the same time as Korea sells robots to China to equip its car assembly plants; Thailand will design and etch circuits on silicon wafers, while Malaysia "packages" them into complete chips that can be attached to a motherboard; Vietnam will sell broccoli to China, while buying Chinese soybeans; and Singapore will provide marketing services to Hong Kong while airing TV commercials created in Hong Kong. Economists call this *co-specialization*—a competitive environment in which different companies specialize in different parts of the value chain and/or exchange specialized products and services across borders. In a co-specialization environment, trade flows in both directions between two countries even in the same industry.

The emergence of co-specialization in Asia represents a fundamental change in the competitive environment. Companies won't be able to rely on being in a location that is advantageous for a particular industry as the primary factor that differentiates them from competitors. Differences in quality and cost between countries will still exist, but they will be insignificant compared to the differences between individual firms. By focusing on achieving high productivity in a particular activity or on devising specialized products and services that are virtually unique, the leading companies in this new Asia will open up a huge competitive advantage. The laggards won't be able to match them, no matter how favorable their home-country environment might look. This has already happened in industries like semiconductors. It is not really where you are from that is decisive for whether you can compete in semiconductors: Companies from China, Malaysia, the Philippines, Singapore, Taiwan, and Thailand, for example, are all in the business. Being in the right location doesn't guarantee success. What matters is that you have the skills, knowledge, experience, and capabilities to make your company excel at supplying a particular part of the chain, such as circuit design, photolithography, or back-end packaging or become a world-beater in producing certain types of chips, such as DRAMs (Dynamic Random Access Memories) or RISC (Reduced Instruction Set Computing) processors.

In this next round of competition, this pattern will be repeated in industry after industry. The cozy world of national advantage in Asia will give way to one in which the sharp edges of productivity and differentiation are what counts. And as this shift takes place, it will drive a fourth far-reaching change in the Asian competitive environment: Former national fiefdoms will be replaced by increasingly pan-Asian competition.

Demise of National Fiefdoms

Both the Asian and the European economies share a common postwar heritage of division into highly segregated national markets, separated from each other by a mix of tariff and nontariff barriers, cultural and language differences, divergent choices about local standards, and regulatory differences between countries. Within this environment it generally made sense for companies to approach each national market as a separate competitive playing field. This behavior was reinforced by various forms of preference given by governments to their local companies through the allocation of licenses, preferential access to finance, and other kinds of direct and indirect support.

Likewise, multinationals historically approached Asia as a collection of separate national markets. Understanding that during the 1970s and 1980s most governments favored a high degree of self-sufficiency and import substitution, multinationals also sought incentives and tax concessions by offering to establish subsidiaries with a fairly complete range of capabilities right from production through to sales and service in each country where they operated. The result was a series of relatively independent national markets, each served by its own distinct set of suppliers comprising local firms and multinationals' subsidiaries inside the country.

Forty years ago, what is now the European Union embarked on a sustained and determined effort to dismantle this structure of fragmented national markets and country-by-country competition. This project gathered pace with the "Completion of the European Single Market" campaign in 1992. In many industries, Asia went in the opposite direction: Not only did the old barriers between national market remain largely intact but also new impediments to cross-border competition were introduced in the form of a growing patchwork of regulation that differed among countries. Agreements to liberalize trade and reduce tariffs, meanwhile, progressed slowly. Regional groupings like ASEAN (Association of South East Asian Nations) tended to emphasize the political agenda first, with trade and economic issues being tackled later.

Fragmented national markets meant that Asian companies typically focused on becoming big fish in their local ponds. Leveraging their local knowledge and relationships in their protected home-country market, a majority of Asian-owned companies chose to diversify their assets across industries to form sprawling local conglomerates with interests in everything from agricultural products to manufacturing, property, and financial services. Moving into a series of different industries while staying within their national borders allowed Asian firms to exploit their strong relationships with local or national governments, maximize their bargaining power with local distributors and suppliers, and access capital from local banks (often without being forced to comply with international borrower standards as the 1997 crisis cruelly demonstrated). The result was a set of national corporate fiefdoms.

Country managers in charge of highly autonomous subsidiaries within the Asian network of foreign multinationals paralleled the behavior of Asian firms. They fought for investment of more resources in their business unit and argued against sharing functions from procurement and manufacturing to distribution and marketing with their sister subsidiaries on the grounds that any such moves would reduce their ability to respond to the peculiarities of the local market. The result was a set of national fiefdoms within many multinationals, paralleling the structure of Asian corporations, despite the multinationals' pan-Asian reach.

But as we entered the new millennium these national fiefdoms—whether they be in the form of diversified Asian corporates who are champions within their home-country borders or the country subsidiaries of multinationals—had begun to come under threat from the rapid growth of cross-border competition in Asia.

A potent cocktail of falling trade barriers, deregulation of national markets, and falling costs of transport and communication is now opening the door to new sources of competitive advantage based on cross-border economies of scale and coordination. The results are striking. Trade between Asian countries is now growing more than twice as fast as Asia's trade with the rest of the world, reflecting a rapid increase in competition between Asian-based companies for other Asian markets beyond their home turf. And perhaps even more significant, Asian companies have invested an average of almost $50 billion every year in building or acquiring operations in other countries since 1995 (despite the setback of the 1997 financial crisis).[10] Much of this investment has been in building beachheads in other Asian markets from which to mount attacks on archaic national fiefdoms.

Indonesia's Indofood is a classic example. During the Suharto era (1967–1998), Indofood's parent, the Salim Group, enjoyed a virtual monopoly on importing and milling wheat—the main ingredient for noodles, a staple of the Indonesian diet. Leveraging this advantage by creating a wide array of instant noodle flavors and brands, it captured 95 percent of the Indonesian market. By 1998 Indofood claimed to be the largest producer of instant noodles in the world. But Asia's $6 billion instant noodle industry had also spawned powerful competitors in other parts of Asia, such as Uni-President of Taiwan and China's Tingyi Holdings. When wheat imports into Indonesia were opened up, these potential rivals, whose international expansion had long been thwarted by the regulation, moved in along with a number of start-ups. Indofood had to compete with unfamiliar rivals. They were unprepared. By 2003, Indofood's market share had fallen 7 percentage points to 88 percent and continues to decline, while the price it is realizing for each pack of noodles is falling by over 1 percent per year.[11]

As local companies break in to each other's home markets, competition is becoming a pan-Asian game. Given Asia's diversity of cultural diversity, this won't mean the sudden rise of homogeneous "Asian" products and services blanketing the continent. But it does mean that Asian companies and the country-focused subsidiaries of multinationals will have to start looking beyond their traditional, local competition and learn to compete with newcomers from across their national borders.

Shifts in the Bases of Competition in the Next Round

These forces of change—(1) the delayed impacts of the 1997 financial crisis; (2) the shift from exports to Asian market demand as the engine of growth; (3) the emergence of China scattering the flying geese; and (4) the demise of national fiefdoms—are coalescing to fundamentally shift the requirements for competitive success in the next round. These shifts, illustrated in Figure 1-1, can be summarized as follows.

From Manufacturing Productivity to "Total Productivity"

In the last round of Asian competition, productivity in manufacturing and the back-room operations of service businesses raced ahead, while productivity in "softer" activities like distribution, sales, and administration lagged well behind (as anyone who has toured one of Asia's gleaming manufacturing plants and then tried to cash a check at a bank or visited a wholesale distribution depot will attest). But in the next round of competition, it won't be enough to rely on high productivity in manufacturing and operations alone. In the future environment—where competition is increasingly for Asian markets rather than export orders, where national fiefdoms are attacked by new competitors, and where Chinese factories set the benchmarks for manufacturing efficiency—one thing that will increasingly differentiate competitors is their total cost of delivering and supporting products and services to Asian consumers. The low productivity that was formerly tolerated outside the factory will become a potentially fatal handicap. The quest to drive up total productivity—measured across each and every activity involved in the chain that ultimately serves the end user—will come to the fore.

From Being "Better" to Being "Different"

We have already seen that as China's development continues to scatter the flying geese it will be increasingly important to become a specialized piece of the larger Asian jigsaw. And as the quasi-monopolies of

FIGURE 1-1

Shifts in the Bases of Asian Competition in the Next Round

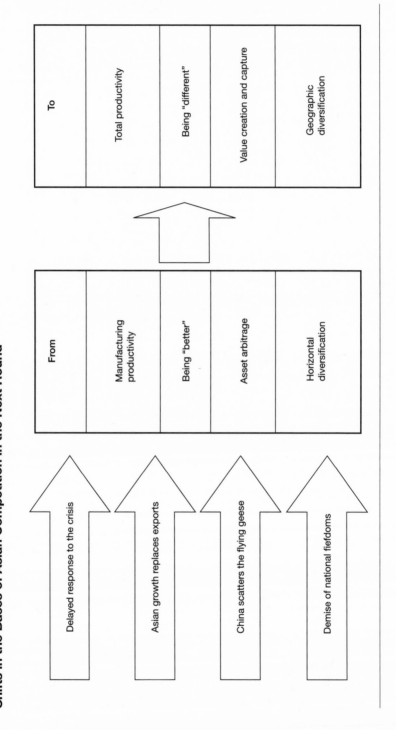

former national fiefdoms disappear, successful companies will need to strive for dominance in particular, specialized segments right across Asian markets. A strategy based on doing the same thing as competitors, but trying to do it better (i.e., cheaper and more efficiently), therefore, will become ever more difficult to sustain. Even the good "jack of all trades" will struggle to find a comfortable position on the new playing field. The new environment will demand that winning companies succeed in pursuing a strategy of being *different* from competitors, as well as better, to decisively set themselves apart from the competition.

From Asset Arbitrage to Value Creation and Capture

Without asset price inflation and "rent collection" to bolster profits, the next round of competition in Asia will be characterized by the need to create and capture new sources of value. This will require many Asian companies to make fundamental changes in their strategy.

To create new value you need a fundamental understanding of exactly what extra features and services customers are prepared to pay for and the depth of operational capabilities required to reliably deliver this more complex offering. That's difficult to do when you have the legacy of a portfolio of businesses that, as one Asian CEO candidly put it: "was created through entering new lines of business we knew nothing about, often for little more than prestige."[12] For the proof, look no further than the experience of the Asian crisis when many well-run, core businesses were threatened by "add-ons," such as property. Like many others, Lai Sun Group, for example, owner of the profitable Crocodile label, brushed with bankruptcy when its property investments collapsed: It had the property assets but not the market understanding and operational capabilities to create value in a market that was very different from its apparel core. Similarly Sime Darby, with a wide spread of businesses and proven capabilities in manufacturing and industrial services, has had to admit that it lacked the operational depth to add value to its Sime Bank. Sime Darby's response was to get out of the business.

But focusing on businesses where you have operational strength alone won't be sufficient to create and capture value. To profit in the new environment, companies will not only need to generate additional customer value but also to signal this extra value to consumers through their brands. Brands, and the improved quality and service necessary to underpin them, will therefore play a much-expanded role in the new era of value-driven competition.

From Horizontal Diversification to Geographic Diversification

Finally, the demise of national fiefdoms and the pressure to spread the extra costs of investment in differentiation mean that the next round of competition will shift from rivalry between conglomerates toward successful diversification across borders.

As noted above, a majority of Asian-owned companies chose to diversify their assets across industries (so-called horizontal diversification). This allowed them to exploit strong relationships with local or national governments, maximize their bargaining power with local distributors and suppliers, and access capital from local banks. But the demise of these national fiefdoms means that more and more Asian-owned companies will be forced to seek cross-border economies to stay competitive. For multinationals it means that the unwieldy list of national subsidiaries many have currently dotted around Asia will need to be refashioned into a much more tightly integrated network. For both groups, therefore, competition will increasingly revolve around the quality of a company's systems, processes, and strategies to coordinate and manage the same business effectively across national borders.

Leveraging Asian Heritage into the Future

In responding to these fundamental shifts in the bases of competition, the obvious strategy might be to imitate what companies in the United States and Europe have done to address similar challenges in their own environments. Ever since the 1997 financial crisis, some commentators have been pressing Asian governments and businesses to create a copy of the U.S. ideal of competition: transparency, a level playing field, prosperity for the fittest, and bankruptcy for those who can't measure up. They blame intransigent governments, "vested interests," and crony capitalists for slowing down the pace of "reform."

This blueprint is part dogma and part wishful thinking. It isn't going to happen, nor should it. To imitate U.S.-style corporate strategies in response to Asia's new competitive game would be to throw the proverbial baby out with the bathwater. Certainly it will be necessary for both

Asian companies and multinationals operating there to jettison some of the baggage of the past. But the winners in the next round of Asian competition will identify the strengths of their Asian heritage and leverage these into the future by building distinctive, new strategies around them. For Asian companies this means carefully separating the strengths of their Asian heritage from the business practices and habits that belong to the era that ended with the crisis in 1997. For Western multinationals it will mean rethinking what they can learn from Asia that can be leveraged both locally and around the world; becoming students as well as teachers in Asia and applying what they learn throughout their global networks, not just in Asia.

The potential strengths of Asian heritage that can be leveraged by Asian companies and multinationals alike, the weaknesses that must be addressed, and the baggage that needs to be abandoned are explored in detail in chapter 2. In defining the challenges ahead in the next round of competition, however, it is useful to briefly sketch out where the potential for leveraging Asian heritage might lie.

Potential Areas for Leverage

One of the striking characteristics of many Asian companies, especially those run by the overseas Chinese, is the ability to move fast when opportunities arise. This is combined with ways of assessing and managing the risk of being first into new markets that differ from those traditionally applied in the West. During the long boom of the 1980s and 1990s, these capabilities were directed primarily toward arbitrage and trading assets; in the next phase of Asian growth, they need to be harnessed to build defensible first-mover advantages when new opportunities are identified.

The rapid growth of Asian demand during the long boom, and the experience of capacity and capability constraints in expanding supply, sensitized Asian managers to the strategy of controlling the "choke points" or "mountain passes" in the supply chain where profit could be extracted. This skill will also be useful in the next round of competition, but instead of looking for choke points created by an overall excess of demand over supply, it will be necessary to identify those activities that have the highest profit potential because they depend on assets, capabilities, and knowledge that are difficult for rivals to replicate.

This, in turn, will require the search for ways of gaining more access to and local control over proprietary, base technology. One way of doing this will be to form more partnerships with small- and medium-sized companies from around the world who have specialist, proprietary technologies to offer. The propensity for Asian companies to "internalize the market" by assembling networks of alliances, meanwhile, is another area in which there is potential to leverage Asian heritage. Despite calls for more transparency and "arm's-length" transactions, competition between complex alliance networks, as we see emerging in industries from telecommunications to airlines, is on the rise in both East and West. If properly harnessed, this potential for competition based on new types of alliances will play to the historic strengths of Asian deal makers.

The strong traditions of service and art that are deeply embedded in many Asian cultures can also potentially be leveraged into future Asian brands and service businesses. Companies like Singapore Airlines, Shangri-la Hotels, Banyan Tree, and Japan's Kenzo and Uniqlo have shown the way. But to exploit this potential in a future environment where strategies for value creation and capture need to replace asset arbitrage as the primary concerns requires much more widespread and sustained focus on building Asian brands.

For all its deficiencies, the era of cronyism (or what Indonesians call "ersatz" capitalism), did develop a subtle understanding in Asia of how to align corporate strategies with government economic and social goals for the benefit of both parties. In the next round of competition, we shouldn't expect Asian governments to stop awarding what many free marketers see as "unfair" advantages to particular companies in the highly competitive game of national development. We can expect Asian governments to be more careful to award preferential treatment only to those companies that can demonstrate a depth of competence and operating experience in the businesses for which they seek government support. But the ability to carefully align corporate strategies with government objectives will remain a key strength. As one senior government official put it: "Western companies keep coming here talking about free trade and opening up our markets as if this must be good for us. We have clear goals to grow certain new, strategic industries. Asian multinationals often have a better understanding of how to align their investments with these goals."[13]

Another aspect of Asian heritage that can be leveraged is the experience Asian companies have gained through years of focusing on commercialization of new technologies and ideas, which were often discovered elsewhere. In some ways the lack of basic research inside most Asian companies is an obvious handicap. But as the range of technologies relevant to any business expands and the dispersion of knowledge that companies needs to access increases, it will be less and less possible for companies to rely solely on their in-house R&D. In this environment, where definition of what constitutes innovation and the nets used to capture new knowledge need to be expanded, Asian strengths in learning from the world and rapidly turning that knowledge into commercial products and services produced on a large scale will arguably become a potential advantage if used in the right way.

Finally, the motto of the most progressive Asian companies has been "It's not what you know, but how fast you can learn." With the demise of rent collection as the primary contributor to profits, we shouldn't expect resources to trump ambition in the next round of competition. If anything, the pace at which companies can learn is likely to become even more important as the new competitive environment demands companies seek higher total productivity and greater differentiation to become different as well as better. Potential therefore lies in finding ways to leverage the traditional focus of Asian businesses on rapidly absorbing new technologies, learning new skills, and understanding new markets.[14]

Faced with the sea change in Asia's competitive environment, however, parlaying the potential advantages of Asian heritage into a successful future presents formidable challenges.

Five Key Challenges in the Next Round of Competition

Winners in tomorrow's Asia will be distinguished by their ability to rise to the following five key challenges: (1) making a step-change in total productivity, (2) building new capabilities for innovation, (3) creating strong Asian brands, (4) extending and integrating their international networks, and (5) reshaping the Asian playing field by driving industry consolidation.

Making a Step-Change in Total Productivity

Making a step-change in total productivity demands a new, broader attack on areas of low productivity that were tolerated during Asia's last boom: inefficiencies in logistics, distribution, supply chains, service and support processes, administration, and management decision making. It will also mean a new focus on maximizing the value added per employee, not just minimizing the cost. Because these changes will require painful adjustment that strikes at the heart of cultures, habits, and orthodoxies that are deeply rooted in corporate Asia, they cannot be achieved simply by copying the processes and systems used in the West. Just as dramatic advances in manufacturing productivity in Japan were achieved through unique approaches developed locally, tomorrow's broader productivity improvements will have to be won by giving an Asian flavor to the new systems and processes learned from abroad. In many Asian companies, these productivity improvements will be necessary to release the resources necessary to invest in innovation, brand building, and reshaping the Asian playing field; thus, they will have to be achieved in record time. This means that yesterday's Asian strengths in moving rapidly to close deals and exploit emerging opportunities will need to be decisively redirected toward achieving a step-change in total productivity.

Building New Capabilities for Innovation

Companies will require new capabilities for innovation to really differentiate themselves from competitors and break out of Asia's current commoditization trap to become "different as well as better." This will demand a change of mentality that allows them to focus on innovation in its broadest sense: to include innovation in all of the firm's undertakings, not just the development of new products or technologies. The winners will also need to develop robust innovation processes that can harness traditional Asian strengths in rapid commercialization and in learning from the world, rather than following the "lone-gun inventor in a garage" model of innovation and entrepreneurship idolized in Silicon Valley.

Creating Strong Asian Brands

Companies will need to create strong Asian brands that are capable of capturing higher value added and building customer loyalty. At the same time, they must leverage the distinctive heritage of Asian service culture and Asian companies' agility and capacity for learning in ways that will shortcut traditional brand-building processes, which normally take decades of massive investment.

Extending and Integrating International Networks

Extending and integrating international networks will be necessary to enable companies to compete as unified, pan-Asian businesses rather than as isolated national champions or a set of loosely connected subsidiaries. The challenge is to go beyond replicating the kinds of international structures Western multinationals have already built around the world, to create distinctive, "Asian-style" multinationals that utilize Asian expertise in assembling and managing networks of alliances, to continue to uniquely align corporate objectives with the goals of Asian governments, and to overcome the disadvantage of being latecomers by shortcutting the standard process of internationalization in innovative ways.

Reshaping the Asian Playing Field by Driving Industry Consolidation

Companies will need to drive industry consolidation using mergers and acquisitions to move from today's fragmented Asian industries to a more efficient structure with improved profit potential. In rising to this challenge, tomorrow's winners will successfully use consolidation to gain control of emerging choke points or mountain passes along the chain of activities between inputs and final users. They will also need to approach the problem of multiple acquisitions and their integration more in the spirit of alliance than of takeover, bringing to bear traditional Asian skills in networking.

Meeting these challenges will require much more than incremental improvement. For many Asian-owned companies winning in Asia's next round will demand major upheavals in both their strategy and organization. For these companies, the trick will be to address these challenges by leveraging their distinctive Asian heritage and capabilities rather than destroying them in quest for change. Nor will Western multinationals operating in Asia be immune. The challenges of Asian next-round competition will call for a strategic rethink among Western companies as they are forced to deal with increasingly formidable competition from leading local rivals who challenge conventional wisdom by building a new and distinctive type of Asian multinational.

Winning in Asia

As we explore the strategies that will win in Asia in the new millennium in the remainder of this book, chapter 2 begins by exploring in greater detail what part of the heritage of Asian companies and the subsidiaries of Western multinationals in the region can be leveraged as strengths in the next round of competition and what aspects need to be jettisoned as deadweight baggage from the past.

The next three chapters explore the key strategic challenges that are ahead: in achieving a step-change in productivity across a broad front, in rising to the challenge of building improved innovation capabilities in Asian companies, and in shortcutting the process of building new and powerful Asian brands that leverage Asia's traditional service, artistic, and cultural traditions.

In chapter 6 we explore the issues faced by companies seeking to build strong international networks from an Asian base or to weld a ragbag of existing subsidiaries in Asia into a unified, efficient Asian business. Chapter 7 examines the potential for leading companies to reshape the Asian playing field by using mergers and acquisition to drive industry consolidation.

Finally, chapter 8 draws these threads together, laying out a set of blueprints for winning strategies in the next round of Asian competition and how successful Asian companies and multinationals in Asia will both need to look different from in the past.

Chapter 2

Asia's Business Heritage: Benefits and Baggage

Faced with the worst glut in global cargo shipping capacity for a decade in 2002, Chang Yung-fa, chairman of Taiwan's Evergreen Group, started placing orders for thirty huge, new container carriers. Many of his rivals at the so-called "Box Club" meetings (gatherings of the International Council of Containership Operators) began to wonder aloud whether he was beginning to lose his grip on reality. Expressing frustration that his Asian rivals seemed to be playing by different rules, one Western former shipping executive exclaimed: "The Chinese and the Koreans are nuts. The whole container-shipping industry is a brothel of bad business practices!"[1]

But Chang begs to differ. As he pointed out in a recent interview: "If taken in a global context then it's true that there is overcapacity, but if you take it in the context of an individual carrier, then the scenario is very different. Evergreen needs new builds because our cargo far exceeds the number of slots we can offer."[2] This is not the first time that Chang has adopted a strategy that many of his Western competitors viewed as unorthodox. In 1991, as airlines' losses mounted, he launched EVA Airways, Taiwan's second airline. Over the first three years EVA Airways lost a total of $90 million. But by the fourth year it broke even, and in 2002 it made post-tax profits of $72 million. Meanwhile, as commentators around the world spoke of the benefits of focus and transparent corporate structures, an Evergreen spokesperson observed: "In the early stages, EVA lost a lot of money and so it had to be supported by the group. Now shipping is not doing so well, so it's only right that EVA should pay something back."[3] Evergreen maintains what some analysts have described as a "fantastically complex web of cross-shareholdings."[4] It runs its ships with a crew of around fifteen, compared with an industry average of twenty-one, and for many years ran much of its fleet at slower speeds, cutting fuel consumption close to half the rate used by competitors. Despite being a Taiwanese company, Evergreen handles a large volume of cargoes from mainland China, flying the foreign flags of its subsidiaries: Italian-based Lloyd Triestino and the British-flagged Hatsu line. It has also carved out new niches on routes to Africa and South America, markets many of its competitors dismiss.

Evergreen illustrates some of the distinctive characteristics of Asia's business heritage and the way it influences the strategies adopted by Asian firms, from acting with the acumen of street traders in seeking out and exploiting new opportunities, through complex linkages between different businesses, to risk assessments that often appear contrarian to Western observers. As a launching pad for success in the next round of competition in Asia, this heritage contains both elements that can be leveraged for future advantage and baggage of the past that needs to be jettisoned. Distinguishing which part of Asian business heritage falls into each of these categories, separating the strengths from the handicaps against the background of the new competitive environment, will be critical. The winners in tomorrow's Asia will be companies that are able to combine traditional Asian strengths with the best business practices that the rest of the world has to offer.

This has obvious implications for what Asian companies need to change versus where they will need to redouble their efforts to exploit time-honored Asian capabilities and mind-sets in new ways. But multinationals too will have to change the way they adapt their global approach to Asia: Some of the adaptations they made to accommodate yesterday's Asia will need to be unwound. There will also be new opportunities to exploit their overseas experience in ways that were thwarted by the realities of Asian competition (such as the barriers between national markets) in the past. The next round of competition will also bring new and extended opportunities for multinationals to learn from Asia and to apply the distinctive knowledge they gain in Asia to their operations across the globe. But to achieve any of this, multinationals will need to mentally separate the benefits from the baggage of Asian business heritage using the yardstick of tomorrow's new competitive environment.

In this chapter, therefore, we begin that separation, seeking to answer the question: What aspects of Asia's business heritage can be leveraged as a source of advantage in the next round of competition and what aspects will need to be abandoned as relics of the past?

Asia's Business Heritage Matters

Some readers may immediately retort: But aren't virtually all the peculiarities of Asian business heritage soon to be relics? Some have argued that, whatever held true in the past, the new Asia will be forced to conform to the international, or even the U.S., model of business. What we have called heritage, they maintain, is little more than the result of intransigent governments, vested interests, and crony capitalists slowing down the pace of "reform." They cite the Asian crisis and the power of "economic fundamentals" as evidence to support their case.

I believe that this view reflects in large part the desire of those, like the container-shipping executive we quoted above, who want the world to play by their rules. To see its fallacy, look no further than the evolution of Japan. In three decades following World War II, it rose to become the second largest economy on earth. And in the immediate postwar era, U.S. policy makers helped "remake" many of Japan's core economic and political institutions using an American blueprint. Yet as we enter the twenty-first century, few would argue that the competitive landscape in Japan approximates a free and open market in which the business heritage of the key players is of little consequence.

Today, much of the Japanese competitive landscape is still dominated by the heritage of powerful corporate players such as Mitsubishi,

Mitsui, Sumitomo, and Toyota, to name just a few. Many of these corporations still sit at the core of groups of loosely associated companies, known as *keiretsu*, or networks of firms located together in a single city. Immediately after World War II, the ancestors of these corporate groups, the *zaibatsu*, were dismantled by U.S. caretakers in the quest for a more competitive market. But within a decade they reappeared in a new form. Certainly the ties between keiretsu members have been weakening in recent years, but the heritage of doing business based on a complex web of relationships lives on. In 2003, for example, Toyota made an $85 million capital injection into the general trading company Tomen, which was facing bankruptcy, and subscribed a further $255 million to preference shares issued by Tomen's main creditor bank, the troubled UFJ. At face value, investing in a failing general trader and its banker isn't an obvious strategic move for Toyota, the world's third largest automaker. So what was the connection between these three companies? The answer: They are all part of a tight network of relationships in the city of Nagoya.[5] So much for convergence toward America's brand of free-market capitalism.

Yes, the Asian environment is undergoing a sea change. But, as the rest of corporate Asia adjusts to these new realities and continues along the path of economic growth, it is no more likely to mimic the U.S. market ideal than has been the case in Japan.

Nor should it! It makes no sense for Asian companies to play the same game, with the same rules, as their counterparts in the United States or Europe. To do so would be to surrender the important advantages they can gain by leveraging traditional Asian business strengths. Similarly, it doesn't make sense for multinationals to ignore Asia's business heritage: Not only would this hamper their abilities to adapt to the next round of Asian competition, it would also close the door on learning from Asia and their chance to leverage these insights globally.

Untangling the Roots of Asia's Business Heritage

Like the diverse Asian continent itself, Asia's business heritage is a complex patchwork, colored by the different cultures and experiences of a fairly disparate group of players. Identifying the common threads that will either need to be discarded or leveraged into future competitive advantage is no easy task. Those common threads do exist, but to unearth them and to ensure they are seen in proper context, we need to trace back to the different "gene pools" from which today's Asian companies have emerged and to understand where they differ, where they have converged, and the characteristics they share.

By studying the backgrounds of the people who built today's Asian companies, those who lead them, and the environments that shaped their evolution, seven corporate gene pools can be identified:

- *Overseas Chinese corporations*—companies controlled by Chinese expatriates located in countries like Indonesia, Malaysia, Thailand, Singapore, Taiwan, and Hong Kong.

- *Korean chaebol*—the large conglomerates that are at last reemerging from the trauma of the 1997 Asian crisis to redefine themselves as a major force both in Korea and beyond.

- *Mainland Chinese companies*—powerful corporates emerging from the People's Republic of China, some majority owned or controlled by agencies of the Chinese government (even though they may be listed on the Hong Kong exchange or other international stock exchanges) and a growing band of Chinese private companies.

- *National champions*—companies that have built sizable operations within the borders of one Asian country, traditionally exploiting their local advantages, but who are now looking beyond their borders.

- *Japanese corporates*—established as major players in the region with formidable technology and systems, seeking a large share of Asia's growth in the face of stagnation at home.

- *Singaporean GLCs (government linked companies)*—companies listed on the Singaporean stock exchange, and sometimes on overseas exchanges, where the government retains a controlling or significant equity stake through its holding company Temasek Holdings.

- *Bumiputera companies*—companies run by indigenous Malays, who enjoy an especially close relationship with their government by virtue of their key role in policies designed to balance the business dominance of the ethnic Chinese in Malaysia.

An analysis of each of these roots of Asian business heritage allows us not only to define the key shared elements of that heritage but also to begin to identify opportunities to leverage it in the future.

Overseas Chinese Corporations

Ethnic Chinese entrepreneurs have been present throughout Asia for many centuries. Mass waves of Chinese migration occurred, however, in the mid-nineteenth century (when over three million people left the Fujian and Guangdong Provinces of China alone); through the early years of the twentieth century, when the so-called deficit economy in many Chinese villages compelled starving families and much of an impoverished nation to seek alternative livelihoods; and through the exodus of millions more during the time of the Communist Revolution in 1949.[6]

Today these Chinese emigrants, and their descendants, have become the major force in business throughout much of Asia including Singapore, Hong Kong, and Taiwan (where they are the dominant ethnic group) and in Malaysia, Indonesia, and arguably in Thailand and the Philippines (four countries in which they are an ethnic minority, sometimes a tiny minority). Their influence permeates every level of business, from the village shop, through subcontractors and medium-sized firms, to business empires with billions of U.S. dollars of sales—such as Cheong Kong/Hutchison Whampoa, Wheelock, and Henderson Land in Hong Kong; Hong Leong and Fraser & Neave in Singapore; Chareon Pokphand and Bangkok Bank in Thailand; Salim and Sinar Mas in Indonesia; Kerry Group and Genting in Malaysia; J G Summit and SM Prime Holdings in the Philippines; and Formosa Plastics and Evergreen in Taiwan.

Even the largest of these companies (most of which are publicly listed) are still today controlled by a single entrepreneur or a small family group. Li Ka-shing of Cheong Kong, Kwek Leng Beng of Hong Leong, the Sophonpanich family of Bangkok Bank, Liem Sioe Liong of Salim, Robert Kwok of the Kerry Group, the Sy family of SM Prime Holdings, Y.C. Wang of Formosa Plastics, are just a few examples.

The experiences and beliefs of these individuals remain a powerful influence on the strategies of these companies and remain deeply embedded in their organization structures and corporate cultures. These structures and cultural characteristics also result in many of these companies being largely invisible to foreigners or casual observers. They seldom appear on *Fortune* 500–type lists because they are not structured as a single company or consolidated group. Instead, they comprise a complex network of controlling interests and cross-shareholdings.

Take the example of Taiwan's Far Eastern Group, whose $5 billion corporate network comprises an inner core controlled by members of the Hsu family around which is a network of eight listed companies and dozens of subsidiaries and associates linked through a patchwork of cross-holdings and controlling interests. Such structures have the advantage of maximizing the family's reach and the diversification of their interests for any given quantum of family equity, as well as enabling external capital to be injected with minimum loss of control.

What some observers have described as "lack of transparency" therefore runs deep. In some cases, this characteristic arises from a desire on the part of overseas Chinese entrepreneurs, conscious of their position as members of an ethnic minority, to avoid conspicuous power or wealth. But it also provides their first key advantage in the battle for Asian markets: Competitors tend to underestimate their resources and capabilities. For their opponents, who can't get a clear picture of their rival, it's a bit like jousting with a ghost.

The importance of such traditional approaches in overseas Chinese companies can easily be obscured by the veneer of modern business. Despite international commodity and foreign exchange traders sitting behind banks of computers, enterprise accounting software, listings on the world's stock exchanges, and shiny annual reports, six rules of thumb that have more to do with heritage and individual beliefs than U.S.-style management and strategic planning continue to dominate the decision making among most overseas Chinese companies:

- *"Informal networks are to be preferred over arm's-length transactions."* Individuals who had left their homeland for an unfamiliar environment naturally turned first to informal networks to get themselves established: kin networks, clan, occupational and trade guilds, or dialect groups (e.g., Hakka or Chiu Chow). As they got started and grew, they used informal family and kin networks to recruit staff and business partners; these recruits were likely to be more reliable and predictable than outsiders who would not be subject to social

control by an extended family or group. Overseas Chinese companies have therefore been built on tight networks of loyal and committed individuals and external partners around a corporate/family
leader who believes in his personal judgment and charisma in a kind
of "benevolent paternalism." Sanctions for failure to make good on
agreements come from being "blacklisted" rather than legal
redress—a powerful force since unreliability or dishonesty rebounds
not only on the individual but on the entire family or clan.[7]

- *"It's not what you know but how fast you can learn."* Arriving in a
  new country as a *sinkheh* (newcomer) from a village in China, it is
  obviously not what you know when you land that is going to make
  you successful. What counts is how well and how fast you learn. This
  thinking continues to permeate overseas Chinese business strategies.
  This means they are concerned with continually learning new competencies; thus, a deal will be markedly more attractive if it promises
  to add to the firm's stock of knowledge. This learning philosophy
  also means these companies are willing to go into new areas of
  business where they don't currently have the full set of competencies
  but believe they can learn what they need to know faster than their
  rivals.

- *"Commercialization rules."* Most of the overseas Chinese companies
  are still effectively controlled by individuals whose training was
  firmly grounded in the nitty-gritty of business. This background
  leads the owners of these companies to emphasize hard-edged
  commercialization of new technologies, ideas, and systems as the
  key to success. While inventive people or those with technical
  knowledge and specialist skills are valued, their status and contribution is always judged in terms of commercial impact. Among senior
  management, the qualities of loyalty, reliability, knowledge of the
  company's basic values, and commercial acumen (sometimes
  referred to as "knowing the smell of money") are prized—a fact that
  reinforces intense focus on commercialization and the expertise to
  make it happen.

- *"Better to be always first than always right."* Most overseas Chinese
  companies have been built on constant adaptation and reaction to
  their business environments rather than on single-minded pursuit

of a grand product or market vision. The founders were resourceful in finding opportunities for arbitrage and trading, sometimes working as middlemen between people in their ethnic network and European colonists or Western buyers (as in Malaysia, Singapore, and Indonesia). They tend to see business as a series of deals rather than as minutely planned, long-term campaigns. Speed in decision making is seen as critical. The Singaporean entrepreneur, Kwek Hong Png, summed up this common sentiment: "Your ability to judge the business situation is very important. Once I am clear about a business deal, I will say 'OK, go ahead, proceed.' There is no need to discuss further. To succeed you have to be able to make judgment. You have to tell yourself that the opportunity is rare—if you postpone your decision once, then twice, the opportunity will soon be lost."[8]

Behind this behavior lies an approach to managing uncertainty that is at variance with Western textbooks on analyzing and managing risk. This approach has three elements. First is the idea that moving fast puts time on your side—time to make mistakes and to learn from them. As one CEO put it, "When you go in early you're not always right, but you have time to correct. If you're a latecomer you have to 'hit a hole in one.' There isn't any time for detours and mistakes, unless you get it right the first time you'll never catch up."[9] The second idea is that, when an opportunity is only beginning to emerge, it is more feasible to start with a "low-cost bet." Later on when the market is established and competitors are lining up to come in, the risks associated with each dollar of investment may have gone down but the stakes required to play have often gone up. When both of these aspects are factored in, it's far from clear that the risk is reduced by waiting. A third idea is that the key to managing risk is to limit the "worst-case" scenario rather than lavishing attention on trying to predict the most likely, "average" outcome. For Western-trained managers brought up on risk-adjusted net present value, this idea of simply putting a floor under the nightmare scenario and then stepping into the dark might be an anathema.

- *"Control the bottlenecks in the chain."* Behind every product or service lies a chain of activities, stretching from raw materials of unprocessed information, through creation of the key product

components or service packages, distribution, and customer inter-
faces. Along this chain there are bottlenecks, the proverbial "mountain passes" of the activity chain where control is concentrated in a
handful of companies. These "passes" or "bottlenecks" may be represented by activities requiring proprietary technologies or specialized
skills, distribution networks, or raw materials in limited supply.
Those companies that control the passes have the leverage to command a high share of the total profit available in the chain. This
leverage was especially great in Asia's last round of competition as
rapid growth built up pressure on the bottlenecks. Historically these
bottlenecks in Asia were in the supply of key components. That is
why companies such as Taiwan's Acer computer began by focusing
on manufacturing motherboards, leaving the assembly to local
competitors. When the bottleneck moved to efficient logistics,
customization, and "just-in-time" delivery, Acer shifted its focus to
controlling the new bottleneck. In the next round of competition
the bottleneck will move yet again, this time to elements like proprietary technologies, brand building, and systems.

• *"Modern tools and technologies can coexist with traditional social
relationships and notions of service."* This overlap gives overseas
Chinese companies a high degree of adaptability to different circumstances and local environments. Many of the overseas Chinese
companies have aggressively introduced the latest technology,
rationalized and restructured their administrative and compensation structures, and even moved to U.S.-style budgeting and financial reporting systems. Hand in hand with this modernization,
however, they have continued to reinforce the family model (bringing only selected outsiders into their core network of relations),
building mutual reciprocity, and reaffirming *ganqing* ("feeling for
each other") as the basis of business relationships. This has led to
"traditional Chinese" management coexisting with modern, Western
management techniques. Singapore entrepreneur Lau Ing Woon
explained this mix this way: "We are fairly modernized. Each of my
family members has clear responsibilities. We have an authority
chart, defining who is the president, manager, and other positions.
In Singapore two brothers are in the same company; one other in
our Malaysian company and three others in Indonesia. Therefore

seven of us bothers are allocated to different places, each person occupying a specific position doing specific jobs."[10] Comfort with this coexistence has also enabled some overseas Chinese companies such as Shangri-la Hotels and Banyan Tree to successfully combine traditional Asian notions of service with modern information technology (IT) infrastructure and systems to create unique service experiences for customers.

Some have argued that as the next generation of overseas Chinese business families take over, many trained in Western business schools, these behaviors will be upended.[11] But there is little evidence of this. Look at companies like the Lippo Group, where day-to-day management has shifted to James and Stephen Riady, sons of the overseas Chinese businessman Lee Mo Tie (who later took the Indonesian name Mochtar Riady). The new generation is certainly introducing Western management tools more rapidly, including sophisticated financial management techniques, but these are absorbed into the existing approach to business rather than supplanting it.

This business heritage creates both strengths and weaknesses in overseas Chinese companies facing the next round of Asian competition.[12]

Benefits and Baggage in the Heritage of Overseas Chinese Companies

Benefits. Among the strengths of traditional overseas Chinese business practices and strategies that can be leveraged into competitive advantage in the next round of competition are: expertise in making and managing alliances with a network of parties; a focus on rapid learning; capabilities in commercialization of new ideas and innovations; controlling emerging bottlenecks arising in tomorrow's growth; combining Asian service traditions with modern technologies, and adaptability to changing circumstances and local environments.

In leveraging these potential strengths, overseas Chinese companies enjoy an ability to move quickly and flexibly when they see an opportunity. Once a decision is made, they rapidly move into implementation—elaborate consensus building in the middle-management ranks is unnecessary because they act on direction from the top. These companies are also consummate deal makers. But behind each deal are a carefully nurtured set of relationships with governments, partners, suppliers, and, often, customers that help mitigate the risk. Some of the old adages of the successful "rice trader" have also been projected into these modern business empires: Keep your inventory, assets, and cash turning fast; generate a margin on each transaction, but profit from volume.

Baggage. Unless reformed to create a new kind of company, however, some aspects of this business heritage will act as a handicap to winning in Asia in the next round. It often militates against long-term investment in intangible assets, so that as overseas Chinese companies face the changing environment we described in chapter 1, few have the benefits of strong brands or proprietary technologies. They are widely diversified across different businesses, which means that the resources they have available to invest in building deep, specialist competencies in each business are spread thinly. This isn't problematic when the key to success is availability of a competitively priced, standard product or service in volume. But when winning demands specialist, customized products and services that are clearly differentiated from competitors' offerings, continued lack of focus and depth of competence threatens to hold these companies back.

Finally, unreconstructed reliance on the clan structure, highly personalized management style, and local networks will hamper these companies extending and integrating their international networks. Like Lau Ing Woon, many overseas Chinese companies have expanded internationally by sending family members to build and run overseas subsidiaries in various locations. The result is integration at the strategic and senior management level, based on shared beliefs and family ties, but only limited integration at the day-to-day, operational level. In an increasingly integrated Asian and global economy, this limits both the degree of operations synergies these companies can achieve, as well as the efficient transfer and integration of systems across borders.

Korean Chaebol

Despite the painful restructuring that began in the aftermath of the 1997 Asian financial crisis and was finally brought to a head with the global economic slowdown in 2000–2001, the huge and diversified *chaebol* remain a dominant force both in the Korean economy and in a number of key Asian and global markets. Samsung, Korea's leading chaebol by 2002, had assets of $54 billion and produced the world's largest volume of both memory chips and flat panel displays; it ranked as the second largest maker of DVD (digital video disc) players and the third largest maker of mobile phones. LG Inc., with assets of $40 billion, was the world's largest producer of air conditioners and CD-ROM (compact disc read-only memory) drives. Even after the high-profile dismemberment of Hyundai, traditionally the number one ranking chaebol, its Hyundai Motor spin-off had assets of $28 billion in 2002 and had quadrupled its car exports to the United States since the crisis.[13]

Like the overseas Chinese companies, the way Korean chaebol approach business has been heavily shaped by their history, beginning with the Japanese occupation of Korea. During the occupation, Japanese corporations and individuals had accumulated significant assets in Korea. With the end of the Korean War in 1953, these sequestrated assets were distributed on favorable terms to a handful of promising Korean entrepreneurs, forming the bedrock of today's chaebol. Following a military coup in 1961, the new government turned to these companies to become the primary instruments of Korea's push to export-oriented industrialization. They were given preferential access to cheap loans from state-owned banks, licenses, and tax incentives, and raw material prices were controlled to boost their margins. They were encouraged to develop in capital-intensive, heavy industries like shipbuilding, steel, and chemicals and succeeded in carving out a substantial share of the world market in these sectors for Korea. In the mid-1970s, the chaebol were urged to create general trading companies (modeled on the Japanese Sogo Shosha or "trading houses" like Mitsu and Mitsubishi) and formed new networks of alliances to source raw materials and promote Korean exports. They moved aggressively into the international construction business in Asia and the Middle East. By the late 1970s, the chaebol had become so large and dominant that, for decades, the government felt it was impossible to curtail their activities without seriously damaging the Korean economy.

As they continued to grow, the chaebol became the ultimate in diversified conglomerates. Prior to the restructuring that began in 2000, almost all of the top chaebol had interests in the auto industry, semiconductors, shipbuilding, construction, chemicals, pharmaceuticals, health care, trading, home appliances, hotels and leisure, energy, telecommunications, retailing, real estate, and media. Authority was highly centralized within the chaebol in the hands of a founding family, despite their public listing.[14] Dilution had been minimized by using high levels of debt to finance expansion, with debt-equity ratios reaching 195 percent at Samsung and over 225 percent at Hyundai. Many of the subsidiaries had little experience of competing in the open market because intragroup transactions accounted for between 36 percent and 42 percent of total sales in the leading chaebol.

Strategic choices and key resource allocation decisions are made by the "President's Planning Office" in most of these companies. New businesses and major expansion projects are generally set up by members of the central management team. Yet there was little evidence of cooperation such as joint R&D across subsidiaries, which often vied for resources within the group.

Low cost of capital, by virtue of cheap state loans, and corporate rivalry between the chaebol for size and market share fueled heavy investment in projects with a low rate of return. In the space of a few years in the early 1990s, for example, the chaebol brought onstream six integrated petrochemical complexes, which more than doubled the total Korean capacity in ethylene at a time when world prices were declining and excess capacity was widely predicted. Such long-term, capital-intensive investments resulted in the chaebol becoming locked into a huge, but often low-yielding, asset base.[15]

Different History, Shared Characteristics

Despite their very different history, then, the Korean chaebol share a number of characteristics with their overseas Chinese corporate cousins. They are experienced managers of alliances and networks that include governments, banks, technology providers, and overseas suppliers and distributors. They have the same aversion to transparency and arm's-length transactions despite continual pressure from the international community.

While the chaebol tend to be highly centralized and have often been described as "militaristic" organizations, this gives them formidable capabilities in large-scale, rapid execution of the business projects they decide to pursue. They therefore have the speed, if not always the flexibility, characteristic of the overseas Chinese. They have a similarly strong focus on learning capabilities as a key source of competitive advantage and are able to quickly absorb new technology from outside Korea and to commercialize it in cost-competitive products churned out in large volumes. This capability is supported by access to a large pool of quality, relatively low-cost Korean engineers and scientists. The willingness of their staff and management to travel and work overseas for the chaebol, even in environments that might be considered hardship postings, has made them highly adaptable. As a result, they have proven skills in operating in developing markets from Eastern Europe and Russia to Latin America, and in less developed parts of Asia such as Vietnam and Myanmar.

Against these strengths their legacy has left the chaebol with significant gaps in their strategies, processes, and capabilities. Foremost among these is the fact that their approach to business does little to help differentiate their offerings. Although the chaebol have increased their R&D spending in recent years, their historic emphasis on learning rather than innovating leaves them heavily dependent on foreign sources of new technology (especially Japan). Their access to a supply of differentiated components is also limited because the chaebol have generally been poor at promoting the development of a strong network of Korean subcontractors outside their "in-house" suppliers. They have also tended to rely heavily on price as a competitive weapon in the global market—playing "catch-up" by offering well-established technology at prices below Japanese or Western competitors rather than competing through investment in brands and service excellence. This tendency has been aggravated by a mentality that put the quest for sheer size and volume ahead of profitability as the measure of success. As a result, their ability to invest in these capabilities as they enter the next round of Asian competition has been constrained by the burden of their massive, but low-yielding, asset bases.

Mainland Chinese Companies

A third distinct gene pool consists of companies with their home base in mainland China. As China scatters the "flying geese," they are becoming an increasingly powerful force in Asian competition.[16] This group comprises three subgroups:

- The more progressive of China's state-owned enterprises (SOEs), many of which have listings on foreign stock exchanges or so-called

Red Chip listings in Hong Kong. Examples include China Merchants (with interests in shipping, marine paints, industrials, and toll roads), the Chinese oil companies Sinopec and China National Offshore Oil Company (CNOOC), and China Ceroil (China National Cereals, Oils, and Foodstuffs Import and Export Corporation).

- The new breed of largely privately owned businesses in China, which have expanded aggressively and a number of which have become leaders in their industries, like the domestic appliance producer Haier Group, Legend Holdings with a 31 percent share of China's computer business by 2001, and Hope Group in agribusiness.[17]

- The Chinese government's overseas trade and investment vehicles—like China International Trade and Investment Corporation (CITIC), China Resources, and China Overseas Shipping Company (COSCO)—which have built significant subsidiaries overseas. China had already set up more than 5,000 companies in 130 countries, investing more than $6 billion by 1996.[18] CITIC's subsidiary, CITIC Pacific, for example, is the twelfth largest listed company in Hong Kong, with a 25 percent interest in Cathay Pacific Airlines and a huge property portfolio; COSCO is the world's largest container-shipping company by volume.

Whether public or private, these companies have a close relationship with national, provincial, and municipal governments in China. CITIC, for example, was established in 1979 with just twenty staff. But it had a mandate from China's State Council, to whom it directly reports, to import technology and managerial expertise, to conduct economic and technological cooperation in China and abroad, and to establish domestic and international financial and trading businesses. By 2002, it had an estimated $30 billion in assets, including interests in an Australian aluminum smelter and one of Canada's largest pulp and paper companies, as well as CITIC Pacific in Hong Kong.

CNOOC, meanwhile, enjoys the exclusive rights to Sino-foreign oil and gas joint ventures offshore. It is estimated to be one of the world's most efficient oil producers, with a breakeven at $9 per barrel. With licenses issued for the exploitation of only 50 percent of China's offshore oil area, the company has huge growth potential and plans to invest $4.3 billion in expansion by 2004.[19]

Among the private Chinese companies, Haier Group is a prime example of the new force of competition emerging from mainland China. It was founded in 1984 when entrepreneur Zhang Ruimin took over the failing Qingdao Refrigerator Factory from the state. Over the next fifteen years, Zhang was able to grow the company, both organically and through a further eighteen acquisitions, to sales of over $2.5 billion, which dominated the Chinese market in refrigerators, freezers, air conditioners, and washing machines. Its market share in these sectors not only outstripped its Chinese-owned rivals but also the subsidiaries and joint ventures of every foreign multinational operating in the market. Haier had built a strong brand and was acknowledged to have the best distribution system and sales force for white goods in China. Building off its strength in China, Haier also moved aggressively into export markets, distributing through 30,000 outlets in more than 100 countries, as well as establishing manufacturing facilities in the Philippines and in the U.S. state of South Carolina.[20] Haier's expansion was supported by the Chinese government (including access to bank loans and licenses) as part of efforts to encourage the emergence of Chinese-based multinationals.[21]

Relationship-Based Competitors, Backed by Commercial Focus and Rapid Learning

Given their important role in modernizing and restructuring the Chinese economy, these mainland Chinese companies clearly benefit from both direct and indirect support of the Chinese government, ranging from access to bank financing through exclusive licenses and lobbying power in negotiations such as China's entry into the World Trade Organization (WTO). Competing by building and leveraging relationships and alliances is their natural predilection. They also benefit from their huge Chinese home market, the scale of which gives them negotiating power in sourcing everything from raw materials through to technology licenses—bargaining power they are not ashamed to harness in the service of driving down their already low costs.

Contrary to some of the stereotypes of firms emerging from a socialist state, the leading mainland Chinese companies are extremely commercial, constantly striving to discover ways of reengineering products and processes to make them cheaper—a skill honed in what has become a fiercely competitive Chinese domestic market over the last decade. They are also fast learners, the best of which are rapidly not only mastering advanced production technology but also the art of building effective sales and distribution networks, at least in the Chinese environment. Rapid learning, for example, propelled China's Baosteel to number two among the world's steel producers in terms of operating performance (measured in terms of twenty specific criteria, including efficiency and workforce skills, by a U.S. steel consultancy).[22]

But like their overseas Chinese and chaebol counterparts, mainland Chinese companies also suffer from the baggage of unwillingness and inexperience in developing proprietary technology and, with a few exceptions such as Haier, in building resilient brands. Meanwhile, they are even further behind in developing the mind-sets and skills, structures and systems necessary to support the creation of an efficient and integrated international network that goes beyond passive investment in foreign assets.

National Champions

Despite diverse ethnic roots, national champions all share one key feature: They have built powerful competitive positions in home markets that, either for reasons of market structure or institutional barriers, have been largely isolated from cross-border competition.

Take the example of Jollibee, which dominates the fast-food business in the Philippines. Despite competition from McDonald's for over fifteen years, it maintains stronger brand awareness in the Philippines than its global rival and has some 600 outlets (30 percent more than McDonald's). Starting from its base in ice cream parlors, Jollibee entered the fast-food business with McDonald's look-alike facilities and kitchens. Their secret of success was a product range better adapted to the Filipino palate than the global hamburger, with many more varieties of chicken and garlic and soy sauce in the burgers.

Not surprisingly, national champions are particularly strong in businesses like food or services, where subtle local adaptation is critical and markets tend to be localized so that domestic firms can prosper, or in industries that have been heavily protected by tariffs. Good examples are San Miguel or Ayala Corporation (respectively the largest beer, spirits, and food supplier and one of the biggest property developers in the Philippines) and Indonesia's car and motorbike maker, Astra (now controlled by the Cycle and Carriage Group of Singapore).

Potentially Valuable Traditions, but Locally Imprisoned

Like their cousins in other Asian gene pools, national champions are skilled in building and managing relationships and alliances, as well as in rapidly learning from partners. These skills have their roots in unmatched relationships with their local governments, but they have been applied to the alliances with other companies from Asia and elsewhere to facilitate entry into new businesses and to strengthen existing ones. A good example is Ayala's partnership with Singapore's SingTel and Germany's Deutsche Telecom to develop its Globe Telecom subsidiary, which has brought new capital, technology, and international marketing experience into the business.

Many of these companies have also embraced and built on the strong service traditions of their local culture, combining these adeptly, as we saw in Jollibee, with modern business practices and processes imported from abroad. Likewise they have demonstrated strong capabilities in importing foreign technologies and profitably adapting and commercializing them in their local environment.

But relying on this business heritage alone is unlikely to be sufficient to compete in the new Asian environment of intensified cross-border competition. Unless they reinvent themselves, Asia's national champions risk being left stranded, lacking the mind-sets, structures, and capabilities necessary to leverage their strengths internationally, yet facing increasing pressure from international players who are combining the benefits of scale and reach with an increasing capability to adapt their operations sensitively to local markets. The future may also bring a cruel reminder that being a leader in a protected national market doesn't mean your capabilities are world-class.

Again, Jollibee is a prime example. In its first phase of internationalization (from 1993–1997), Jollibee established 23 stores, scattered across 10 countries. Lacking the critical mass to gain customers' attention in each of these isolated markets, and with little scope for sharing local fixed costs among stores, each was operating at half the estimated minimum efficient scale. Moreover, Jollibee's business formula, so successful in the Philippines, proved poorly suited to a number of overseas markets. It has since adopted a more conservative international expansion, focusing on centers of Filipino expatriate population like Guam, Brunei, and the Middle East. But like other national champions, Jollibee still faces the risk of becoming boxed into a corner as Asian markets integrate and barriers to cross-border competition fall.

Japanese Corporates

Despite a seemingly chronic deflationary spiral in Japan itself, Japanese companies will continue to be key players in the Asian competitive game by virtue of their massive numbers, scale, and technological strength. Their wider influence increased as Japanese companies began to export to meet the rapidly growing demand in Asian markets in the 1980s and early 1990s. In the process they established powerful distribution networks across Asia for both finished products and high-specification intermediate inputs like chemicals and plastics. In a second phase they began to shift production to other Asian economies in the quest for lower-cost locations to undertake labor-intensive, relatively standardized parts of the value chain. Companies such as National-Panasonic, Fujitsu, and Sony, for example, all moved significant parts of their assembly processes to Taiwan and Southeast Asia and, more recently, to China. In parallel, many have built global sales and supply networks.[23]

It would be wrong to conclude, however, that the export prowess of Japanese companies and the spread of their manufacturing networks across Asia and beyond have turned them into cosmopolitan organizations. The way they do business still reflects the extreme centralization of decision making back in their head offices in Tokyo, Osaka, or Nagoya. Their strategies and modus operandi, therefore, continue to be heavily influenced by their Japanese heritage.

As a result, despite being further along the development curve than many of their Asian corporate sisters, Japanese companies share a number of common characteristics with the gene pools we have discussed above. They tend to compete through a network of allied companies rather than as individual firms. Historically this was through the zaibatsu and their successors, the keiretsu. But as some of these links have weakened, Japanese companies have established new networks of alliances to help them compete. Consider NTT DoCoMo's approach to developing its mobile telephony services. It began by establishing close alliances with what it describes as its "family of equipment suppliers" including Fujitsu, NEC, and Hitachi to ensure that equipment capability, technology, and handset supply kept up with its strategy for expanded services. It then went on to form relationships with IBM Japan and SAP Japan to explore mobile business solutions; with Hewlett-Packard (HP) to improve mobile multimedia delivery; a joint venture with Mitsui, NEC, and Nissan to develop car navigation systems; a strategic alliance with Coca-Cola Japan and trading house Itohchu to link mobile phones with vending machines; alliances with Sony and SEGA in mobile games; and a joint venture with Sakura bank in mobile e-payments, to name just a few of the more than thirty-five alliance networks NTT DoCoMo established between 2000 and 2002.[24] This predilection for alliances extends to working closely with governments both in Japan and elsewhere.

Like many of their Asian counterparts, Japanese companies also have a well-honed capacity to commercialize new technologies quickly. Recounting how Japan developed a lead in the use of carbon fiber in a wide range of applications, for example, one Japanese executive remarked : "[W]e were able to start quickly because we first deployed the new carbon material in a low-risk application, fishing rods, and worked up from there through learning by doing."[25] In the United States, he observed, the use of carbon fiber was pioneered in military jets—a high-risk application that meant experience was difficult to accumulate and diffusion of the technology to other applications was slow. Ask yourself why it was the Japanese that put so-called fuzzy logic in the humble washing machine to create products that were brimming with sensors and software and a capability to adjust automatically to different fabrics years ahead of their U.S. and European competitors.

Contrary to their stereotypes, Japanese companies have also proved to be highly innovative in some areas. True, they may not be the cradle of Nobel Prize–winning breakthroughs. But consider Total Quality Management, Total Productive Maintenance, and "Just-In-Time" supply chains—all arguably innovations with a more far-reaching impact than discoveries that grab the headlines. This is innovation "Asian style," where, as the head of R&D for another leading Japanese company put it, "We talk about 'discovery creativity' and 'applications creativity'; they are equally respected."[26]

Finally, Japanese companies often have the advantages of well-specified and minutely documented procedures that help them to deliver above-average quality and product performance and to rapidly build efficient manufacturing plants throughout Asia. They also enjoy the benefits of disciplined and well-qualified Japanese management cadres, many willing to work for the company throughout Asia, often in isolated locations with poor infrastructure. The downside, however, is that such tightly prescribed processes and mind-sets risk becoming inflexible baggage as they move into the next round of Asian competition. This problem will be aggravated in the future unless their headquarters start to loosen their viselike grip on decision making and allow for greater local autonomy.

Singaporean GLCs

Since Singapore became an independent country in 1965, the government has developed a stable of GLCs (government linked companies) that, while listed on the local stock exchange, are substantially owned and controlled by the state holding company, Temasek. Temasek draws its capital from Singapore's huge compulsory, state-run pension scheme to which employees contribute during their working life. By 2002, the combined market capitalization of listed companies within the Temasek portfolio stood at $40.3 billion and included companies ranging from the bank DBS to Keppel Corporation, SingTel, and Singapore Technologies and national icons such as Neptune Orient Lines and Singapore Airlines.

Far from the caricature of lumbering and inefficient state-run giants, most of these companies have proved formidable competitors in local, and sometimes international, markets. While they often take broad strategic direction from the government (such as encouragement to achieve technological self-reliance through increased R&D or to expand overseas), they are run largely free of day-to-day interference by politicians and civil servants by independent management and outside directors.

At the same time, Temasek's portfolio management has ensured that there is little competition or overlap between the GLCs (each GLC specializes in its own core area) and a historic focus on growing operations in Singapore (to create local jobs and value-added) rather than expanding overseas. As a result, the business heritage of the GLCs incorporates a dangerous dichotomy. Within the GLCs sits well-developed technocratic competence in the full range of functional areas from financial management to operations and marketing. Along with this they have a lack of familiarity with, and in some cases even distaste for, cutthroat competition as well as inexperience in international markets and in understanding the vagaries of the business and regulatory infrastructure elsewhere in Asia.

The downside of this heritage has come to light since the Singapore government began in the late 1990s to encourage the GLCs to expand internationally, with the long-term goal of building significant, Singapore-based multinationals.[27] A flurry of deals followed, including SingTel's acquisition of Australia's Telstra; DBS's acquisition of banks in Singapore, Thailand, Hong Kong, and the Philippines; NOL's acquisition of American President Lines; and Singapore Airlines' purchase of a 49 percent stake in Virgin Atlantic Airways. The results have often been disappointing, suggesting the need for strengthened capabilities in internationalization.

Bumiputera Companies

The Bumiputera (literally "sons of the soil") companies are those controlled by ethnic Malays. They form a separate competitive force on the Asian scene by virtue of their close ties with government policies designed to redress the disproportionate control of business by the ethnic Chinese in Malaysia.[28] The support provided to these companies is analogous to what in the United States is sometimes described as positive discrimination.

In 1971 the Malaysian government enacted its "New Economic Policy" aimed at encouraging the development of Malay-owned businesses. This was partly in response to the 1969 ethnic riots that led to many deaths and to the fact that an estimated 62 percent of corporate assets were in foreign hands (a legacy of colonial rule), while ethnic Chinese and Indians controlled a further 34 percent, with only 4 percent in Bumiputera hands.

British colonial businesses, such as Sime Darby and Guthrie Corporation, were acquired by the Malaysian Government Trading Corporation (*Perbadanan Nasional Berhad*), in Sime Darby's case by buying a controlling interest on the London Stock Exchange. When they were subsequently listed (Sime Darby was listed on the Kuala Lumpur Stock Exchange in 1979), control was transferred to Bumiputera entrepreneurs.[29] Other budding Bumiputera enterprises were assisted through preferential award of licenses, government contracts, and access to finance and information.

Take the example of Renong, one of Malaysia's largest conglomerates. Until late 2001, when it was effectively renationalized, Renong was controlled by Malay businessman Halim Saad. Halim began his career at a state-run property company headed by Daim Zainuddin, who later became the country's finance minister. Striking out on his own in 1985, Halim gained control of United Engineers Malaysia (UEM), a troubled machine equipment maker. Three years later, UEM won the $2.4 billion build-operate-transfer contract to construct one of Malaysia's biggest infrastructure projects: the north-south tollway. By 1990 Halim took control of Renong, backing UEM into the company along with a string of businesses owned by the ruling party, the United Malays National Organisation. Helped by the daily cash flows from the tollway and borrowings of over $5 billion, Renong built a group of thirteen listed companies in telecommunications, construction, hotels, banking, media, and oil and gas.[30] Renong proved unstoppable until its patron, Daim Zainuddin, left the government in 2001.

Technology Resources Industries (TRI), run by Tajudin Ramli, is another Bumiputera company that was given a boost from the Malaysian government, which awarded TRI with one of the first licenses for provision of mobile telecommunications services. Its market capitalization rapidly increased to over $2 billion, enabling it to buy a controlling interest in Malaysia Airlines for $720 million in 1994 (which it subsequently sold back to the government in 2001).

An obvious aspect of the Bumiputera companies' heritage is their reliance on the preferential treatment, and sometimes monopoly rights, they receive as part of government policy. Some of these companies, like Sime Darby, have moved beyond that narrow reliance on government preference to develop a depth of management skills and systems to add to their connections and strong balance sheet. This transformation has enabled Sime Darby to successfully extend its business throughout Asia and Australia and across a wide variety of industries from plantations to heavy equipment, manufacturing, and property development. But others, like Renong and TRI, have not been able to broaden their base of competitive advantage much beyond the initial preferences they were awarded. TRI, for example, notched up three straight years of losses and a mountain of debt before it was forced to sell its controlling interest in Malaysia Airlines back to the government (at almost triple the prevailing share price).[31] Meanwhile, when Renong faced bankruptcy during the 1997 Asian crisis, Halim Saad engineered a deal for UEM to inject cash into Renong for a 32 percent stake. He agreed to buy the stake back for around $700 million in July 2001. When he failed to make the payment, the government ousted Halim and renationalized both Renong and UEM by purchasing outstanding shares to the value of $974 million—a move that came within one week of the resignation of Halim's long-term mentor, finance minister Daim Zainuddin.

Those Bumiputera companies with a continued reliance on preferential treatment and local connections and without a broader set of competitive advantages have been unable to successfully expand internationally. To grow, they have therefore diversified across industries within their home country, often resulting in loss of focus and an inability to build deep operational competence in particular businesses. This makes them vulnerable to specialized competitors with world-class technology, systems, and processes in the next round of Asian competition. Moreover, being duty-bound to act as a virtual arm of the government when called upon can also impose costs that will hamper their ability to compete in the next round. A number of observers have suggested that the investments of Bumiputera companies include unprofitable "trophy" projects that have more to do with national policy than business. When the government decided it wanted to acquire TRI to maintain its assets in Malaysian hands, for example, it persuaded another Bumiputera company, Telekom Malaysia, to act as the buyer.

Latent Potential in Asia's Business Heritage

The gene pools that have shaped Asia's business heritage are obviously diverse. But our analysis also makes clear that there are a number of widely shared capabilities, strategies, and mind-sets that characterize a broadly "Asian approach" to competition. This approach includes positive elements that Asian companies can potentially harness to improve their chances of winning the next round of competition as well as baggage from the past that must be jettisoned if these characteristics are not to handicap Asian companies in the changed environment that is now emerging.

The positive features of Asian business heritage that we have seen repeated across the gene pools we discussed include:

- *Skill in building and managing networks of alliances with companies offering complementary resources and capabilities, suppliers, governments, and even competitors.* In the past, many of these alliances were aimed at reducing risk, maintaining family or personal control, and currying preferential treatment. But this heritage has latent potential to be redeployed to help speed up the rate of productivity improvement and to contribute to innovation and brand building. These skills will also have a role to play in forging a new route to internationalization, smoothing the path to industry consolidation, and winning over governments that fear loss of national sovereignty or owners who see loss of control when a company is acquired outright as a sign of defeat.

- *Capability for rapid learning and the practical application of new ideas.* In the past this capability was largely directed toward "catch up." In the future it will need to be directed toward innovation, finding ways to improve productivity across a broader front, building new brands, and shortcutting the traditional process of international expansion.

- *Speed, flexibility, and first-mover opportunism.* These capabilities have been accumulated through the deal-making, "rice-trader" approach through which many Asian companies grew and diversified. Provided they can be repurposed, these same qualities will have a key role in the next round of competition if they can be redeployed to help exploit opportunities to drive industry consolidation and to speed up cross-border expansion and the organizational restructuring necessary to support it.

- *Commercialization know-how.* This strength has been a recurring theme across many of the Asian gene pools we examined above. Historically it was mostly focused on the task of commercializing technologies, products and services already proven elsewhere in the world in Asian markets. In tomorrow's environment this capability can be extended to leapfrog competition by commercializing and scaling up innovations sourced from overseas as ideas and early protypes, not just offerings already proven elsewhere. These same skills can also be deployed to increase the tempo of "Asian-style innovation" where creativity is focused on developing new applications and processes, not just on blue-sky discovery.

- *Identification and control of choke points.* As mentioned in chapter 1, this strategy was common to the success of many Asian companies in Asia's rapid growth phase where capacity bottlenecks frequently emerged. Since the 1997 financial crisis, however, a chronic capacity glut has rendered it ineffective. But in the next round of competition, new potential choke points will arise, not in basic manufacturing capacity but more likely in the opportunity to profit from controlling key technologies, distribution channels, and brands. To take advantage of these opportunities will require similar skills but a new mind-set about where to look for future choke points.

- *Service traditions.* Recall that leveraging strong Asian service traditions combined with modern technology is an already established capability, especially among today's "national champions" and the "overseas Chinese" companies. In the future, companies that can harness these service traditions will enjoy the advantage of a distinctive base from which to build tomorrow's brands in an environment where creating and communicating differentiation is increasingly critical for success.

- *Adaptability.* A final hallmark that spanned many of the Asian corporate gene pools examined above was adaptability both to rapidly changing circumstances and to subtle local differences in consumer behavior, competition, and government objectives, even when this required strategies that Western observers viewed as highly unorthodox. This heritage can have an important role in winning in the next round of Asian competition. However, it will need to be parlayed into a capability to rapidly and effectively adjust to new geographic environments while reaping the synergies available through integration as successful cross-border expansion and industry consolidation become critical aspects of the competitive playing field.

Along with these potential strengths of the Asian business heritage that can be leveraged to create future advantage, our assessment highlights some of the mind-sets and habits formed in the past that will need to be abandoned. These include:

- *Overcentralization of decision making.* Overcentralized decision making is already hampering international expansion by thwarting the transformation of Asian companies into effective and efficient international organizations (the fact that Japanese companies still suffer from this malaise after decades demonstrates just how difficult it is for Asian companies to break this heritage).

- *A focus on size and asset accumulation, rather than productivity.* This is likely to undermine profitability following the the end of "rent collection" and militates against the step-change in total productivity necessary to establish a solid platform for competing in the new Asian environment.

- *Diversification driven by opportunism, rather than capability.* While higher levels of diversification may be justified by less developed and efficient Asian capital markets than exist in the United States and Europe, the widespread Asian heritage of extensive diversification starves individual business units of the resources necessary to develop deep, specialist capabilities.[32] This is likely to be increasingly damaging in a future environment that demands high levels of differentiation, innovation, and branding and the specialist capabilities to support them. Diversification also diverts capital away from international expansion by individual businesses and from investments designed to drive industry consolidation.

- *Underinvestment in intangible assets.* As we saw, the heritage of many Asian companies is to favor investment in hardware, manufacturing capacity, and property. But in the emerging Asian competitive environment described in chapter 1, it will be judicious investment in intangible assets—such as intellectual property, proprietary technologies and products, systems, and brands—that wins out.

- *Sheltering behind national barriers.* This repeated theme in Asian business heritage is one that increasing cross-border competition and the demise of national fiefdoms will render untenable in the future.

Leveraging the potential benefits of Asian heritage, combining these traditional strengths with world best practice, and jettisoning destructive baggage from the past to create a new breed of Asian company that is capable of winning in the next round clearly presents formidable challenges. These are addressed in the next five chapters. Before turning to those issues, however, a few words on the implications of Asian business heritage for Western multinationals who will also compete in Asia's next round are opportune.

Implications for Western Multinationals

In assessing the implications of Asia's business heritage for future competition, Western multinationals are faced with three key questions:

- In what ways will the strategies and structures Western multinationals put in place to compete in yesterday's Asian environment need to change to win in the next round? Western multinationals will, in a sense, need to reassess the suitability of their own heritage in Asia.

- What will be the right balance between exploiting their distinctiveness in Asia versus seeking to emulate and harness some of the traditional advantages of local companies?

- What can Western multinationals learn from Asia's business heritage that they can leverage elsewhere in the world through their global networks?

The precise answers will vary by industry and also depend on the way any particular multinational has evolved its Asian operations. A few generalizations, however, are possible.

First, most Western multinationals operating in Asia have optimized their operations to reflect the past fragmentation of Asia into discrete national markets. Barriers to trade, investment, and information exchange made it sensible to establish self-sufficient subsidiaries in each main market, whose primary links were back to headquarters, rather than to their Asian sisters. Multinationals will have to break the bonds of this heritage if they are to prosper in tomorrow's more economically integrated Asia.

Second, multinationals have tended to leverage only a very narrow set of Asia's traditional capabilities in the past; mainly in the areas of reliable, cost-efficient manufacturing and routine service operations such as running call centers. In the future the activities multinationals undertake in Asia, and the way they go about them, will need to be broadened to enable more of the traditional strengths of Asian business heritage (such as commercialization or the management of complex alliance networks identified above) to be harnessed. This will improve the odds of their subsidiaries winning in the new Asia and possibly globally. Some companies have already started to make this shift. Citibank, for example, has tapped into the experience of its Singaporean unit in commercializing new product concepts to develop, launch, and roll out innovative services around the world.

Third, most Western multinationals in Asia have been set up to be effective "teachers" rather than A-grade "learners." But in the future, Asia's potential as a source of distinctive knowledge and as a lead market in which to sense emerging consumer needs and changing customer behavior promises to be just as important as its attraction as a growing market for multinationals' existing products and services. Witness the fact that the global lead markets in use of broadband mobile telecommunications today are Japan and Korea. Meanwhile, some of the major innovations in the design and manufacture of mobile handsets (soon to become mobile terminals)are happening in China. Western multinationals will be at a disadvantage in winning the next round of competition in Asia if they are unable to reposition themselves to learn from Asia, as well as to teach.

For Asian companies and Western multinationals alike, the challenges of leveraging the strengths of Asia's business heritage into the future, combining this with world best practice, and jettisoning the baggage of the past to create new breeds of company capable of winning in Asia's next competitive round are formidable. It is to these challenges that we now turn.

Chapter 3

Stepping Up to the
Asian Productivity Challenge

Established in 1906, Li & Fung had long prospered as a traditional Chinese trading house, using its local knowledge and close relationships with suppliers and governments to mediate between Chinese suppliers of products like clothes and toys and U.S. and European retailers. By the late 1990s, its major customers had come to include The Limited Inc, Warner Brothers, Britain's John Lewis Partnership, and Spain's El Corte Ingles.[1] Against the standards of its competitors, both Western-owned companies (such as Jardine Matheson and Inchcape Buying Services) and a string of Chinese-owned rivals, it was regarded as efficient. But as the forces of globalization began to hit hard in the aftermath of the 1997 financial crisis, the brothers Victor and William Fung, who run the Hong Kong–listed company, realized that Li & Fung's productivity was too low, and its value-added too limited, to ensure continued success.

Since both Victor and William had studied at Harvard Business School (Victor subsequently joined its faculty before returning to Hong Kong), it might have been tempting to try to address the challenges of productivity and value-added simply by importing supply chain management software from the United States or by morphing the company into a "B2B" (business to business) portal. These options were dismissed as inadequate to win in the future Asia they saw emerging. Instead, the brothers decided to reshape the business into a new kind of company: one that would be able to revector cutting-edge U.S. technology to match the unique demands of Asian competition, while leveraging off the strengths of an organization that Victor described as being "rooted in Chinese values."[2] To achieve this feat they went back to first principles, asking themselves: "What would globalization mean for Asia?"

The key implication for Li & Fung, they decided, would be the emergence of the sort of co-specialization environment we described in chapter 1—an Asia where different suppliers focus on ever more specialized slices of the value chain, exchanging and recombining specialized materials, components, and services across borders in the course of assembling a final offering to the customer. Co-specialization, in turn, would mean an explosion in complexity: Supply chains that once consisted of five links would in the future have dozens, or even hundreds, of pieces that needed to be coordinated. Even a seemingly straightforward clothing order from a U.S. retailer, for example, would involve spinning, weaving, dyeing, zipper manufacture, sewing, and financing and accounting, all undertaken by specialist companies, involving different locations spanning every corner of Asia, and all having to dovetail with logistics, marketing, and design input provided by yet more specialists. The existing Asian logistics, coordination, and administrative processes would not be able to cope; productivity would plummet as a result.

A new, winning strategy emerged from these insights. It was based on the recognition that, as William Fung put it: "Somebody's got to pick up all these pieces and put them back together. There's always been a supply chain, but no management of it."[3] Superefficient manufacturing at each individual stage would no longer be sufficient to deliver cost-competitive products. The entire chain would need to be reengineered to deliver world-class productivity. This would require a dramatically improved coordination and a step-change in the efficiency of neglected "support activities" ranging from capacity planning to order taking and scheduling and an organizational structure and incentives that could help unlock knowledge in the heads of the army of people involved.

Li & Fung decided that its future lay in squarely facing this productivity challenge and driving out inefficiencies from Asia's supply chains. Of course, they use the full power of both the Internet and cutting-edge supply chain management software. But rather than simply mimicking the solutions adopted in the United States and Europe, Li & Fung has succeeded by creating an organization that is capable of integrating these with local knowledge, Asian alliance management skills, and overseas Chinese opportunism and first-mover advantage (a combination that Victor Fung jokes is like "a machete in one hand, a laptop in the other"). This enables the company to integrate the tacit knowledge of its 3,600 staff, traditional Asian strengths, and best-of-breed technology and processes to develop an efficient network that spans right from the design studios of U.S. retailers to village women with sewing machines in Bangladesh. Such a combination has allowed Li & Fung to outperform, and then acquire, its former rivals Inchcape Buying Services and Dodwell. It has also grown faster than any of Asia's leading B2B portals such as Alibaba or Global Sources, which rely on state-of-the-art technology alone.

Making supply chains more efficient is at the core of Li & Fung's business. But many other companies will have to implement strategies to achieve a similar step-change in productivity across a broad front including supply chain management, logistics, sales, and administration. This all-out push to improve productivity will be necessary because, in the new competitive environment that is emerging in Asia, world-class efficiency in manufacturing or basic service operations alone won't be enough to succeed in the next round.

In this chapter we will look at how that challenge can be addressed. It examines why productivity improvement will be critical to the next round of competition, identifies the mind-sets and processes that act as enemies of Asian corporate productivity today, and outlines the strategies companies can use to achieve the kind of step-change productivity improvements required. Just as in the case of Li & Fung, I argue that Asian companies can use cutting-edge technology to leverage their traditional strengths and turn Asian productivity from a handicap into a source of competitive advantage.

Productivity Improvement Is Now Critical

The first step toward achieving dramatic improvements in productivity is for companies in Asia to recognize that they have a productivity problem. In the past, denial was made possible by low labor costs. More than a decade of growth at average rates two or three times that of the United States or Europe also helped breed complacency. But it is worth remembering that growth in output and national income can be fed from two different sources: either by sucking in more inputs or through increased productivity. A rigorous study by researchers at the Brookings Institution concluded that the bulk of Asia's growth during its long boom came from what they called "accumulation"—absorbing more inputs—of capital, of technology, of natural resources, and of a growing, better-educated labor force.[4] They went on to conclude that "TFP (Total Factor Productivity) played a surprisingly small role in East Asia's success."[5]

While the TFP methodologies have been subject to lively academic debate, other researchers including Alwyn Young and Paul Krugman have independently pointed out that the vast bulk of Asia's growth could be traced back to massive infusions of capital and a larger, better-educated workforce.[6] Like gluttons, Asian economies and companies gorged themselves on resources without much concern for how much was going to waste on the way and whether those resources were being put to the most productive use. Expansion was the name of the game, often at almost any cost. The result is that today, Asian businesses are nowhere near as competitive as they should be given their relatively low unit labor costs because much of their potential advantage is squandered through low productivity.

Data from the World Bank, meanwhile, suggest that throughout the 1980s and early 1990s, Asian companies lost ground to their cousins in the United States and Europe, where productivity was the major driver of growth. In South Korea and Taiwan over the same period, for example, productivity improvement (measured across all activities, not just in manufacturing plants and "service factories") accounted for less than 15 percent of overall growth in gross domestic product (GDP), compared with nearly 50 percent for the United States and over 70 percent for Germany.

Anyone who has walked into a traditional Asian bank branch to cash a foreign currency check, even in Japan, can testify to this. Compared with the United States or Europe, most of these branches are heavily staffed but still inefficient. In Thailand they call it "no *tom yum gung* service," in reference to the fact that many a worker has missed a meal of that famous spicy and sour soup, having spent their entire lunch hour standing in a queue at the bank.

To understand the size of this productivity challenge at the corporate level, I assembled a sample of the top thirty companies by market capitalization in each of three regions—North America, Europe, and Asia—and compared them on a rough and ready productivity measure: turnover per employee. In North America, each employee supported $388,000 of turnover. In Europe the figure was almost $275,000. For our sample of the top thirty companies in the *Asiaweek* 500, turnover per employee averaged under $250,000—some 36 percent below the North American figure.[7] In some sectors, the gap was even larger. Turnover per employee in the top telecommunications companies, for example, was $149,000 in Asia, compared with $531,000 in the United States.[8]

Defenders of Asian corporate productivity often argue that lower turnover per employee reflects a sensible choice to use more staff and less capital in a region where wage costs are well behind the United States. If this were the case, however, we would expect the productivity of that supposedly carefully targeted capital investment to be exemplary. But our calculations show that capital productivity in Asia also lags well behind the United States. Based on our sample, the productivity of capital investment in the Philippines is 52 percent behind the U.S. average, 31 percent behind in Malaysia, close to 25 percent behind in Singapore and Taiwan, and 15 percent behind in South Korea.[9] And recall that these statistics don't include the long tail of laggards: It's a comparison of Asia's leading companies with the largest U.S. companies.

Although these statistics represent only top-line measures from a limited sample, their message still comes through loud and clear: Even the top Asian corporations generally aren't world-class in either labor or capital productivity. This message is reinforced by the fact that the dollar total returns to shareholders delivered by Asian corporates over the decade 1993–2002 ranged from 2 percent per annum for the Korean chaebol to negative for companies headquartered in Japan, Indonesia, Thailand, and China. This compares with annual rates of return averaging between 5 percent and 15 percent in Western Europe, the United States, and Russia (figure 3-1). Given the size of this gap, productivity improvement represents both a huge opportunity and a tough management challenge.

In addressing that challenge it makes sense, of course, to start in the areas where the problem, and the potential, is greatest. The first step, therefore, is to pinpoint the productivity "black-spots" on which to concentrate the most attention.

Productivity Black-Spots in Corporate Asia

One of the contrasts that strikes most visitors to companies in Asia is that shiny, world-class, lean manufacturing operations often sit side by side with overstaffed offices and warehousing and distribution methods that seem to have changed little for decades. In a country packed with electronics companies, Japanese office workers pass mountains of paper documents around consensus-building loops, each person showing his approval by affixing his *hanko* (personal stamp). The technology to attach a *hanko* to an electronic document exists, but few offices use it yet. These anecdotal impressions are confirmed by the data on the variations in productivity growth across different sectors during the recovery from the Asian financial crisis (table 3-1). In all three countries studied, productivity growth rates in the transport and trade sectors (the latter includes distribution, wholesaling, and retailing) were only one-third to one-half the rate achieved in manufacturing. Productivity growth in the financial sector, meanwhile, was negligible (or in the case of Malaysia, actually slightly negative). Productivity black-spots seem to be most common in nonmanufacturing areas like distribution and logistics, sales, and financial services.

A recent study of Taiwan's service sector supports this contention that service sectors are the productivity laggards. Of the total increase in value-added in Taiwan's service industries over thirty-five years, additional capital invested accounted for 40 percent of the growth; next

FIGURE 3-1

Asia's Relative Shareholder Returns

AVERAGE ANNUAL TOTAL RETURNS TO SHAREHOLDERS 1993–2002 (%)

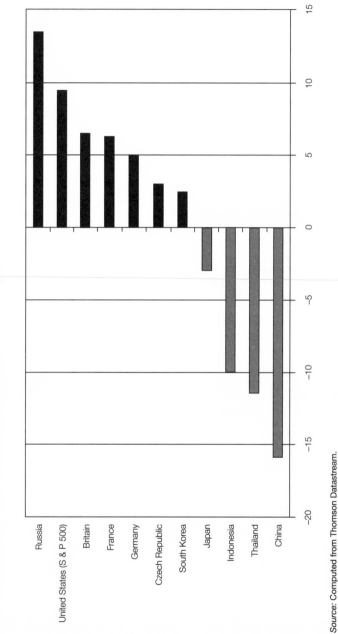

Source: Computed from Thomson Datastream.

TABLE 3-1

Estimated Productivity Growth in Selected Sectors in 1999

	Manufacturing	Transport	Trade	Finance
Malaysia	9.1	3.2	3.2	−0.4
Singapore	16.2	8.7	6.8	N/A
Taiwan	9.5	N/A	4.3	0.6

Source: Computed from data presented by Abdul Rahman Ibrahim and Ab.Wahab Muhamad, "The Productivity Framework, Productivity in the Service Sector and the Productivity Paradox," in *Productivity Measurement in the Service Sector* (Tokyo: Asian Productivity Organization, 2001), 77–82.

was additional labor, accounting for 32 percent; and finally came total factor productivity, the smallest contributor at 28 percent.[10] Another study, this time for Japan by the McKinsey Global Institute, found that productivity in the auto, steel, machine tools, and consumer electronics industries was around 20 percent higher than the average for U.S. and European competitors.[11] By contrast, similar research found that Japanese productivity in retailing and distribution was 50 percent below the U.S. level, while health care was 7 percent below.

This low productivity also carries over to customer service, inventory management, and finance and administration within Asian manufacturing companies. Comparing stock-outs, inventory turnover, and debtors-to-sales ratios for Asian companies versus world benchmarks, another McKinsey study found that Asian performance lagged behind by between 35 percent and 55 percent (figure 3-2).[12]

There are good reasons why Asia's productivity problem mostly lies in areas outside manufacturing and routine, back-office service operations. First, high productivity is often largely "built in" to the equipment that composes modern manufacturing lines or the information technology (IT) systems that drive the back office of service activities. Productivity improvement in these areas can therefore be "bought" by investing in up-to-date technology. In areas like the distribution chain, sales, frontline service, and supplier management, there are few standard solutions; investment in technology is only a small part of the issue. In these areas, major improvements in productivity can only be achieved by painstakingly refining processes through experience, better management, training, and cultural change. It takes time, the right skills, and accumulated experience.

FIGURE 3-2

Black-Spots in Asian Supply Chains

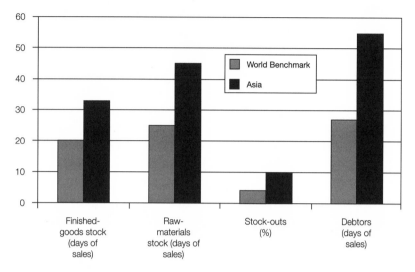

Source: Based on estimates by McKinsey Global Institute.

Second, the historical preference among Asian companies is for investment in tangible assets ("hardware") like property, machinery, or even computer equipment rather than in intangibles, including soft systems, training, and process development. The lack of investment in this organizational software has resulted in the productivity of activities outside manufacturing and back-office service operations lagging behind.

Third, productivity of the distribution and supply chains and front-line customer service and support often depends on the quality of local infrastructure, including transport and communications systems, and even the efficiency of service provision and decision making by government authorities. Gaps in Asian infrastructure, inefficient and poor-quality supply of complementary government services, and poorly capitalized distributors and retailers who are unwilling to invest all impede productivity improvements in parts of the chain outside the direct control of corporate managers.

Finally, unionization (especially in Korea and the Philippines) and an implicit social contract between large corporates and governments support a level of "disguised unemployment" with the aim of preserving social stability in some Asian countries. As a result, some service activities have become virtually "no go" areas for productivity improvement. Legislation in Japan and Thailand that effectively maintains a highly fragmented retail sector, for example, hampers both improved efficiency retailing itself as well as burdening many manufacturing and service companies with the costs of dealing with an inefficient retail distribution network.

Some of the baggage of Asian business heritage that we identified in chapter 2 has continued to reinforce these barriers to productivity improvement. The most obvious example is the historic focus among Asian companies on size and asset accumulation, at the expense of productivity. The fact that diversification has largely been driven by opportunism has also meant that while companies had the assets and licenses in place to operate, they often lacked the specialist capabilities necessary to maximize their productivity. A prime example is Thakral Corporation, once one of Singapore's most prosperous trading houses.

Thakral built its business wholesaling Japanese-made stereos, television sets, and videocassette recorders throughout Southeast Asia and China. But in the late 1990s boom, the company diversified into businesses ranging from a string of retail stores in China, through property development in Australia, to a joint venture in Internet technology consulting—areas in which it lacked all but superficial capabilities. At the same time, it failed to invest in the systems to improve the productivity of its core distribution network and to develop new competencies, such as foreign exchange management expertise, that were becoming necessary to compete. Burdened with the debt it had taken on in the course of expanding and diversifying its asset base and with margins squeezed by a failure to reduce its cost base in the face of more intense competition from companies in Korea and China, Thakral's share price plummeted from $8 per share to a few cents by 2002. Failure to focus its investment on improving the productivity of its core business had cost Thakral dear.[13]

Productivity problems arising from lack of targeted investment have been further exacerbated by the traditional centralization of decision making in many Asian companies that has hampered the evolution of organization structures that would have facilitated improvement in the total productivity of the supply chain.

Together these factors have permitted five "enemies" of productivity improvement to persist:

- *Functionalism*—organizational structures that create a set of isolated functions like sales, distribution, operations, and marketing so no one focuses on whether the overall delivery or service pipeline really works for the customer.

- *Pipeline fog*—no one knows what is happening in the distribution pipeline of wholesalers, retailers, agents, maintenance service, brokers, and so on that is not directly under the control of the company, nor whether an individual customer is actually profitable after all these "costs to serve" are included.

- *Squandered lead time*—while we know that "time is money," we are much more careful to avoid wasting money than we are about unnecessary delays and extra lead time.

- *Wage illusion*—headcount and wage rates dominate staffing decisions, not employee value-added.

- *Traders' curse*—by focusing only on purchasing from the cheapest supplier, the potentially detrimental impact that a poor supplier can have on productivity is ignored.

An understanding of these enemies of productivity needs to shape management priorities for tackling Asia's productivity gap. Each is therefore worth brief discussion in turn.

Functionalism

As we saw in chapter 2, many Asian companies are comprised of strong functional departments, such as sales, marketing, operations, finance, and product development. This type of organization structure makes sense when the goal is to build strong capabilities in each separate function: It gives focus and coherence to the team; it facilitates learning and development of best practice; and it provides a clear career structure that helps to attract and motivate staff. But the flip side of this coin is that functional structures often fail to maximize the performance of the overall chain of activities that serve the customer. So while each functional contribution might be performed effectively, there are so many handovers along the chain that overall productivity and service tend to fall through the cracks. No one has overall responsibility for maximizing the productivity and service delivered by the chain from the time an order is received to the time the customer settles the bill and starts using the product or service.

Take the simple example of checking in to a hotel room. You only see a few frontline staff at the reception desk. But the productivity of the whole process of getting settled in your room depends on a myriad of other functions: whether the sales department logged your reservation properly; the efficiency with which the finance department's system checks your credit card; whether housekeeping has cleaned the room in time for your arrival; whether the maintenance department has fixed any defects; and so on. The finance department might pride itself on having developed an excellent system for double-checking your credit so that it almost never suffers a bad debt. But this same system might well impair the productivity of the front desk staff (and keep you waiting as well) by adding extra steps. The housekeeping department may have devised a brilliant process for cleaning rooms sequentially so as to save time walking between rooms. But because this doesn't fit the arrival times of new guests, cleaners end up rushing from one emergency job to another because the right rooms aren't ready for arriving guests. The cleaners' productivity (and your satisfaction) plummets as a result.

This simple example demonstrates the fundamental point: When the emphasis shifts from building basic capabilities to driving up productivity levels for an end-to-end process, functionalism is poorly suited to the job. Functional structures served Asian companies well in the last round of competition when building capacity and capabilities at a rapid rate was the key source of advantage. As we move into the next phase, where productivity improvement is the priority, the functional structures prevalent in Asian companies today will have to be augmented or replaced.

Pipeline Fog

As we saw earlier in this chapter (table 3-1), productivity growth in transportation and logistics, and wholesale and retail trade has lagged far behind that in manufacturing. Inefficiency in these areas directly lowers the productivity of supply chains throughout Asia. But worse still, it sets in train a destructive cycle that impairs the productivity of other companies that depend on the chain to serve their customers.

These negative, "knock-on" effects, where low productivity in one part of the chain in turn undermines productivity in performing subsequent activities, work in two ways. First, because the distribution and service delivery chain is often unproductive and unreliable, the product and service companies that supply it can't forecast accurately, nor can they smooth out their workflow. They have to hold excess stock or extra capacity to compensate for the shortcomings of those downstream in the chain. This reduces their productivity.

In manufacturing industries, the following negative spiral often ensues: Errors forecast lead to the need for increased buffer stocks; these replenishment orders clog up capacity, so lead times increase; this means having to forecast further into the future, which in turn increases forecast errors. To satisfy demand, more and more orders then have to be expedited as "special runs," increasing downtime and reworking, and preventing efficient scheduling—factors that together dramatically undermine productivity. *Pipeline fog*—the inability to get accurate visibility of stock levels, costs incurred, and service levels within your distribution channels—can thus result in companies becoming permanently locked into a cycle of production instability and low productivity. Similar destructive cycles can impair productivity services industries whose distribution agents or brokers are unable to furnish the information necessary to plan capacity, workflow, and appropriate staffing. Imagine trying to run a productive airline or railway service without knowing how many tickets had been sold or how many cargo pallets were going to show up that day.

Pipeline fog can also undermine productivity by obscuring the true picture of what is going on even inside a company's own boundaries. Struggling to keep afloat immediately after the 1997 Asian crisis, the Hong Kong retailer Circle K, for example, found itself severely handicapped by cash registers that weren't networked between stores, so it lacked visibility of the total stock it was carrying within its chain. Individual store managers also ordered products directly from different suppliers, resulting in multiple, disruptive deliveries throughout the day—distracting staff and undermining customer service.[14]

The second knock-on effect of pipeline fog arises because it thwarts proper control of what it ultimately costs to serve an individual customer. The total "cost to serve" for any individual customer comprises a complex amalgam, including:

- Costs of delivery of products or services

- The cost of returns of products or refusal to accept scheduled services

- The costs of educating the customer about a particular product or service

- The cost of customizing the product or service to individual needs

- The costs of paperwork required to deal with a customer (including tendering or quotation costs)

- The costs of credit, late payment, or bad debt.

Many of these costs are actually driven by the behavior of the wholesalers and retailers and the quality of their own internal processes and controls. Failure to collect accurate and timely information from the customer, for example, can drive these costs up dramatically through returns, replacement, reworking, error correction, and retraining. Again, overall productivity is severely undermined as these effects ricochet back through the supply chain.

The challenge of controlling cost to serve is, therefore, heightened by the fragmentation of retailing and corresponding underinvestment in retail systems throughout much of Asia. In China, for example, there are an estimated 17.4 million retail outlets and the five largest account for just 0.7 percent of the market. Even in Japan and Hong Kong, there are 13 and 10 retailers, respectively, per 100 households, compared with around 5 in the United States. The result, as the group manager of Swire Beverages, which is responsible for distributing Coca-Cola throughout many provinces in China, put it: "Visibility of sales and inventory is typically poor, with limited data on what products have been sold and where."[15] Consequent high costs to serve undermine total productivity.

In financial services, pipeline fog can be even more problematic because it threatens to undermine risk control as well as operational efficiency. When Singapore's DBS bank took over the Bangkok-based Thai Danu bank in 1997, for example, it found that existing systems in the branch network were so poor there was no visibility of the total indebtedness of any given customer because loans made by different branches were not cross-referenced. It was therefore possible for one branch to extend additional credit without being aware that the customer was in default on a loan from another, sister branch. Soaring numbers of nonperforming loans were one result. The productivity of both the bank's capital and its staff plummeted as it struggled to sort out the resulting mess.

While these pervasive types of pipeline fog persist, Asia's productivity will be stuck in the doldrums. Actions to dramatically improve visibility along the total supply chain from cash or raw material through to end-user are critical to closing the productivity gap.

Squandered Lead Time

A number of recent studies have analyzed the total time elapsed between receipt of an order or service request and when the customer finally received the completed goods or services in a number of Asian companies. The results are staggering: On average, orders were being worked on only between 5 percent and 0.5 percent of the total time they spent making their way through these companies' systems. The remaining 95 percent to 99.5 percent of elapsed time, customers' orders or service requests spent waiting in one or more of the following queues:

- Waiting to be input into the system

- Waiting to be specified, costed, and priced

- Waiting to be prioritized

- Waiting to be scheduled

- Waiting for the rest of their batch to catch up

- Waiting for orders ahead in the queue

- Waiting to be invoiced

- Waiting to be picked from a warehouse

- Waiting to be delivered

To quote the manager of Swire Beverages again: "In reality, relative to the U.S. or European industry benchmarks, [in Asia] most so-called 'fast-moving consumer goods' are 'slow moving.'"[16] These extended lead times undermine the productivity of Asia's supply chains. They result in delays that mean workers and equipment further down the chain are left idle while they wait for materials, components, or services to be delivered. This reduces capacity utilization and hence productivity of both capital and labor.

Longer lead times force companies to forecast further out into the future, aggravating the problem of forecast errors undermining productivity. And they introduce the need for more stocks and buffers in the system, which in turn reduces the efficiency of the whole supply chain.

Squandered lead time is, therefore, another important dead-weight cost that reduces Asian productivity. Companies in the United States and Europe have spent the last decade focusing on driving these costs out of their processes and investing in systems to make this possible. By contrast, process improvements and IT investments in Asia have been insufficient to tackle the challenge of reducing lead times and improving supply chain efficiency to comparable levels. In a recent survey of Malaysian firms, for example, more than half the respondents reported that their existing systems were unable to fulfill the requirements of their customers.[17] If Asia is to close the productivity gap, it must not only address this deficiency but do so at an accelerated pace.

Wage Illusion

The fact that expanding capacity to keep up with demand was a top priority in many Asian companies during the growth phase of the 1980s and 1990s led to an emphasis on rapid recruitment of new staff at competitive wage rates. To avoid losing market share, managers faced strong pressure to "throw people at the problem" in the scramble to keep pace with rising demand for their products and services.

Underlying this behavior was an implicit assumption that leveraging Asia's low wage rates would automatically ensure competitiveness. With wage levels less than one-quarter of comparable rates in Europe or the United States, staff productivity seemed to warrant only secondary concern. But this assumption that low wages by international standards automatically meant cost-competitive operations has turned out to be a dangerous illusion. As we move into the next phase of competition, three fundamentals have changed that render companies caught by this "wage illusion" exposed: (1) the China factor, (2) rising "overhead" costs, and (3) productivity improvements in the United States and Europe.

The China factor is the first of these. The emergence of China as the "factory of the world" is putting intense pressure on Asian countries that relied on low wage rates as a primary source of advantage in the past. And even within China herself, companies drawing labor from expensive cities and provinces on the eastern seaboard are facing increased cost competition from less-developed regions. With low wage rates evaporating as a source of competitive advantage, the focus has to shift to value-added per employee. To compete with the wage levels of less-developed Chinese regions, higher relative wages will have to be more than offset by additional value-added per staff member; in short, by a step-change in productivity that reestablishes a company's cost advantage.

It's very difficult to gain this productivity-driven advantage compared with low-cost locations in China in manufacturing or routine service operations. China can now buy world-class equipment, production lines, or IT systems and has a large pool of qualified engineers to run them. Companies in competing locations will have to look for productivity and cost advantage in areas that require "soft skills," processes and tacit knowledge that it will take time for Chinese organizations to perfect. Chinese competition is yet another force pushing the need for productivity improvement outside routine operations to the fore.

The second factor laying bare the risks of wage illusion is the increasing proportion of costs that are now lumped into the catch-all we call overhead. Today, overhead often accounts for upward of 40 percent of total costs. But in most of these overhead functions, it's not the volume of activity that drives productivity (how many pieces of paper you shuffle in a day), but the quality of decision making. This is true for activities that range from high-level strategic decision making to tasks like production scheduling that may seem routine; apparently routine tasks often hide a multiplicity of complex trade-offs that, if made wrongly, massively jack up costs and undermine customer service. The real costs are driven by the quality of decision making, not by wage rates.

The final factor that is making wage illusion more dangerous is the relentless, cumulative improvement in productivity that has been achieved by fifteen years of intense focus on nonmanufacturing productivity in the United States and Europe in every activity from retailing to logistics and administration. The resulting improvements in these areas in the West have been dramatic. Productivity enhancement in these areas has been given extra impetus through widespread use of outsourcing of administrative and support services. Outsourcing has allowed stepwise improvement in productivity—allowing companies to access the benefits of focus, expertise, and scale economies by using specialist suppliers to replace subscale, in-house activities. Today, outsourcing, and the productivity improvement that it achieves in support services, is still in its infancy in Asia, hampered by a mix of lack of qualified suppliers, incomplete legal and administrative infrastructure, and managerial suspicion. As a result, support services remain a black-spot that undermines Asian cost advantage compared with the United States and Europe.

Traders' Curse

As we saw in chapter 2, one of the strengths of many Asian companies is their entrepreneurial deal-making culture. One of the benefits is the keen prices at which they are able to purchase the products and services they require as input to the business. But this "trading" mentality to the supply chain also has drawbacks. First, looking narrowly at the purchase price may result in lower productivity and increased costs at other points along the chain. Cheap raw materials or inadequate support services, for example, can easily lead to higher downtime, more reworking, or customer dissatisfaction. Second, concentrating on getting the lowest purchase price can obscure opportunities to drive unnecessary costs out of the supply chain through cooperation (driving buffer stocks out of the chain by better information sharing, for example).

The management consultants McKinsey & Company estimate that an average Asian company can gain a one-off improvement in total supply chain productivity of 10 percent, followed by ongoing gains of between 3 percent and 5 percent per annum, by moving from "traditional purchasing" to best practice supply chain management.[18] This includes redesign of products, services, and internal processes so that they can integrate materials, components, and support services more smoothly; improved specification of supplies; cooperation on new product development; better and more timely exchange of information with suppliers; and optimization of logistics and material flows.

Surrendering these potential gains in productivity through a sole focus on deal making amounts to a "traders' curse." To break out of this productivity straitjacket requires a shift from concentrating on purchase costs to the total cost of a product or service over your whole value chain and the life cycle over which it interacts with your business.

Tackling these five enemies of productivity—functionalism, pipeline fog, squandered lead time, wage illusion, and traders' curse—obviously presents a challenging managerial agenda. A step-change improvement in productivity, however, is an essential foundation for winning in Asia's new competitive environment.

Efficiency "Asian Style"

Treading the well-worn path toward productivity improvement across a broad front already traveled by many U.S. and European companies, however, won't be the way to win in the next round of Asian competition. A strategy of mimicking approaches to increasing total productivity used elsewhere risks consigning Asian firms to thankless cycles of perpetual catch-up. It also surrenders the opportunity to leverage some of the distinctive strengths of Asian business heritage that we identified in chapter 2.

Three such opportunities for achieving a step-change in total productivity "Asian style" stand out:

- *Using new technologies to leapfrog global competitors*—redirecting Asian companies' traditional eye for first-mover advantage, their capabilities in commercializing new technologies and rapid execution toward today's productivity problem.

- *Deploying world-class systems in support of traditional Asian relationship management*—by using state-of-the-art software and systems working in the background to inform dealings with customers and suppliers and broaden channels of communication.

- *Engineering a new type of supply chain, based on networks*—creating a new alternative to the linear, "production line" concept of supply by harnessing Asian strengths in assembling and managing alliances.

Each of these initiatives will be deployed by winners in the next round of Asian competition in shaping strategies that both attack the enemies of Asian productivity improvement identified above and begin to build new and distinctive sources of productivity advantage. At the same time, some elements of Asian companies' traditional strategies and organizational structures will need to be abandoned, including past emphasis on asset accumulation, opportunistic diversification, and fixation with costs rather than value-added.

Strategies for a Step-Change in Productivity

This redefinition of Asian-style efficiency will require new Asian organizational structures, new approaches to managing the delivery pipeline, a shift from speed in commissioning new capacity toward speed of response to customer orders, revised ways of assessing the contribution of employees, and the evolution of a new type of networked supply chain management.

New Asian Organizational Structures

As discussed above, the functional organizations that dominate many Asian companies today have largely served their purpose: that of successfully building a strong set of capabilities in key functions such as sales, finance, operations, and so on. It is now time to move on and to implement structures designed around seamless processes, each aimed at creating value for the customer. This will necessitate the breakdown of existing functional boundaries—a change that requires considerable managerial determination and courage to fight the entrenched interests of "functional barons." But the rewards in improved productivity are large. Much of the Japanese consumer products company Kao's improvement in margins in recent years, for example, has been made possible by restructuring that ended the dominance of its historically all-powerful functional groups.[19]

Rather than follow the path trodden by many Western companies that created divisional, strategic business units and then matrix organizations, however, there is a strong argument for Asia to leapfrog these structures by going straight to modern, so-called front-end/back-end structures in the interest of gaining a step-change increase in productivity.[20]

The central feature of these organizations is a "front end" structured around a series of teams that focus on understanding the needs of particular customers or customer segments (such as hospitals, semiconductor manufacturers, or airlines). These front-end units are then charged with creating a customized bundle of products and services to satisfy these needs and with acting as a single "champion" for the customer in dealing with the company. This structure is linked to a "back end" made up of units whose job it is to efficiently supply the constituent products and services that make up the bundle (whether sourced in or produced internally). Each back-end unit focuses on mastering the technologies, processes, and supply chain that will enable it to efficiently deliver the specific component, product, or service it is mandated to supply to the front-end units.

These new structures are not a panacea. They bring their own problems: Back-end units complain that they risk becoming isolated from the marketplace or that they end up cross-subsidizing other products and services in the bundle; front-end teams lament that they are forced to spend too much time haggling over transfer prices and that, unless their customers are huge, they don't receive sufficient attention and customization from their back-end internal suppliers. But leading global companies such as IBM and HP that have implemented such front-end/back-end organizations in recent years have enjoyed significant improvements in productivity and margins.

In overcoming the drag on productivity that their existing functional organizations impose, therefore, Asian companies have a threefold opportunity. First is the potential to improve productivity by going straight to front-end/back-end organizations. This would enable them to leapfrog many of their Western competitors whose legacy of traditional multinational or matrix structures impede such a shift. Second is the opportunity to leverage their traditional strengths in running efficient manufacturing or basic service operations by applying these same skills to the entire "back end" of these new organizations that encompasses the full set of supply chain activities, including those beyond the proverbial "factory gate." Third, releasing the constraints of existing functional organizations opens up new opportunities to deploy traditional Asian strengths in deal making and service provision into front-end organizations that are focused directly on the customer.

One company that has taken steps to reap these opportunities is San Miguel Corporation, the Philippines' largest beer maker. Starting in 1998, it restructured its beer operations to create front-end units focused solely on improving productivity in its distribution system. A doubling of the number of wholesalers it served helped drive down unit costs as the fixed costs of the network were better spread. Even more important, however, was a series of new distribution contracts designed to directly promote the productivity of San Miguel's channels, including incentives and credit terms specifically designed to increase rate of sale and improve stock turn. The brewing end of the business, meanwhile, was restructured to focus on efficiency and quality of supply.[21] Profitability was transformed as a result.

New Approaches to Management of the Delivery Pipeline

A second important set of initiatives required if Asian productivity is to make a step-change improvement must be aimed at clearing today's pipeline fog, so that companies have a "line of sight" to the end customer and much better control over costs to serve.

Just as with front-end/back-end organizations there is potential to improve productivity in Asian delivery pipelines by borrowing from the state-of-the-art abroad. Investments in customer relationship management (CRM) systems, for example, can play an important role in facilitating improved visibility and control. Recent surveys suggest that Asian companies spend around $1 billion per year on CRM systems. But although this is expected to grow fivefold by 2006, even such a dramatic increase would still leave spending on these systems at only one-half the $10 billion U.S. companies were already investing in 2001.[22] And if these investments are to deliver significant improvements in productivity, managers' view of their potential role will have to be expanded. In another recent survey by OgilvyOne in Singapore, most respondents focused on the software implementation issues associated with CRM systems rather than on the productivity benefits from better visibility of the delivery pipeline, costs to serve, customer profitability, and customer behavior.[23]

To build a productivity advantage, therefore, Asian companies will need to go far beyond simply importing and implementing customer and pipeline management software already in use in the United States. The keys to success will lie in combining these systems with traditional Asian relationship management strengths to use the new technology to strengthen existing relationships with distributors and customers, not to supplant them. This means using the new systems to open up new and broader channels of communication with distributors and customers. To reap the full potential for improved productivity, the aim must be to help intercept changing customer preferences, to reinforce their purchase decisions and anticipate future needs, and to communicate customer and distributor feedback widely throughout the company. As a manager at Swire Beverages, which works with 215,000 active retailers, put it: "We have introduced systems to track sales by product from each individual outlet daily and to integrate sales and inventory data with information on distribution and production capacity.... But to use these tools to maximum advantage the company will need to further enhance its ties with its retail partners, understanding their customer base and needs more fully."[24]

More generally, Asian managers will have to place more emphasis on the efficiency of their distributors and agents to ensure that high productivity in manufacturing and routine service operations isn't negated by inefficiency in the delivery pipeline. After all, the price paid by the end user has to support the whole chain. An unproductive delivery pipeline therefore squeezes the margins available to others. To meet this challenge, new types of alliances with distributors and agents, innovative delivery channels that remove layers in the chain, and possibly investments in the greater capability to deal direct with customers will be required. Airlines, for example, will have to look more aggressively at improving productivity in the networks of travel agents who distribute air tickets or replacing them with Internet booking engines or efficient call centers. Manufacturers, meanwhile, will have to link more seamlessly into the activities of their distributors and users and, where feasible, deal more directly with their customers. Most of these initiatives, again, offer opportunities to leverage Asia's relationship heritage in new ways and to deliver traditional service qualities more efficiently.

From Speed of Expansion to Speed of Response

As we saw in chapter 2, Asian business has a long tradition of speed in deal making, grasping emerging opportunities, and getting new capacity up and running. In the next round of competition, it needs to replicate this speed in the way it responds to customer orders, tackling the productivity losses associated with squandered lead time. This means learning how to track where time is being expended as closely as cash

expenditures are monitored today. It means setting up systems to measure total lead times and to pinpoint where that time is being squandered
through delays—creating a "time budget." Employees need to be made
responsible for the extra lead time their part of the process is contributing to the total, including the knock-on effects on others. Standard tim-
ings need to become as commonly used as standard costs.

Recall the problems the Hong Kong retailer Circle K faced back in the
late 1990s: low productivity from its in-store staff and frequent stock-
outs despite high inventory levels. By focusing on time budgets and
investing in appropriate systems and processes, Circle K was able to halve
its average transaction time from twelve seconds down to six. It also
achieved a reduction in the time it takes each store to turn over its inventory from almost a month to under two weeks.[25]

Once management has a handle on lead times, the next step involves
systematically and relentlessly removing the bottlenecks that contribute
to delays. Scheduling, prioritization, batching, workflow, and inventory
management systems all need to be reexamined to drive out delays
that undermine productivity. Successful implementation can pay rapid
productivity dividends. The Japanese consumer electronics company,
Sharp, for example, extended its cost-control systems to encompass
time-based budgeting in its Osaka operations in 1999. Within two years
it increased the rate at which it was able to instantly fulfill customer
orders from 77 percent to 88 percent while cutting inventory by over
30 percent.[26]

A New Approach to Assessing Employee Contribution

It is time to reexamine the low-productivity jobs companies in Asia
created in their rush to keep up with booming demand in the 1990s. This
means the value-added of every employee and job must be systematically
reassessed. Historically many Asian companies have assessed and
rewarded employees on the basis of whether procedures are being followed reliably and diligently by employees whose wage rates are competitive with the market. But employees who score well on these measures
may still be caught in a trap of low productivity. This is because they
measure effort and compliance, rather than the ratio of input to output.
To root out low productivity, companies in Asia instead need to be asking questions like:

- Why are we doing that task at all?

- What value is it adding?

- How could the same result be achieved in a more efficient way?

Therefore it won't be sufficient to implement arbitrary "across-the-board" cuts in headcount; this risks cutting the proverbial bone and muscle as well as unproductive fat. The existing processes in many Asian companies, especially in "overhead" areas like administration, accounting, or customer service will need a "root-and-branch" overhaul so that waste and low productivity can be *designed out* of the system. This goes for managerial roles as well. Asian companies will need to place greater emphasis on the quality of decision making among their managerial ranks and set rewards and penalties accordingly.

But rather than importing processes and performance measurement systems wholesale from overseas, the trick will be to design new ways of assessing and improving employee value-added while retaining some of the strengths of Asian organizational cultures discussed in chapter 2. The experience of Li & Fung, the company we described at the opening of this chapter, points the way forward. Historically many of their managers had been charged with controlling the entire process of sourcing and manufacturing within a specific country. They were assessed and rewarded on their success at managing the sources from that country. But such a job structure limited their value-added by discouraging them from searching for even better sources outside their national borders. It also undermined the level of flexibility Li & Fung could offer—another key source of value-added to its customers.

Having implemented new, U.S. informational technology that enabled information about Li & Fung's entire network to be accessed with a few keystrokes, the company reassigned its managers to customer groups and not countries, "telling them to focus on the product and work with our entire network to source from the region instead of just on country."[27] The bonus system was revamped to reflect customer and product profitability. But alongside this new emphasis on value-added, rather than conformance, some of the traditional Chinese heritage remained. Fung emphasized, for example, that: "If managers don't succeed, however, we don't necessarily get rid of them right away. We understand the nature of the business and sometimes during a downturn a manager can do poorly for a few years. Our father taught us the value of loyalty, however, and we will keep a manager on or move [him] around if poor results are a consequence of something other than [his] efforts."[28]

At the same time, Asian managers will also have to abandon the natural desire for internal control and take a closer look at the potential benefits of outsourcing activities where value-added per employee is below industry norms. As the technologies and expertise required to perform support services efficiently become more advanced, Asian companies will find their in-house services are subscale and obsolete. Outsourcing noncritical support services allows a company to access economies of scale through pooling volume with others and to amortize the cost of investments in building state-of-the-art capabilities that only specialists can afford to make. The fact that outsourcing of support services remains in its infancy in many Asian companies represents a continued drag on productivity improvement.

A New Type of Networked Supply Chain Management

The final fertile area in which managers need to look to close the Asian productivity gap is in supply chain management. This means lifting their sights far beyond traditional definitions of "purchasing." Minimizing total cost of a product or service supplied to the company across all activities it touches and across the full life cycle over which it impacts users needs to become the objective.

This means building a cross-functional supply chain management team; it means upgrading capabilities of the staff involved from a base of clerical and negotiation skills to include the capabilities for respecification, process redesign, and working with suppliers to improve the design of products, services, and information exchange. It means linking supplier management to the product design process. It means bundling purchases across functions and business units to increase volume leverage. It means agreeing on a road map of supplier improvement, not just a set of specifications and prices for next quarter. It means benchmarking against leading industries like electronics manufacturing to set targets for productivity improvement.

Many of these initiatives to improve supply chain efficiency have already been implemented by companies in the United States and

Europe. But they have been deployed within the context of what is still a linear, "production line" view of the supply chain between raw materials or raw data and the final product or service offering. Asia's opportunity may be to increase total productivity still further by extending the concept to a supply network that crosses industries and alliance partners as well as activities and geography; driving out the multitude of inefficiencies in the existing Asian supply chain in the process.

Take the example of Singapore-listed Noble Group. It purchases iron ore from Bahir in India, then charters shipping capacity to take it to Qingdao in China, where an alliance partner turns it into cold-rolled steel. This is reloaded onto another ship chartered by Noble and supplied to users in Japan, South Korea, and Australia. The required working capital is financed by Noble Finance, and insurance en route is provided by its risk-insurance arm, Trade-Vest Risk Services.[29] Just like Li & Fung, Noble assembles and manages a more efficient chain by building a complex network of suppliers, alliance partners, and associate companies. Charoen Pokphand—the Thai group discussed in chapter 1 that has revolutionized productivity in the Asian agribusiness supply chain by assembling a network of farmers, retailers, and food-service businesses with its own seed and breeding stock supply, feedmills, and food-processing plants—is another example. These new, Asian-style supply networks may provide the blueprints for driving productivity improvements in Asia that go far beyond what can be achieved simply by replicating the methods used in the United States and Europe, creating a new source of advantage that plays to Asian strengths in deal making and alliance management.[30]

Stepping Up to the Challenge

The appropriate mix of these strategies and initiatives that is required will clearly vary by company, industry, and country across Asia. But the fact remains that to compete in this new millennium, Asian companies need to make a step-change improvement in their productivity outside the confines of already efficient manufacturing and routine service operations. This chapter has laid out the priority areas for attack: functionalism, pipeline fog, squandered lead time, wage illusion, and the traders' curse. In tackling these black-spots, investment and technology will play a role. But even more important is a change in mind-set: the recognition that productivity in "soft," overhead areas, and in parts of the supply chain pipeline traditionally left to others, is where the real scope for productivity improvement lies in Asia. Equally, the winners in the next round will be those companies that accept that the productivity rewards will come not just from shiny new equipment or the latest expensive software, but instead from relentless and detailed enhancement of the way things are done. This means that in the quest to step up to the productivity challenge there are opportunities to create new sources of competitive advantage by combining traditional Asian strengths with technologies, systems, and processes imported from abroad to create uniquely profitable hybrids. These opportunities include using new technologies combined with capabilities for rapid learning and adaptation to leapfrog global competitors, deploying world-class systems in support of traditional Asian relationship management, and engineering a new type of supply chain based on complex alliance networks.

So are these opportunities only relevant to Asian corporates? Unilever's experience in Thailand suggests not. Despite more than thirty years operating in the country and a close relationship with its packaging supplier, Starprint, for example, Unilever decided to focus on making a step-change improvement in this aspect of its supply chain. Through a new alliance with Starprint that synchronized supply by sharing both production planning information and actual planning rates, combined inventory was cut by 40 percent and lead time was reduced by an impressive 60 percent, while was faultless delivery reliability was maintained.[31] Winning in the next round of Asian competition will require Asian companies and Western multinationals operating in Asia alike to step up to the Asian productivity challenge.

Chapter 4

Ramping Up Asian Innovation

With notable exceptions, such as Sony of Japan or Creative Technology of Singapore, Asian companies and the local subsidiaries of multinationals have mostly been importers of new technologies and innovative products and services. This is not because, as some have argued, Asia is fundamentally less creative than the West.[1] Look no further than the fact that four of the great inventions that changed the world—gunpowder, the compass, papermaking, and printing—all originated in China. A more persuasive reason is that, during the long boom that came to a sudden halt with the 1997 financial crisis, it probably did not pay most Asian companies to develop new, basic technologies nor to invest a lot in developing their own, innovative products and services. Rapidly growing demand for standard products and services, supplied at lower cost and improved quality, meant that strategies based on quickly absorbing and leveraging tested technologies, product designs, and service packages made commercial sense for Asian companies. Innovation breakthroughs, whether they be in new types of products or services or fundamental technological breakthroughs, were not core to most Asian companies' business models; they were an "optional extra" if resources and time allowed—which, generally, they didn't.

But as we saw in chapter 1, the basis of competition in the next round is shifting from being "better" to being "different." Innovation therefore needs to become high priority for Asian companies. Trying to innovate the way it is done in the United States, however, is likely to fail in Asia. Mimicking foreign ideals of the innovator or importing "proven" innovation processes wholesale from elsewhere doesn't play to Asian strengths. Instead, tomorrow's winners will redefine both the innovation playing field and the innovation process in ways that defines a unique Asian innovation style. Just as with achieving a step-change in productivity, this will require strategies that combine learning from the world with the best of Asian business heritage in the innovation arena.

This chapter tackles the issues involved. It begins by detailing the critical roles of innovation in the next round of competition: as a powerful tool to help Asian companies break out of the chronic "commoditization trap" into which many have descended and as a way to benefit from the growing demands among Asian consumers for products and services that are not only "new" but also more convenient and more customized to their individual needs. It then goes on to explore how Asian companies can respond to this innovation challenge: by redefining the innovation playing field, by managing risk by creating a portfolio of innovation options, by stimulating a flow of innovation by challenging internal orthodoxy and through targeted acquisitions and learning from the world, and by leveraging Asia's unique knowledge base and proven commercialization skills. To determine how this Asian-style innovation process can be ramped up, however, we first need to understand the root causes of Asia's current innovation deficit.

Asia's Innovation Deficit

Innovation is notoriously difficult to measure. However, indicators such as R&D spending as a ratio of GDP show that, at the national level, most Asian economies allocated a much smaller proportion of their growing income to innovation than developed Western countries, and even compared with Eastern European nations (figure 4-1). Notable exceptions were Japan and South Korea, where the ratio of R&D spending to GDP outstripped the United States for the decade of the 1990s. Even in Singapore, the share of national product allocated to R&D was one-half of that in the West and similar to the level of investment by Eastern European economies.

This pattern is evident at the corporate level as well, with Asian-owned firms being especially parsimonious with spending on R&D. This deficit has translated into a low proportion of innovative products and processes in Asian companies' product offerings. A recent study of 109 manufacturing firms (around half Asian owned and half foreign) conducted by Wong Poh Kam of the National University of Singapore, for example, found that nearly half the Asian-owned companies derived in excess of 75 percent of their sales from products or processes more than three years old. Only 13 percent of these companies had ever had a patent issued in their name, while 50 percent had an average product life cycle greater than three years (table 4-1).[2] It also appeared that the operations of multinational companies in Asia were only marginally more innovative on these measures.

FIGURE 4-1

R&D Spending As % of GDP, 1987–1997

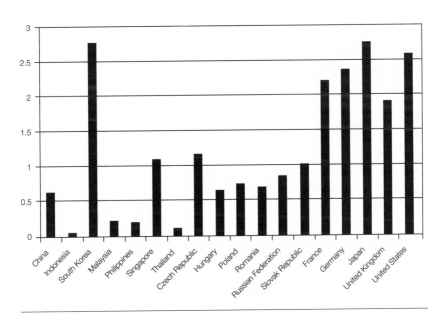

TABLE 4–1

Innovation in Asian Companies' Products and Processes

	Asian-owned firms (%)	Foreign-owned firms (%)
75% of sales or more derived from products that are over three years old	43	35
75% of sales or more made using production processes that are more than three years old	51	36
One or more patents issued	13	17
Average product life cycle of greater than three years	50	62

Source: Computed from Wong Poh Kam, "Technology Acquisition Pattern of Manufacturing Firms in Singapore," *Singapore Management Review* 20 (January 1998): 149–161.

These statistics support a contention that few experienced Asia-watchers would doubt: Asia today has a striking innovation deficit compared with its global competitors.[3] But as we noted in the introduction to this chapter, this does not reflect an inherent lack of creativity or potential for innovation. The reality is that, over recent decades, it simply didn't pay most Asian companies to allocate a significant slice of their investment resources to innovation.

As we saw in chapter 2, many Asian companies became profitable by exploiting their "resource-based" advantages, such as access to competitively priced raw materials, low-cost labor, government permits, and local knowledge. By importing foreign technology, product designs, and systems they could leverage these same advantages successively across a wide spectrum of businesses. But this strategy militated against investment in R&D and innovation: Being nonspecialists they lacked the international scale in any single business to spread the costs of innovation. Where focused global competitors could afford the high fixed costs of developing new products and processes, diversified Asian firms could not. They were better off buying technology and licensing innovation at marginal costs from those who had already developed it as part of their core business.

A second reason why investing in innovation often looked unattractive to Asian firms was their lack of local capabilities to innovate successfully. Even where the basic scientific and engineering skills and market knowledge necessary to innovate were available, most Asian companies had little experience in the process. And they rightly understood that building the know-how to support an effective innovation process was likely to prove challenging. Those who did take the plunge, such as HP in Singapore, found that building a even a baseline product innovation capability required more than four years of intensive investment in people and process development, according to its former CEO, Koh Boon Hwee.[4] Having to build the capabilities from scratch, therefore, made investment in innovation an expensive proposition—a disincentive that led many Asian companies to import innovative products, services, and technologies or imitate ideas from elsewhere.

A third reason is that, as long as most Asian economies were in catch-up mode, local companies could afford to let innovation take a back seat. Today, some of Asia's markets are on the leading edge of using new technologies. Japan and Korea, for example, were the first countries to develop the market for wireless Internet services: In 2000 they accounted for 90 percent of world users, compared with 5 percent in Europe and 1 percent in the United States. But only now as the game moves from catch-up to the frontier of pioneering new markets have innovation capabilities become an essential ingredient in winning strategies.

Fourth, government spending on R&D and innovation in most Asian countries was low. Even the more developed economies in Asia rank poorly on this measure when compared to the United States and developed countries in Europe. In 1999, government R&D expenditure accounted for 0.27 percent of GDP in Singapore, 0.10 percent in Thailand, and 0.42 percent in Malaysia. That same year the U.S. government allocated 0.84 percent of GDP to R&D, while France, Germany, Finland, and the United Kingdom allocated 1.08 percent, 0.82 percent, 1.05 percent, and 0.67 percent, respectively. Moreover, U.S. and European government R&D spending spreads far beyond the narrow confines of defense, health, and infrastructure to include environmental control, energy, transportation, industrial production, space exploration, and university research grants. This broad-based R&D spending by governments generates important spillovers for the corporate sector. U.S. steel and bearings producer, Timken, for example, recently secured a $2 million grant for research into "memes" (contagious ideas that replicate like a virus, passed from mind to mind) as part of a government contract run in conjunction with a number of university departments. In Asia, for the most part, companies have benefited much less from these kinds of positive spillovers as an indirect source of funding for innovation.[5]

For all these reasons, large investments in R&D and innovation didn't make economic sense for many Asian companies in the past. But as we move into the next round of Asian competition, the resulting innovation deficit has left Asian companies with two major problems. First, many are stuck in a "commodization trap" where lack of differentiation among rival suppliers forces them to compete primarily on price. This means their margins are continually being squeezed. Second, because their innovation processes are underdeveloped, they are unable to satisfy Asian consumers' rising demand for variety and novelty, which now characterizes Asian markets.[6] Understanding these two problems is essential to help define exactly what kind of innovation capabilities Asian companies will need to develop to address them.

The Commoditization Trap

During the 1990s the amount of investment in adding new capacity in Asia was staggering. Fueled by cheap money from local and international banks, along with funds from equity investors around the world eager to share in the "Asian economic miracle," investment was growing almost exponentially year after year (as figure 4-2 dramatically illustrates). The drive for market share and scale economies was paramount: "If you don't win share in the takeoff phase of your market," so the argument went, "you can never dislodge your more aggressive rivals when the market starts to mature." The key to winning share in a growth market was having sufficient capacity available to supply. Falling costs with larger-scale investments provided an added bonus, allowing aggressive investors to win customers with more competitive pricing. The game was about raising capital, buying or cloning proven technology, and bringing new capacity onstream quickly.[7]

When this merry-go-round stopped abruptly in 1997, many Asian companies found themselves deep in a *commodization trap*: with massive excess capacity and a group of Asian rivals all using similar technologies, at large-scale, with similar costs, producing almost identical products and services. They were essentially set up to deliver large quantities of

FIGURE 4-2

Roots of the "Commoditization Trap"

CUMULATIVE INVESTMENT IN CAPACITY: EAST ASIA (EXCLUDING JAPAN)*

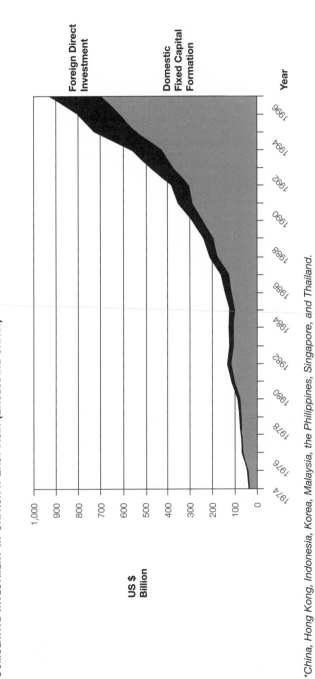

*China, Hong Kong, Indonesia, Korea, Malaysia, the Philippines, Singapore, and Thailand.

Source: Data drawn from United Nations website <http://unstats.un.org/unsd>.

commodity products and services in a situation where supply now far outstripped demand.

With little to differentiate their products and services from rivals, and no real technological advantage in their processes and systems, companies had no choice but to sell on price. Cutthroat competition and chronically low margins were the result. They were locked into a competitive stalemate: big competitors all with too much, large-scale capacity desperately trying to fill it by selling at close to marginal cost.

The Korean chemical companies, mostly part of the *chaebol* we discussed in chapter 2, are a classic case in point. They temporarily triumphed through rapid sales growth and ever-increasing scale in the quest for sheer size. But even during the boom, profitability was falling as the drive to fill up each new plant put pressure on prices. Years after the market collapsed, excess capacity in the industry still stood above 25 percent. Losses mounted.

Many companies hoped simply to survive long enough until the next economic upswing lifted them out of the profit mire. But the more forward-looking Asian companies have come to realize that such a strategy condemns them to something tantamount to purgatory: It means they can only make adequate returns during booms in the cycle when capacity is scarce, and even then their profitability will be limited by their lack of differentiation from competitors.

Some have decided to escape the commoditization trap by selling out to companies that can use the capacity to produce differentiated products and services. Korean companies that invested heavily in chemical plants like Daesung, Hanwah, and Samsung, for example, sold capacity for carbon black, whitening agents, lysine, structural resins, hydrogen peroxide, and chemical pesticides to Western companies including Degussa, BASF, BOC, and Novartis. The difference, as BASF Chairman Fred Baumgartner observed, is an ability to bring to this capacity innovative new products and technologies and sell these at a price premium because, as he put it, "we care less about size than about profit."[8]

In other areas Korean chemical companies have decided to stay the course, but their strategies have changed. LG Chem, for example, now focuses on bringing innovation to specialty chemicals, to engineering polymers, and to developing high-technology products such as mobile phone batteries, polarizing films used in computer monitors, and chemical products to make the next generation of electric cars. As Kim

Jong-pal, executive vice president of LG Chem, put it, "This reflects a shift in LG Chem's business away from commodity chemicals towards more attractive, high-end products, based on research and development rather than capital investment."[9] To build its innovation capabilities in these areas, LG has formed technology and R&D joint ventures with both Dow Chemical and Rohm and Haas and has taken three years of substantial losses to get the new business established and to pass breakeven.

The message is clear: If your company has fallen into a deep commoditization trap, waiting for the next cyclical upturn isn't a strategy for long-run profitability. As we saw in chapter 1, even when demand recovers, Asian producers will be faced with competing against massive, and ever lower-cost, Chinese capacity. The Asian game has changed. Innovation is now a key ingredient, even in industries that used to be seen solely in terms of competition through increased capacity and greater economies of scale.

The need for innovation to break out of the commoditization trap is equally pressing in many service businesses. Take the case of television broadcasting. Today there are more than a dozen satellites beaming programs down on Asia, in addition to many terrestrial channels. Capacity and bandwidth alone are no longer competitive strengths. Increasingly the winners will be those with fresh and innovative content: programming that attracts ever more demanding viewers. CNBC Asia, for example, introduced an interactive short message system (SMS) service that allows viewers to send questions to the channel and have their questions answered on air; Sony's innovative AXN "Action TV" channel has gained a large and loyal following.

This need for innovation to break out of the commodization trap is reinforced by the second major problem we identified above: As we enter the new millennium, Asian consumers are rapidly becoming more demanding.

New Demands by Asian Consumers

Primary consumer demand—from the first-time purchasers of everything from cars to washing machines and mobile phones—accounts for a large part of the market when an economy first takes off. During this phase, consumers are willing to accept standardized, basic consumer goods. If you have never owned a refrigerator before, the most basic box that keeps food cool at reasonable cost is acceptable. But once consumers move on to become second- or third-time purchasers, they look for features: the exact performance, styling, color, and so on that suits their individual needs. Consumers begin to demand higher product quality and variety, not simply more volume.

Whirlpool's experience when it entered the Chinese market for domestic appliances a few years ago is a good example of this change. Contrary to its initial expectations, it quickly found that Asian consumers rejected last year's American designs and technologies. Instead, they demanded environmentally friendly chlorofluorocarbon-free refrigerators, washing machines with state-of-the art electronic controls, and integrated, wall-mounted air conditioners instead of the standard type that hung precariously from a window space.[10]

The same is true of fast-moving consumer goods (like food or cosmetics) and services: Once your basic needs are satisfied by the range of products and services you consume, you start to look for particular varieties, flavors, sizes, presentations, and so on or for services customized to your individual needs. Even Asia's humble instant noodle now comes in more than twenty different flavors and a range of packaging from paper to Styrofoam cups, not to mention pink "Valentine's Day" and red and gold "Chinese New Year Limited Edition" varieties.[11] These trends are a simple fact of life that goes right back to Maslow's hierarchy of needs: As consumers become richer, they want better and more customized offerings, not more of the same.

These trends are now reaching far beyond Asia's wealthy elite. Throughout much of Asia, the mass market has now reached a stage of development where consumers are no longer satisfied with reliable but standard, often boring, products and services. Even in China and India, countries with huge rural populations (estimated at 900 million and 700 million, respectively) that have been little touched by consumerism, there are hundreds of millions of urban consumers who are now sophisticated buyers who demand goods and services with the innovative features, variety, and customization that fit their individual needs. Companies unable to provide more innovative, flexible products will literally be left on the shelf.

In parallel, a new generation of Asian consumers is entering the market. Unlike their parents, today's so-called X and Y generations have never lived through real hardship; they were born into a consumer society. As a result, they take abundance of goods and services largely for granted. Their choices reflect a complex mix of demand for higher-quality, fashion, a desire to express more individualism, and a "what's new?" mentality. While the precise implications of serving this new consumer generation will vary by industry, it is safe to say that they will demand even greater variety, customization, and innovation from suppliers than today's mainstream consumers.

Despite all these changes, the Asian consumer is unlikely to abandon his or her traditional nose for value. Nor are Asian business buyers going to forget their historic emphasis on costs. The convergence of new demands for nonstandard, customized products and services with a continued emphasis on value for money means that the kind of innovation Asian companies will need to escape the commoditization trap won't usually be "weird and wonderful" new inventions. Rather than falling into a love affair with Silicon Valley–style invention and garage entrepreneurship, therefore, the winners in the next round will be those who make a careful reassessment of exactly what kind of innovation is likely to bring competitive success in a uniquely Asian context.

Redefining Innovation

Much of the publicity and newspaper headlines around innovation focus on fundamental breakthroughs and Nobel Prize–winning research. But more often than not, the lion's share of the value of new ideas, products, services, and processes is captured by those who find innovative ways to commercialize, standardize, and engineer these inventions for volume and reduced costs. The first important step in meeting the innovation challenge faced by Asian companies, therefore, will be to choose their playing field both in terms of the products and services and the stage in the chain of innovation activities on which to focus—in short, to redefine what kind of innovation it makes sense to target in the next round of Asian competition.

Here it is useful to think about innovation as a chain involving three core activities, each with a different focus: (1) breakthrough, (2) extension, and (3) improvement.

Breakthrough Innovation

Breakthrough innovation involves activities that are often closer to art than science. This is the realm of discovery, ideas, and basic research.

The results tend to be random and the payoffs long. Success in this area requires not only access to the most talented researchers in their fields, with a massive depth of knowledge and experience, but also global linkages to research institutes and other development sites working on similar problems around the world. It doesn't necessarily make sense to start on the road to meeting the innovation challenge with investment designed to yield breakthroughs. But that doesn't mean the idea of innovation has to be abandoned. In fact, few new products and services in the world are developed and launched by the people that created the original inventions or technologies that underlie them. Many innovative companies effectively outsource this initial stage in the chain by licensing everything from new science to new molecules with the potential to be turned into innovative pharmaceuticals or new materials. Many of the final product and process patents, however, may be theirs.

Some Asian companies, such as Charoen Pokphand, Creative Technology, and Merlion Pharmaceutical, have been highly successful playing in the field of breakthrough innovation. It is instructive, however, that these three companies have done so by choosing fields of research that leverage off unique local advantages that give them a head start in these domains compared with rivals operating outside Asia.

In the course of its shrimp-farming activities, the Thai agribusiness group Charoen Pokphand, for example, has accumulated extensive knowledge and experience of aquaculture in the tropic climatic zones of Asia, including feed formulation, control of water quality, toxicology, and protein production and disease in sea life. Leveraging on this knowledge and work being undertaken in tropical biology research institutes in Thailand, the company successfully developed a new, hybrid strain of fish, known as "Tabtim," that is especially well suited to high-productivity aquaculture in tropical conditions while delivering appealing taste and other eating qualities like firm texture. Its genetic engineering research, meanwhile, is focused on genetically modified orchids, another species in which the local environment provides unique experience that can be leveraged.

Singapore's Creative Technology is the source of breakthrough innovation in audio and multimedia devices linked to personal computers (PCs). Founded in 1981 by local entrepreneur Sim Wong Hoo, Creative began experimenting with PC audio, producing the Sound Blaster card in 1989 that set a new industry standard and by 2000 accounted for 70 percent of the word's soundcard market. More recently the company came forth with its revolutionary NOMAD range of MP3 portable digital audio players, devices the size of a Sony Walkman, capable of holding music equivalent to 150 compact discs. Again Creative's playing field turned out to be well chosen because its breakthrough innovation goals were able to leverage off well-developed local knowledge of how to design PC devices and circuit boards and a continuous flow of related technology coming into Singapore from the electronics multinationals operating there.

Merlion Pharmaceutical, a company that emerged from an alliance between Glaxo Smith Kline and the Centre for Natural Products Research in Singapore, has isolated over 400 naturally occurring, active compounds for use in the development of new pharmaceuticals, many of them involving cutting-edge science. Over one-half of the cancer and anti-infective drugs in use in 2002 contained one or more of these compounds. This breakthrough innovation playing field is more commonly associated with companies based in the United States or Europe. But in Singapore, Merlion has a unique advantage to leverage: access to a library of over 500,000 unique extracts collected from bacteria, fungi, plants, and marine organisms occurring naturally in North and Southeast Asia.

The moral of these examples is clear: Focusing on breakthrough research is one way for Asian companies to meet the innovation challenge they face. But if you decide to adopt this strategy, start by picking a playing field where you can leverage unique local advantages: experience in tropical agriculture in the case of Charoen Pokphand, a core of local knowledge around circuit board design in the case of Creative Technology, and a library of organisms endemic to Asia in the case of Merlion.

Innovation by Extension

Innovation by extension involves taking an existing product or service concept and extending the functions or sources of value it offers to the customer (by making it more convenient to use, for example). This offers an attractive alternative to many companies compared with projects aimed at breakthrough innovation. Not only is the probability of success generally higher and the payback period usually shorter, but focusing on extension helps a company build its innovation capabilities and processes. It can therefore help establish a solid foundation for more stretching innovation goals in the future.

Many Asian companies have a strong history of importing technologies or product concepts and adapting them to local conditions (part of the heritage we discussed in chapter 2). These selfsame adaptation skills can be redeployed to facilitate extension innovation. Take the example of Nongshim, a Korean manufacturer of noodles. Nongshim built its business by repositioning traditional, packaged noodles as "an inexpensive meal to cook at home." The key to this repositioning was the use of a Japanese technology, which Nongshim adapted to produce products with highly spiced, Korean flavors. As imitators entered the market, commoditization of this base business led it to search for ways to reposition its product yet again, this time as an "anytime, anywhere snack." Leveraging its experience in adaptation, it came up with an innovative, instant noodle snack product prepackaged in a facsimile of a traditional Korean bowl (using synthetic resin instead of the ubiquitous white polystyrene cup). Having unlocked new sources of customer value by combining convenience with a higher-quality, traditional look, it was able to charge a price premium that represented a threefold improvement in margins.

Likewise, SK Telecom's *n.Top* service has made it one of the two most innovative providers of mobile telephone–based services in the world (along with NTT DoCoMo's *i-mode*). *n.Top* offers automated location-finder services for everything from restaurants to ATM machines, as well as news, sports, weather, entertainment, banking, e-mailing, and scheduling. But the basic underlying technology is a standard, second-generation (2G) mobile telephone network. The service is a classic, innovative extension of well-known technology. Clearly, choosing extension innovation as the playing field can still allow a company to revolutionize its profitability and successfully break out of the commoditization trap. Unlike breakthrough innovation, however, it may offer more opportunities to leverage Asian companies' heritage of excellence in commercialization.

Improvement Innovation

A third innovation playing field is to focus on improvement of existing products or services without significantly extending either functionality or value-added. This kind of "improvement innovation" may not grab headlines or Nobel Prizes, but it can still open the way to significant business enhancement. It should not be dismissed as a less creative, poor cousin. Quite the contrary, a focus on improvement innovation may reflect the best fit between perceived potential for innovation in a business, scope to leverage off existing knowledge and heritage capabilities, and willingness to invest.

A classic example of the power of improvement innovation is the success of Citiraya Industries, a Singapore-based company that makes its money out of recycling electronic waste. Citiraya offers a one-stop service for recycling and processing of electronic scrap and rejected electronic products, recovering precious metals such as gold, palladium, and silver. Its business model is fundamentally the same as the family *karang gumi* (scrap trading) business from which it emerged. It began with standard technology imported from Japan. But key to Citiraya's success has been improvement innovations: the idea of an integrated, one-stop service for its customers; a relentless stream of advances in processing technology that have dramatically improved yields (it now recovers 150 grams of gold from every ton of waste); and an Enterprise Resource Planning system adapted from manufacturing industries that allows it to provide a seamless, worldwide network for its multinational customers.

The company leveraged local knowledge accumulated in Singapore's electronics manufacturing industries by using it to help innovate efficient ways to deconstruct the very products its sisters were so good at putting together. Citiraya now operates in Brazil, China, Germany, India, Italy, Malaysia, the Philippines, Taiwan, Thailand, and the United Kingdom.[12]

Another Asian firm that has succeeded on the basis of improvement innovation is Thailand's Aapico, which now designs, supplies, and tests jigs—the machines that hold car parts in place for welding—for DaimlerChrysler car plants around the globe. It started in the late 1980s producing low-technology jigs that incorporated manual clips. But a series of improvement innovations took it through hydraulic jigs to today's state-of-the art electronic jigs capable of use in high-precision manufacturing operations. Even top-end jigs don't involve proverbial rocket science, but Aapico is regarded as having developed what is "probably the best concept design for low volume tooling in the world."[13]

None of these innovations involved development of breakthrough technologies. But by clear focus on innovative improvements to the existing systems, the results were just as dramatic. They also had the added advantage of exploiting an aspect of Asia's business heritage that affords equal respect to "discovery creativity and applications creativity" (as we put it in chapter 2)—a respect that is often lacking in the West.

The boundaries between breakthrough, extension, and improvement aren't hard and fast. But the key point is this: Don't assume that rising to the innovation challenge means investing in blue-sky research or a dramatic shift in your product or target markets. Innovation does not have to involve a leap into the great unknown. It can occur at every level and every activity in a business. Choosing a realistic innovation playing field—and one that plays to your unique strengths, local knowledge, and business heritage—is a key first step.

Betting on Innovation

Whatever mix of breakthrough, extension, and improvement innovation a company chooses, however, it will obviously still be exposed to residual risks. Most managers are only too well aware of the risk that investment may not generate viable innovations and the risk that changes in the market environment render promising innovations irrelevant or unprofitable. But in balancing the potential benefits against the risks of investment in innovation companies also need to take into account the risk that their existing business model will become obsolete, leaving them stranded.

Successful companies often get ahead of their competitors by focusing their efforts on a particular segment of customers or geographic market so that they come to know more about the behavior and needs of these potential buyers than anyone else. They design a profit-generating engine, based on a particular price, margin, and cost structure, that is in turn underpinned by a set of investments in the capability to source, produce, distribute, and support a product or service these customers value. Over time, this profit engine is continually fine-tuned, often reaping economies of scale, scope, and learning along the way. But this strategy also carries an important source of risk: the risk that a company's market offering becomes irrelevant to customers or its technologies and processes are rendered obsolete. The sea change in Asia's competitive environment discussed in chapter 1 means this risk of obsolescence is now high for companies in Asia.

Failure to manage the risk of obsolescence in the face of a changing environment can have devastating consequences. Consider the experience of the veritable trading house, Inchcape. With a strong trading base in Southeast Asia, its geographic reach extended through to the Americas, the Caribbean, India, Europe, and Africa with interests in over 500 companies in 44 countries. It became a professional distributor, marketer, and seller of products and technologies of its "principals" (the owners of the branded products and services it traded) and as a provider of specialist services. But as the principals for whom Inchcape acted as agent became more familiar with the behavior of local markets, wanted more control over their market positioning, and built up the scale necessary to cover the fixed costs of their own local operations, they began to integrate forward into Inchcape's business. As a traditional "trader," it had few places to turn. With finely honed trading skills, but lacking the breadth of capabilities to add value in other ways, its strategic options were tightly circumscribed. The result was a long period of downsizing that saw it retreat to become a specialist motor vehicle distributor with a limited network and a much smaller-sized business. Contrast that with Li & Fung and Noble (discussed in chapter 3), which remain growing and profitable trading companies today, in part through investment in innovation that opened up new options to prosper in a changing environment.

By opening up new options on the future, investment in innovation across a broad swathe of activities cuts the risk of being left strategically stranded like Inchcape.[14] Historically Asian companies have coped with this risk by diversifying across industries. But this won't be possible in Asia's new environment, where investment will have to be focused on fewer businesses to build the depth of capabilities necessary to compete. Another way of spreading risk is now required. The solution lies in building a portfolio of innovation options that allows risk to be diversified across technologies and market trends instead of industries.

Building a Portfolio of Innovation Options

Entrepreneurial start-ups often bet their investment in innovation on a single technology or set of assumptions about how the market will develop. But most established companies are rightly uncomfortable with "betting the farm" on a single outcome. The solution is to be found in investing in a portfolio of innovation options that cover the main technological and market discontinuities that the company believes it may face.

Take the example of NTT DoCoMo. In late 2001, the company faced a switch from second-generation to third-generation (3G) mobile telephone services that had been described as the biggest gamble in business history. Not only was it unclear which of the competing 3G technologies (W-CDMA, CDMA2000, or TD-CDMA) would become the industry standard, it was even less clear what 3G services would be popular among users and ultimately profitable for NTT DoCoMo. Would, for example, consumers pay for video capabilities to receive mobile TV, or would demand for still pictures or the display of Web pages prove to be the "killer application"?

NTT DoCoMo prepared a matrix of the major alternative ways demand for 3G might potentially develop. Faced with these many uncertainties about where it should invest in innovation, it could have decided to wait and be a follower. As the leading mobile company in Japan but facing competition from powerful global competitors like Vodaphone, however, such a strategy would risk dramatic loss of market share while it struggled to catch up with the innovators. At the same time, it was uneconomic for NTT DoCoMo to launch a set of services covering every eventuality (investment costs to cover all the cells in the matrix would be crippling).

The solution was to make investments in a set of innovation projects that would enable the company to test the technical feasibility and market acceptance of the most promising services such as mobile banking, remote medical diagnostics, video mail, or mobile TV. The company would then be in a position to rapidly scale up particular services as it became clearer which way the market was evolving, or in response to competitive threat. NTT DoCoMo invested enough in mobile TV to understand its technical feasibility, for example, but did not launch it immediately.

By investing in a set of these innovation projects, NTT DoCoMo created a portfolio of options on the future. It could choose to exercise any one of these options at a later date by investing the additional capital necessary to launch it into the market and scale it up into a full-fledged business. In this way the company was able to spread its risk across alternative technologies and services, while conserving its capital by limiting the initial investment in each.

Innovation options can be held in one of the following three forms:

- *An idea* for a new opportunity that has been thought through but not tested.

- *An experiment or pilot* that has been conducted to test a new business model or market proposition.

- *A venture* where the pilot has been launched as a stand-alone business, but not yet scaled up or rolled out into a full-fledged division.

The choice of whether to maintain an option on the future as an idea, experiment, or venture involves a trade-off between cost on one hand and speed on the other. If the option is maintained as an idea, we minimize the cost of the option—maintaining an idea does not involve much investment. But the speed with which we can exercise that option and its power as a launching pad for a new business are limited because we have not tested the idea or developed it into a business venture. By contrast, if we decide to develop every option we want to maintain in our portfolio right through to the point where it has been launched as a venture, the total investment required could be huge. Developing the option through to the venture stage, however, enables a quicker scale-up when we detect that the environment makes it opportune to exercise the option. It makes sense for a company to invest in innovation projects that create a portfolio of options on the future at different stages of development.[15]

Recall the case of Charoen Pokphand (CP). They invested in understanding genetic engineering and genetically modified (GM) foods by conducting research on orchids. The primary reason was not because orchids are likely to become a big part of their $15 billion of sales. Rather they were investing in the option of understanding GM technology. They kept this option at the stage of a set of experiments designed to improve CP's knowledge about the new technology. In their view, it didn't pay to grow this option into a full-scale business yet, or even to launch it as venture, because the market wasn't ready.

Some of CP's other innovations, like development of the Tabtim fish mentioned above, have been pushed more quickly through the cycle, allowing them to be fully tested in the market. But they have not yet been developed into a full-scale business. Before that, there is still more to learn. Yet other CP innovations, like new strains of seeds, chicken breeding stock, or innovative processes for maintaining the health of farmed prawns while maximizing their growth rates, have been rapidly deployed in their mainstream, full-scale agribusinesses. Together these different investments in innovation form a powerful portfolio of options for future expansion and development. Their portfolio gives CP a high level of flexibility to maintain its competitive advantages depending on the way market and technological conditions unfold.

Generating and maintaining a portfolio of innovation options, therefore, makes particular sense for Asian innovators given their rapidly changing environment. It is also a natural extension of the traditional way overseas Chinese companies have gone about managing risk. As we saw in chapter 2, these companies, rather than shying away from risky opportunities, have sought to reduce their exposure by limiting their initial investments and maximizing their opportunities to learn before making further commitments. Creating a portfolio of innovation options that can be exercised through further investment at a later stage is an analogous approach.

By treating investment in innovation as the creation of a portfolio of options, risks can also be diversified, and success no longer rests on correctly predicting the continuance of any single trend or the success of a particular technology. Of course, depending on the way the future environment unfolds, not all of these options will be exercised. However, those that are discarded won't have been wasted. Instead they will have served the useful purpose of insuring against an uncertain future. After all, we don't say fire insurance was a waste of money because our house didn't burn down!

Stimulating a Flow of Innovation

To develop a rich portfolio of innovation options requires quality raw material: access to a strong flow of ideas for new or improved products, services, and processes; knowledge about emerging technologies; and complementary know-how. This raw material can be accessed in four main ways: (1) by challenging internal orthodoxy, (2) by accessing underexploited pockets of knowledge scattered around the world, (3) through new types of alliances, and (4) through targeted acquisitions. All four have a potentially important contribution to ramping up Asian innovation.

Challenging Internal Orthodoxy

Every company has a set of internal *orthodoxies*—assumptions about the behavior of its customers and competitors, the economics of its business, and the keys to success—that are implicit and therefore never questioned.[16] These orthodoxies constrain innovation because they act in the background to automatically exclude new ideas before they even get considered. In the past, for example, most companies in the business of mobile telephony implicitly assumed that mobile phone technology was for people to communicate. This orthodoxy seems so self-evidently correct that it wasn't questioned for decades (after all, if mobile phones aren't for people, who are they for?). But think again: What about using mobile phone technology to allow products sitting on a shelf or on the back of a truck to communicate their location automatically to an inventory-control computer sitting in the central warehouse? Today, the use of mobile telephony technologies to allow inanimate objects to communicate is revolutionizing logistics. In 2003 for example, Gillette, the U.S. razor blades and batteries group, began using radio frequency identification tags to allow individual products to communicate their location, whether on a retail shelf or in a shipping container. Gillette's initial order was for 500 million units.[17] Yet just a few years ago the innovations that have opened up this huge new market weren't even considered by leading companies in mobile telephony because of a deep-seated orthodoxy that implicitly ruled them out of consideration.

After years of successful expansion, many Asian companies have developed a strong sense of "what works" in their businesses. They are therefore replete with deeply embedded orthodoxies that exclude important possibilities for innovation. In strategy discussions with several Asian airlines, for example, the author discovered that it was an article of faith that passengers have to face forward in an aircraft—a constraint that greatly hampers innovative use of space. This was revealed as a dangerous orthodoxy when British Airways (BA) stole a march on Asian carriers (who prided themselves on offering superior comfort) by reconfiguring its cabins to provide business-class passengers with flat beds at minimal loss of seats. BA achieved this innovation by breaking out of the "schoolroom, face forward" orthodoxy, having its passengers face backward as well as forward, as is common in trains.

The heritage of highly centralized organization structures and reward based on reliable execution in many Asian companies (identified in chapter 2) serves to reinforce damaging internal orthodoxy. Challenging orthodoxies can play an important role in stimulating the flow of innovation necessary to win in the new Asian environment where companies need to be different as well as better. Consider a few examples. At the Japanese auto-parts maker Denso Corporation, managers believed that automation of production lines had reached its limits because of an inability to cope with volatile demand and unpredictable life cycles. Their conventional solution was to put humans back onto the assembly lines. But an engineer at a plant in Nagoya, Shuichi Hashimoto, and his team overturned the orthodoxy that automation couldn't be flexible by designing robots that could move around, stop at the right point, and change their posture to cope with variations in throughput and rapid changes in product design.[18]

Faced with problems of how to build electric motors small enough to power micromachines used to clear cholesterol from human arteries, Kazushi Ishiyama and his team broke orthodoxy and dispensed with the electric motor altogether. They came up with a device like a magnetized rotating screw that could be spun and steered from outside the body by means of a three-dimensional magnetic field. A Chinese researcher working in Singapore, Zheng Zhongming, was presented with the problem of how to efficiently decontaminate soil from industrial sites. The orthodox view, using microbes to eat the contaminants in soil, was nonpolluting but slow; chemicals were faster, but the effluent was just as polluting. Zheng's answer was to wash the soil with a nontoxic solution and then unleash a fungus to detoxify the contaminated effluent. Growing in a liquid, the fungus worked at a much faster rate than on the soil itself.[19]

Breaking orthodoxies is not only an effective way to stimulate technological advance, however. VIA Technologies, one of Taiwan's most successful semiconductor makers, prospered by overturning Intel's business orthodoxy that successive generations of chips should be increasingly powerful. Started by an ex-Intel engineer, Chen Wen-chi, VIA's breakthrough was an innovative chip-set that was less powerful but much cheaper to produce.[20]

So how should other Asian companies go about stimulating innovation by challenging their orthodoxies? One way is to get staff at all levels to ask themselves the question: "What are ten things you never hear customers say about your company or industry, but wish they would?"[21] You never hear bank customers, for example, say how much fun it is to visit a branch! This kind of questioning should help banks ask what it is about the banking experience that their customers find unappealing and how they could redesign their customer interface to make it enjoyable. Another example: You seldom here people remark that packaging is easy to open. One reason is that a common orthodoxy among makers of packaging is that their job is to keep products well sealed. As a result, they tend not to pay enough attention to opportunities afforded by innovating packages designed for easy opening.

Some other questions useful in unearthing orthodoxies that can be challenged to stimulate innovative ideas include:

- *Who is not buying my product or service and why?* That's how Fuji and Kodak came to supply disposable cameras, overturning the orthodoxy that only people who had a camera with them could be customers.

- *What stands in the way of potential customers easily accessing my product or service?* Overturning the orthodoxy that Asians would only buy insurance face-to-face from an agent led to the innovation of financial services companies selling insurance over the telephone and the Internet.

- *How can we deliver the familiar functionality to customers in a new way?* Overcoming the orthodoxy among electronics companies that text had to be typed in through a conventional keyboard was necessary before SMS messaging could emerge.

Challenging their heritage of orthodoxies, however, will only take Asian companies part of the way toward ramping up the rate of innovation to the level required to win in the next round of competition. The flow of internally generated ideas will need to be combined with insights and knowledge drawn from the rest of the world. As we saw in chapter 2, learning and integrating global best practice is one of the historical strengths of many Asian companies. But to leverage this capability to help fuel innovation, it will need to be deployed in a new way.

A New Approach to Learning from the World

Licensing and learning technologies and innovative products, services, and processes from abroad has served many Asian companies well in the past.[22] But at best, a license is likely to bring you to competitive parity with its owner and other licensees. Many licensers tightly restrict their licensees from changing the technology or product any way, and mastering a new product or technology that is licensed is often very different from understanding how to develop it further. You might achieve minor innovations in the course of adapting borrowed technologies or ideas. These strategies may help make you better, but they aren't likely to make you much different. Almost by definition, relying on others is more useful for catch-up than for innovation.

On the other hand, trying to innovate by relying on technologies and market understanding drawn only from around your home territory puts you at a severe handicap. You are likely to face critical gaps in the knowledge you need to win. You risk missing important customer trends emerging overseas. Despite strong engineering skills, for example, Korean automobile makers were unsuccessful in sophisticated export markets until after they were able to infuse design expertise drawn from overseas into their product development processes.

Relying solely on homegrown sources of innovation also leaves you exposed to competitors coming from left field with unfamiliar tactics that catch you by surprise. Myopic competition, innovating using local knowledge, perfecting your product or service to meet the needs of customers in your home market, and benchmarking yourself against domestic competitors have become high-risk strategies. They will become even less tenable as Asia's historic national fiefdoms crumble.

If neither licensing nor replicating what you have learned from others, nor relying solely on your home-grown innovation capabilities are sufficient to compete in an era where innovation becomes critical to Asian success, then what is required? The answer lies in the ability to access underutilized knowledge scattered around the world—not existing product designs or proven technologies—and to combine this with your distinctive local knowledge base to create something new and unique.

Beyond Catch-up Learning

Accessing knowledge that can fuel innovation is very different from learning existing best practices. For knowledge that helps you master best practice, you can go to the existing "capitals" of you industry. But acquiring knowledge that will allow you to innovate, making you different from competitors, requires searching out emerging pockets of knowledge that competitors haven't yet spotted. It also means that it's not enough just to access well-documented technologies because in the information age these are readily available to all. The knowledge that will set your company apart is precisely the know-how that is difficult to move—in people's heads and difficult to understand outside its local context—because that is the knowledge that your competitors probably lack.

To use this knowledge to contribute to innovation, meanwhile, you have to be able to subtly combine (or "meld") it with your distinctive, local expertise to create products, services, or processes that, by definition, haven't yet been invented. That is very different from learning to replicate and adapt something that already exists elsewhere.

The experience of Shiseido, the Japanese cosmetics and skin care company, shows what is involved. Shiseido found its market share and margins under threat as competitors used their exclusive perfume brands to gain loyalty from distribution. But the knowledge base around fragrance development and marketing Shiseido needed was underdeveloped in Japan. The company was only able to successfully innovate in this area through a sustained effort to internalize new knowledge from France, including starting production in Gien, close to other leading fragrance makers. But it also searched out less conventional sources of knowledge by buying two prestigious Paris beauty salon chains, Carita and Alexandre Zouari, so as to observe trend-setting customers firsthand. It also decided to hire as CEO of its newly starting perfume company in France a woman who had been the marketing head of Yves Saint Laurent Parfums (quite a departure for a Japanese company that was used to appointing expatriates to head up its major overseas units).

By melding what it had learned from multiple sources of fragrance knowledge in France with its local expertise in cosmetics formulation and manufacture in Japan, Shiseido was able to revitalize distribution for its cosmetics business in Japan. It also became an innovative and very profitable player in the perfume business with products like Eau d'Issey and the Jean Paul Gaultier line.[23]

Licensing perfumes or even technologies from France wouldn't have made Shiseido an innovator. At best, it might have caught up with its international competitors. Innovation using only the knowledge available in Japan would have left it lagging way behind the world's best. But by accessing underexploited knowledge about perfumes, combining this with existing in-house expertise, and learning how to develop and market new fragrances, Shiseido was able to become a world-class innovator in its business.[24]

Prospecting for Underexploited Knowledge

To identify and access knowledge that will take them beyond competitive parity and fuel innovation, Asian companies will need to become global prospectors capable of finding hotbeds of emerging technology or bellwether customers that foreshadow future trends. This means drawing on new sources beyond those Asia used in the catch-up phase. Indicators of underexploited knowledge and technologies include:

- *Leapfroggers.* These are new groups of customers who aren't hampered by previous product experiences or an installed base of product. New knowledge is more likely to be generated in markets unencumbered by legacy technologies. North America wasn't the right place for Asian companies to look for emerging smart-card technologies, for example. The canny prospectors instead scoured Europe, where cards with magnetic strips were much less established and smart cards were leapfrogging traditional credit cards as a result.

- *Locations where technologies are converging.* Here, mutually reinforcing innovative trends are likely to create a new knowledge base. Everyone looks to Silicon Valley as a source of emerging technology in chips and software. But the pharmaceutical company Glaxo Smith Kline, stole a march on the competition in the race to develop drugs using the new technique of "combinational chemistry" when it recognized that it too should be looking in the Valley rather than in the traditional capitals of the pharmaceuticals industry. The reason: Silicon Valley was the place where technologies were converging between computer science, robotics, miniaturization, and biotechnologies.

- *Lifestyle leaders.* Bellwether consumers whose behavior can be used to predict future trends in the global market tend to be concentrated in particular locations around the world. It's probably not surprising, for example, that Scandinavia's rapidly changing lifestyles bred Ikea's success in modern, affordable furniture. Innovation in Asian companies can benefit from intercepting such trends before their competition.

- *Government/university science centers.* Many of these have underutilized technologies, resources, and skills. It is estimated, for example, that there are over 15,000 scientists working on biotechnology research at China's seventy-four national laboratories within its universities and research institutes.[25] Paradoxically, because of the historical divides between Chinese state-owned enterprises and their cousins in academia, much of this technology and knowledge is underexploited.

- *Regulatory differences.* Such differences can facilitate the rapid advancement of knowledge in particular areas. China, South Korea, and Singapore are likely to be productive places to look for innovative ideas emerging from stem cell research due to a more open regulatory environment than, say, traditional biotechnology centers in Europe and the United States where regulations are more restrictive.[26]

Of course it's one thing to identify underexploited pockets of knowledge that could fuel innovation, it's quite another to access it. The problem of tapping into these new pockets of knowledge is particularly acute because, as we have already mentioned, the knowledge that will likely result in innovation that will set you apart from competitors isn't that which is well documented or on the Internet. Rather, it's the messy knowledge that is in people's heads and is difficult to interpret without understanding the local context, much like the subtle know-how Shiseido had to access about what makes a successful fragrance.

Tapping into new pockets of knowledge that are useful for innovation usually requires more than short-term visits, "study missions," searching the Internet, or a visit to the patent office. To tap into the poorly codified knowledge in people's heads that is bound up in an unfamiliar, local context generally requires close and sustained interaction with local partners. Fortunately, this plays to one of the strengths of Asian corporate heritage: know-how in alliance management. Many of these native skills can be parlayed into the use of alliances to promote innovation. But to be really effective in assisting innovation, some things about the way Asian companies have used alliances in the past will need to change.

New Types of Innovation Alliances

Historically the division of responsibilities between Asian and overseas partners has been based on the local partner providing access to distribution, market knowledge, permits, relationships, and local resources. The foreign partner typically contributed the core products, technologies, and systems. Alliances formed by the Japanese car makers with Astra of Indonesia, by Daewoo and Hyundai of Korea, and by Proton's early relationship with Mitsubishi are all examples of this type of arrangement.

Such relationships often lead to some technology and knowledge transfer to local partners.[27] But in most cases, the local partner failed to develop the depth of capabilities necessary for independent innovation. To meet the innovation challenge, tomorrow's alliances will need to be different. They will have to be explicitly designed to bring together knowledge from both parties to create something fundamentally new, rather than to adapt and implement a tried and tested formula or proven technology imported from abroad. This will require each partner to have already established a strong set of innovation capabilities and processes through which to leverage the innovation potential of the alliance and a structure that allows joint discovery.

These "new style" alliances are beginning to emerge. Charoen Pokphand (CP), for example, has used its alliances with the leading British food retailer, Tesco, to incorporate Tesco's intimate knowledge of the European consumer preferences, packaging, and supermarket logistics into CP's innovation processes. The aim was to innovate a new "Kitchen of the World" concept that would allow CP to supply beautifully presented, table-ready chilled foods for sale in the world's supermarkets. But this was only possible because CP had already established an effective innovation process and accumulated its own, distinctive knowledge to bring to the party.

To use alliances for innovation rather than catch-up, Asian firms will also need to become participants in international alliance consortia at the early stages of the development of innovative products and technologies. Samsung, for example, recently became a partner with established innovators like Sony, AOL, and Compaq to invest $88 million in a project managed by the chip designer Transmeta to develop low-power-usage chips for use in battery-powered products. Like a caravan crossing the desert, these firms will ally during the development phase. But they will then separate and take the resulting technology and apply it to their own innovation processes. Again, this requires a strong existing portfolio of innovation and the processes to utilize new technology independently as a prerequisite to use the alliance as a means of meeting the innovation challenge.[28]

In short, to succeed in the next round of competition, more Asian companies will have to move from passively sourcing innovation through alliances to become active, independent players capable of using new-style alliances to bolster their own product development and innovation processes.

In some cases, however, the technologies and know-how Asian companies need to innovate effectively won't be on offer from alliance partners (many of whom will want to keep them proprietary). Here, carefully targeted acquisitions have a key role to play.

Targeted Acquisitions

Forward-looking Asian competitors are using a strategy of targeted acquisitions to gain access to specialist knowledge and technologies they need as input to their innovation processes. Of fifty-three acquisitions by Asian companies in the United States and Europe reported in the press during the first half of 2000, for example, 68 percent were designed to access new technologies and know-how that could be used to stimulate innovation.[29]

The acquisition of an 80 percent stake in the British sports car producer, Lotus, by Malaysian car maker Proton (*Perusahaan Otomobil Nasional*) in 1996 is an early example. The former alliance between Mitsubishi and Proton had recently been concluded, leaving Proton without a source of innovative technology and design skills. Lotus, a low-volume, niche car maker, but with strong engineering and design expertise, offered a source of key knowledge to help Proton introduce innovative models.

In addition to a purchase price of £51 million, Proton invested a further £7 million to upgrade the engineering facilities at Lotus's British headquarters. A team of Proton engineers was dispatched to work jointly with Lotus staff on the development of a luxury family sedan to upgrade Proton's existing range. By 2001 the investment bore fruit when Proton released the Satria Gti model to great acclaim. The car, which embodied substantially upgraded features and technology, had been developed by the joint team working at Lotus. Proton then went on to incorporate some of these innovations to upgrade its entire range. According to Robert Tickner, a senior manager at Lotus Engineering, the acquisition has had "a significant impact on Proton's ability to make and market" an improved range of cars.[30]

Acquisitions designed to improve innovation capabilities are, however, fraught with risks. Seeking to gain access to new technology to upgrade its product line, for example, Samsung acquired a 40 percent stake in the U.S. personal computer producer AST for $378 million. Soon after Samsung took control, culture clashes led to a rash of departures among senior engineers and management. While Samsung had been unable to integrate AST smoothly into its innovation processes, AST's losses widened, forcing it to invest a further $260 million to keep the company afloat. In 1998, after three years of mounting losses, Samsung disposed of the company, having made little progress in bolstering its stream of innovation and nursing a large writedown.

Before making an acquisition as a vehicle to help address the challenge of innovation, it is critical to resolve the following issues:

- *Why am I acquiring the whole company rather than hiring individuals or licensing particular technologies?* Acquisitions only make sense when the knowledge or technology is tacit (i.e., not well codified) or is deeply embedded in the systems and culture of the company so that it can't easily be extracted by other means.

- *Where do the competencies and knowledge I need reside?* Are they in the heads of a few people or in broadly shared experience or systems broadly shared across the company?

- *How will I effectively transfer or utilize the competencies and knowledge I need?* Knowledge that can only be understood by experience or cannot be understood outside a particular local context is difficult to integrate into you own stream of innovation.

- *How do I need to change my own organization to make it more receptive to learning from the company we have acquired?* This question is particularly important if the acquired company is smaller or less financially successful.

Targeted acquisitions can, therefore, be used to help stimulate innovation and fill critical gaps in the knowledge base required to develop new products and services. To achieve these goals, post-acquisition integration must first preserve the knowledge base being acquired and facilitate the proper links with the acquirer's existing capabilities. But beware of seeing an aggressive acquisition program as the easy route to ramping up innovation: Mixed success to date would suggest the complex integration required to use an acquired company as an innovation arm is something many Asian companies have yet to master.

Rising to the Innovation Challenge

In the last round of competition, innovation was an optional extra for most companies operating in Asia; their sources of advantage emphasized low costs, reaping the benefits of economies of scale, and building capacity to supply rapidly growing demand. Against this background, Asia's innovation deficit is neither surprising nor irrational. The returns for making substantial investments in innovation were often low compared with the opportunity costs of resources and managerial attention.

But as the Asian competitive environment enters a new phase, lack of innovation has left many companies stuck in a commoditization trap where margins are continually squeezed by lack of differentiation. The need to break out of this trap combined with growing demand from Asian consumers for more innovative offerings means that ramping up innovation will need to become a top priority in the next round of competition. Just as control of efficient manufacturing capacity was a profitable choke point in the past, control of proprietary processes and innovative product designs and service formulas will be a key choke point for extracting profit in the future. Yet innovation is clearly a risky business, especially for firms that lack the depth of experience and capabilities to invest in it efficiently.

To meet this new innovation challenge, Asian firms need to abandon the "inventor in the garage" metaphor of innovation and target a mix of breakthrough innovation, extension, and improvement that leverages their own historic strengths in commercialization and creative application of promising technologies and ideas. The risks of betting on innovation need to be diversified across alternative technologies and possible changes in customer behavior by building and actively managing a portfolio of innovation options on the future.

To develop a strong portfolio of innovation options, new strategies will be required. Today's highly centralized and execution-focused organizations will need to make decisive moves to challenge their internal orthodoxies and thereby release their self-imposed constraints on innovation. A new approach to learning from the world will need to leave licensing and catch-up learning behind and allow Asian companies to begin identifying and accessing technologies that are only just emerging and underexploited pockets of know-how scattered around the globe. New types of alliances, specifically designed for joint discovery, rather than adapting existing technologies and products, will need to be established. Finally the role of acquisitions will need to be expanded. In the next round of competition, acquisitions will need to be used as a source of new technologies and know-how to fuel innovation, not only as a way of securing additional capacity or market share. Using acquisitions in this new way will require even more careful acquisition integration.

This changing role of innovation in the next round of competition also has far-reaching implications for multinationals operating in Asia. The competition to launch innovative products and services and deploy new technologies in Asia is certain to heat up. Multinationals will therefore be forced to exploit their innovations into Asia more fully and more rapidly.

To better keep up with advancement, fashion, and new technologies and processes emerging from tomorrow's more innovation-focused Asia, multinationals will need to ramp up their own innovation activities in Asia. Multinationals will also need to become more open to the idea of their "Asian periphery" becoming a key participant in their global innovation process. Too often in the past, Asia was regarded only as a manufacturing base or as a source of customers in a growing market. Too few multinational companies have seen the potential of leveraging innovations from their Asian operations across other markets. Even those who have done so frequently fail to recognize Asia as an important, ongoing source of innovation. The primacy of the home base and the "parent" organization as the fount of innovation dies hard.

Forward-thinking multinationals are, however, beginning to reassess the potential role of Asia in their global innovation strategies. The global drinks group Diageo, for example, has an innovation group in Hong Kong whose role is to seek out emerging trends and technologies within the region for global innovations. Johnson & Johnson has begun to deploy innovative manufacturing processes designed in Asia across its subsidiaries in the region, rather than implementing solutions born in the West. DHL Asia, meanwhile, created "Jumbo Box," its new "flat-fee" courier solution for bulky items in Asia. It has now been successfully rolled out across the world.

As Asian companies seek to ramp up their rate of innovation, there will also be new opportunities for smaller foreign companies to participate as technology and innovation partners—opportunities that were precluded by old-style Asian joint ventures aimed at exploiting products and service designs already proven elsewhere. Multinationals will need to decide whether to join these new consortia as allies or see them as rivals with whom to compete.

If successful, the ramp-up in Asian innovation will open the way to much higher levels of value creation in Asia, both by local companies and multinationals. But from the corporate standpoint, creating extra value is only the first step toward higher profits. Before it hits the bottom line, that extra value must be communicated to potential customers and captured in higher margins. That's where branding can help.

Chapter 5

Building Asian Brands

Of the top sixty most valuable brands in the world, how many belong to Asian companies? By 2001 the answer was only four. Three of these—Sony, Toyota, and Honda—were Japanese. Outside Japan, only one Asian company had a brand valued in the top sixty in 2001: Korea's Samsung, which ranked forty-second.[1]

This paucity of powerful Asian brands doesn't align with the size and strength that today's top Asian corporates have attained. Given that in that same year, 2001, the region's largest one hundred companies each had an average of over $20 billion in sales and nearly $40 billion in assets, their brands could be expected to figure more prominently.[2] But this mismatch is less surprising once the aversion many Asian business people have toward investing in intangible assets is acknowledged. As we saw in chapter 2, heavy investment in brand building runs against the tide of Asia's business heritage. Asian conventional wisdom about where to allocate investment was forged in an era in which other factors were seen as more important in driving success: an affordable product or service of reliable quality; the volume to drive economies of scale; the right distribution relationships to ensure the product was available to a mass market. As one CEO put it in an interview with the author: "If we have a good product, and make it available, people will buy it." He regarded spending on brand building as a waste of money.

But some companies in Asia are beginning to challenge this conventional wisdom. They are proving that brands can be a powerful weapon in Asian competition and, with the right strategies, that they can also be built a lot more rapidly and cheaply than many have traditionally supposed. A good example is the Singapore-based resort developer and operator, Banyan Tree Hotels and Resorts (Banyan Tree). Its chairman, Ho Kwon Ping, put this new view starkly: "I felt that Asian business would never get anywhere if it didn't own brands."[3] From a standing start in 1994, Ho had catapulted Banyan Tree to number eighteen on the list of Asia's top fifty brands (ranked by the independent consultants Interbrand) in just over five years.[4] This was achieved with total marketing spending of under $2 million per annum, around 7 percent of Banyan Tree's revenues.[5] Its brand strength has been a major contributor to Banyan Tree's success in building a profitable business with average occupancy rates and revenues per room well above its nearest resort competitors, which include properties in Thailand, Indonesia, and the Maldives. To win in the new Asian competitive environment, many more Asian companies will need to follow the lead of Banyan Tree and Asian branding pioneers like it.

This chapter examines the potential role of brand building in helping companies win in the next round of competition for Asia's markets. We begin by discussing the new opportunities for profitable branding that are emerging. Next, we identify the barriers that stand in the way of reaping this potential and explore why these barriers to investment in brand building must be overcome if Asian companies are going to break out of the commoditization trap and improve margins. We explain how Asian companies can shortcut traditional decades-long brand-building cycles and how to go about building a powerful brand without pouring hundreds of millions of dollars into a potentially bottomless advertising pit. We examine how traditional Asian service strengths can be harnessed to facilitate efficient brand building. We also look at the implications for multinationals of a new focus on efficient brand building by Asian companies: new pressures on multinationals to use branding to differentiate their offerings, to improve the cost-effectiveness of their brand spending in Asia, and to find new ways to exploit the power of global or regional brands.

New Branding Opportunities

As we saw in chapters 3 and 4, many Asian companies need to break out of the commoditization trap in which they are caught. Breaking out of this trap doesn't necessarily require higher quality in terms of basic functionality and reliability; many Asian suppliers are world-class in these areas. Instead, what's necessary are higher levels of variety and customization that give both retail and business consumers more choice; products and services that better fit individual customer needs; new types of functionality (like ease of use); and more sophisticated bundling of basic products with new services, information, and customer support. This means generating innovations, whether they are breakthroughs, extensions, or improvements, that can create more value for the customer through becoming different, not just better.

Creating extra value for the customer is a critical first step in breaking out of the commoditization trap and improving margins. But creating extra value for the customer is no guarantee of improved profitability. Obviously only the share of extra value that is actually *captured* in the higher prices or sales hits the bottom line.

Successful branding is an important way of making sure that the extra value being created is also captured. Without it, there is a considerable risk of creating extra value but failing to capture it (ending up in the bottom left quadrant of figure 5-1). A report commissioned by the Hong Kong government in 2002 makes this point, noting that manufacturers who supply high-quality, but unbranded, products or components to branded OEMs (original equipment manufacturers) "capture relatively little of the final price of the goods."[6]

This risk of creating unprofitable differentiation is aggravated by the fact that, as Asian companies seek to differentiate their offerings, the bundle of "attributes" they present to consumers, customers, or clients is apt to become more complex than standard products or services they offered in the past. This creates a need for better communication about what makes a product or service different and why it is worth more: The consumer won't pay for improvements and extras if she doesn't recognize their value! To capture higher prices and fatter margins from a better, more complex and sophisticated product or service, you have to convince the customer she is getting extra value for her money. Successful branding is an important way to communicate that extra value and to

FIGURE 5-1

Value Creation Versus Value Capture

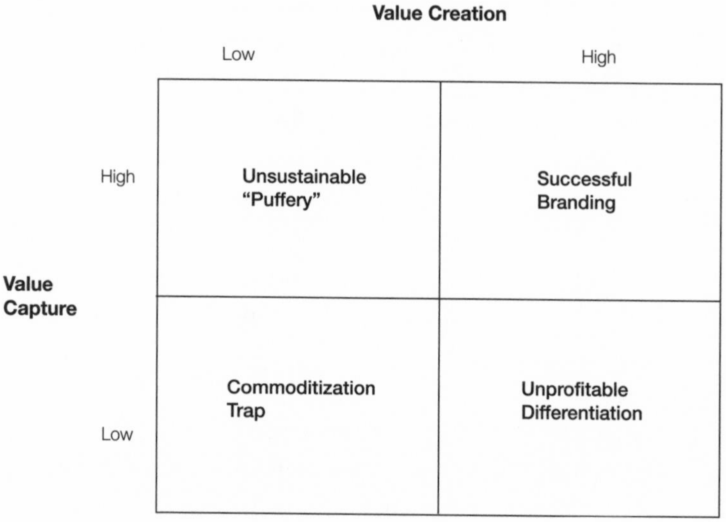

Value Creation

	Low	High
High	Unsustainable "Puffery"	Successful Branding
Low	Commoditization Trap	Unprofitable Differentiation

Value Capture

reinforce customers' willingness to pay more for it (reaching the upper right-hand quadrant in figure 5-1). As Ron Sim, chairman of OSIM, a successful supplier of health equipment (such as the "home massage chairs" popular in Asia) puts it: "Branding is a sincere effort in creating a reputation and promise of value. This must be projected consistently across every customer interface—at the point of sale, at road-shows, as well as in the products and services themselves."[7]

Moving to high value-added, more complex product and service offerings therefore creates more need for brand building. This is not only true for classic "consumer goods" such as clothes or soap powder. It is also true for leisure services like hotels and resorts; professional services such as accountancy, investment advice, and banking; and business-to-business products and services from office equipment to machinery and cleaning to IT outsourcing. When the product-service bundle becomes more complex, it becomes harder for the layperson to judge and compare alternatives, and when consumers perceive a greater risk of making mistakes or choosing a proverbial lemon, they tend to buy on brand. As the old adage goes, "no one ever got fired for choosing a blue-chip supplier." More variety, more customization, more complexity, therefore, mean brand equity will become a more decisive force in the next round of Asian competition.

Now, despite the claims of some of the more zealous marketers who claim to be able to "buy junk and sell premium antiques," it's tough to build a strong brand without some intrinsic differentiation to provide the foundations. For a while, customers may be fooled into paying higher prices for brands that don't deliver real added value. But the "free ride" of capturing value you don't really create (the upper left quadrant of figure 5-1), generally proves a short-lived trip. When consumer retribution comes, it is likely to be harsh: A brand with a reputation for puffery is a costly liability. But within the functional structures that prevail in many Asian companies, brand-building initiatives can easily become detached from the real attributes of the product or the capability to deliver. Successful brands are built on a crystal-clear understanding of why a product or service can create more value for customers and a capacity to deliver that stays in line, if not ahead, of what the brand promises.

Banyan Tree's brand promise of a "sanctuary for the senses," for example, was backed by resorts designed around villas using natural materials, private pools, its signature health spas with soft music and soothing oils, and service standards to match. Maintaining brand integrity required a rigorous, long-term approach. When Banyan Tree was unable to ensure its capability to deliver its brand promise at a Bali resort that it was offered under a management contract, it abandoned the project. As its senior vice president of marketing Edwin Yeow explained: "The physical product of the resort in Bali didn't meet our standards. The owners were unwilling to upgrade the property. . . . If it is short-term profits but long-term regret, we would rather forgo it."[8]

Successful brands, built on strong foundations, can also help to stabilize profits in the face of market volatility. Singapore Airlines (SIA) is a good example. During the 1997 Asian financial crisis, SIA's strong brand, backed by high service quality and tight cost control, meant its revenues and profits held up much better than those of its competitors such as Thai Airways, Malaysia Airlines, or even than China Airlines (from Taiwan, a country much less impacted by the crisis than Southeast Asia). Its unbroken record of twenty-five years of profitability continued, while it generated sufficient cash to go on investing. Since then SIA has proved resilient, even after a fatal crash in Taipei in November 2000 and a crisis in the airline industry initiated by the events of September 11, 2001. Its unbroken record of profitability remains intact, such is the faith of the public in the SIA brand. Some would even argue that the SIA brand has enabled the company to benefit from a "flight to quality" associated with a more nervous traveling public sticking to carriers they trust.

As well as providing a mechanism to capture higher value-added, therefore, branding can also provide a potentially powerful way of coping with the more volatile economic environment that now seems to be with us. As we will see in chapter 6, brands can also provide a powerful vehicle to seek out new customers by moving into overseas markets. If we were confident about a return to the days of rapid and constant growth, with demand reliably outstripping supply in Asia, then maybe brand building would be an optional extra. In the "buyers' market" that seems likely to characterize the next round of competition in Asia, however, it is good strategy both as offense and defense.

Dearth of Asian Brands

At present Asian companies are poorly positioned to take advantage of the opportunities brands offer to capture more value and to improve and stabilize profitability. This is not because of a shortage of homegrown companies with the necessary scale and resources. Companies such as Astra and Indofood of Indonesia, Sime Darby and Hong Leong in Malaysia, Ayala in the Philippines, Cheong Kong in Hong Kong, Keppel Group in Singapore, Siam Cement and Charoen Pokphand in Thailand, to name just a few, all have capabilities that allow them to deliver differentiated products and services. These companies market a wide range of products; have hundreds of millions, sometimes billions, of dollars in sales; and have a plethora of trademarks, logos, and trade names. But they have few real *brands*—marques that have strong brand equity in the sense that customers are willing to pay a substantial and consistent price premium for the brand versus a competing product, brands that the customers associate themselves with, "buy into" the concept of, want to be associated with, and are fiercely loyal to.

The fact that most large Asian companies have a set of trademarks and trade names (images that simply identify the product) rather than true brands (that command a price premium and customer loyalty) shows up in the percentage of their market value accounted for by its "intangible assets"—in other words, what they are worth over and above the value of their tangible assets like property and machines. Clearly the value of intangibles is the sum of many different sources of value, including the value of a company's systems and processes, its competence base, and its access to profitable investment opportunities in the future. But for consumer goods companies, a large proportion of their intangible assets are accounted for by the value of their brands. Here the difference between leading international companies and their Asian counterparts is striking. Consider the data presented in figure 5-2.

In the Western branded consumer goods companies, more than 75 percent of their market value is accounted for by intangibles, among which their brands are most prominent. Even in some of the large Asian

FIGURE 5-2

Intangible Assets in Asian and Western Companies

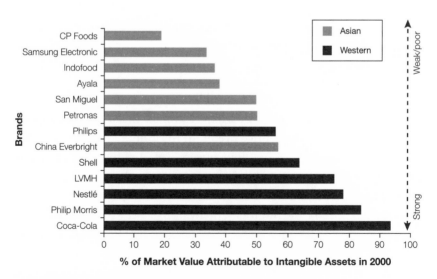

Source: Computed from published annual accounts.

companies that are recognized as brand leaders in their fields (e.g., San Miguel, which owns the powerful Asian beer brand of the same name, and Indofood, which numbers Indomee (the world's largest-selling brand of noodles) in its portfolio, the value of intangibles in their total market value is less than 50 percent and as low as one third. For most other large Asian corporates, the figure is substantially below that.

These statistics reflect the fact that for many Asian companies, with some notable exceptions that we will discuss later, brand building has traditionally been relegated to the back seat of Asian corporate strategy. If the new opportunities to use brands in the next round of competition are to be grasped, this will have to change. To achieve this, however, significant barriers that now stand in the way of successful Asian brand building will have to be overcome.

Barriers to Asian Brand Building

The main barriers to the development of successful Asian brands are to be found in the traditional mind-sets and strategies prevalent in Asian companies that we discussed in chapter 2. To move forward, these must first be recognized and then adjusted. Three aspects of the conventional wisdom of Asian business, in particular, need to change: (1) misperceptions about Asian consumers, (2) trading mind-set, and (3) broad diversification.

Misperceptions About Asian Consumers

Traditionally, many managers have assumed that Asian consumers wouldn't pay a significant price premium for brands. They argued that most Asians were "value-conscious buyers" (or "tightwads"—take your pick) whose choices were based on functionality and price.

In a past era of shortage and low incomes throughout much of Asia, this may have been true. But today, many of Asia's consumers have quite a lot of discretionary income, over and above that required to satisfy their basic needs. Even in poorer parts of Asia, today's consumers often reward themselves or their families and friends with branded "treats"— extra expenditures on branded items that carry a cachet or some other emotional benefit that economists like to call "psychic pleasure."

Try telling LVMH, the supplier of luxury goods including Asia's ubiquitous Louis Vuitton handbags and luggage, that customers won't pay a hefty price premium for brands. Despite the aftermath of the 1997 Asian crisis and the extended slowdown that followed, LVMH has made an average of 18 percent of its global revenues from sales in Asia since 2000, down only slightly from its peak of 26 percent in the boom of 1996. Nike's sales revenues in Asia have grown from less than $300 million per annum in the mid 1990s, to over $1.1 billion in 2001—selling a U.S.-branded product in Asia that is, after all, 95 percent manufactured in Asia.

But it's not only foreign brands that Asian consumers respond to. In Taiwan and Korea, for example, more than half of consumers in a 2002 survey indicated that the "social status" conveyed by the brand was a key factor in buying the right car. In Taiwan the brand most people aspire to is a Ford, but in Korea it's homegrown Hyundai.[9] The most preferred brand of cooking oil in Asia isn't from one of the multinational food giants, but the Asian *Knife* brand, and the hotel brand considered the crème de la crème by more Asians than any other is Asian-based Shangri-la. A survey that tracked behavior over a four-year period from 1999 to 2002, meanwhile, confirmed that Asian consumers were also loyal to their favorite brands.[10]

Clearly today's Asian consumers are responsive to Asian brands just as they are to well-established foreign ones. Provided that a local company can back up its promise to reliably deliver more value, the idea that consumers are deaf to the message is a historical myth.

Trading Mind-set

The second barrier to Asian brand building has been the "trading mind-set" that, as we saw in chapter 2, pervaded the business heritage throughout much of Asia. This trading mind-set focuses attention on asset turn: It doesn't matter if your margins are low, if you keep your assets turning quickly, the rewards from a series of trades will mount up. Long-term investments in building brands, a process that can sometimes take five or more years to secure results, didn't sit easily with this thinking. Why take the risk for such a long-term payoff when there are easy gains from buying and selling assets?

This thinking was reinforced by the strong preference for tangible assets. It's easier to feel the worth of something you can see, touch, and feel, whether it's a gleaming new office building or a wafer fabrication plant. This preference for tangibles was rightly reinforced by the observation that in a region where copyright infringement and intellectual property piracy were often rife, the value of intangibles was questionable. Certainly it can be argued that, at minimum, investment in intangibles like brands was risky in Asian environments where legal protection was hard to enforce in practice. But these rationales for preferring tangible assets over intangibles are now falling away: The ability to effectively protect the value and exploitation of intangible assets from brands to intellectual property is steadily improving; and the boom period of excess demand has been replaced by chronic overcapacity and price wars for standard, commodity products in many Asian markets. As we saw in chapter 1, the days of profits from rent collection and asset arbitrage have also come to an end. In the next round of competition, creating and capturing value—not asset speculation—will be the route to profitability. In this environment the role of brands is key.

To remove the trading mind-set barrier, Asian companies' traditional trading flexibility and "nose for a deal" must be redirected to the task of finding ways to build brands more quickly and more cheaply than conventional wisdom would suggest is possible. The experience of Banyan Tree, where a powerful brand was established in less than five years with only modest marketing expenditures, shows this is possible. Later in this chapter we will explore more fully how it can be done.

Broad Diversification

A third barrier to investment in brand building is the broad diversification across very different businesses and industries that characterizes many Asian companies. It is instructive that most of the world's most effective brand builders are companies that are either focused on a single business (like Coca-Cola, McDonalds, or Singapore Airlines) or a closely related set of businesses (like Unilever, Nestlé, Toyota, Sony, or LMVH). A company that is in twenty or fifty different businesses with little relationship to each other (spanning food, telecommunications, property, building materials, banking, and auto parts, for example) will face a massive disadvantage in brand building compared with its more narrowly focused sister, even if it is large. The reason is straightforward:

Economies of scale and scope in brand building tend to be massive, even compared with activities like production, service operations, and purchasing.

When most Asian CEOs think of branding, they see dollar signs. It's true that at least some ways of building brands, such as heavy advertising in the mass media, involve high fixed costs. A focused company can spread those fixed costs much more effectively than a company that is diversified across tens of businesses, each needing a different brand image and brand attributes. A company that has a portfolio of related businesses (like food, detergent, and personal care product maker Unilever), meanwhile, can redeploy its core competencies in brand building (people, processes, know-how) across brands that share similar basic requirements and approaches, even if the brands for individual products (like Unilever's Persil detergent or Walls ice cream) need to be built side by side.

But a conglomerate like Far Eastern Group (analyzed in chapter 2)—with interests spanning construction, retailing, financial services, textiles, and telecommunications—has few opportunities either to spread the fixed costs of brand building or to leverage a common set of brand-building competencies because the branding requirements of its businesses are so diverse. As a result, the diversified company is at a cost disadvantage when it comes to the process of building brands; it gets less brand value for each dollar of investment. Not surprisingly, then, Asia's heavily diversified companies are loath to compete in an arena where they are disadvantaged. Most have therefore shied away from a wholehearted commitment to building brands and concentrated on developing other forms of competitive advantage where they perceive higher odds of success.

Given that brands are set to play a greater role in the next round of competition, these competitive disadvantages need to be overcome. One way is to become focused on a narrower range of businesses that can either share a common brand or achieve synergies from the transfer of brand-building know-how across a related set of businesses. Another approach is to find ways to build a brand that involve lower fixed costs—an option we will discuss in more detail below.

A new resolve to invest in brand building, however, won't alone be sufficient for success. It is quite possible to embark on a course of, as one commentator aptly put it, "building a brand and losing your shirt."[11] Effective brand building is a subtle skill that requires much more than deep pockets or a willingness to spend. In the next section we examine some of the successful lessons and pitfalls from Asian brand pioneers that can help newcomers improve their chances of getting it right.

Lessons from Asia's Branding Pioneers

Successful Asian brand pioneers span industries as diverse as consumer electronics and computers, through hotels and air transport, to food condiments and pewter. But despite this broad spread and significant differences in the specific strategies and tactics, at least three common lessons emerge from their experience.

Promise Only What You Can Deliver

Strong and resilient Asian brands—whether early Japanese brand pioneers like Sony or more recent branding successes like Samsung, Shangri-la Hotels, Singapore Airlines, Royal Selangor, Lee Kum Kee, or Acer—have all been built on a solid base of underlying differentiation in product or service quality. They have built the capability to deliver their brand promise ahead of the brand.

Samsung is a good example of what is required. "Samsung" long existed as a trademark with wide distribution that included Wal-Mart's ubiquitous U.S. stores. But while it remained a supplier of "me-too" products, often modeled on Japanese innovations, it was not a true brand—in the sense of a marque that consumers sought out, recognized as superior, and were willing to pay a premium to obtain. Eric Kim, Samsung's head of marketing, charts its emergence as one of the global top 50 brands from the time that the company began to produce a range of innovative products, such as Samsung's voice-activated mobile phones and personal digital assistants (PDAs). "Our strategy of moving up-market very aggressively, with clearly differentiated products, has been a major driver of rapid brand improvement" says Kim.[12] Similarly, Sony's brand was built on the foundation of a stream of innovative products like the Walkman, PlayStation, and Minidisk.

Robert Kwok's Shangri-la Hotels and Resorts Group built its brand on a foundation of the "build quality" of its luxurious properties, plus service standards that consistently rate it by independent inspectors as one of the top luxury hotel chains in the world. This is backed by a hotel management school and hotel institute that graduates 1,400 students trained to high standards each year. The Taiwanese computer company brand, Acer (the best-selling computer brand in Asia outside China), meanwhile, was built on a foundation of bringing new technologies to market more rapidly than its competitors. Back when the Intel 386 chip was introduced, for example, Acer had a product based on the new chip in the market ahead of IBM. This technological edge provided an important differentiator that the company (formerly known as Multitech) was able to leverage in building a global brand behind the Acer name.

The family-owned food brand Lee Kum Kee, which sells its Chinese cooking sauces and condiments in over sixty countries, was built on the basis of consistent quality and authentic flavor—attributes that major multinational competitors have been unable to match. Lee Kum Kee has become so synonymous with "oyster sauce" and Chinese recipe sauces that for four consecutive years from 1999 to 2002, it has won the Reader's Digest Asian Gold Superbrand Award and is one of the few Asian food brands that is recognized around the world.

The first powerful message from Asian brand pioneers, therefore, is this: A clear source of product or service differentiation is a prerequisite for building a successful brand. You need something unique to leverage. Without this foundation, brand-building efforts risk degenerating into marketing fluff. Under the critical eye of Asia's value-conscious consumers, a brand that isn't backed up with performance will be quickly identified as a sham. Its also risky to attempt building a brand before you can demonstrate "clear blue water" between you and your competition. As the Samsung example demonstrates, it's not enough to have a reliable me-too product or service as the foundation for building a brand. You have to have a clear source of value-added. Branding can help you capture a share of that extra value, but it can't create value out of thin air.

To Be Resilient, Asian Brands Need to Be World-Class

The second lesson from Asia's successful brand pioneers is that, right from the outset, they aspired to match or exceed "world-class" standards both in their underlying product or service and in their brand execution. Shangri-la, for example, didn't just seek to improve on what was available in the cities they entered. Instead, it decided to set new standards for quality and service, beyond even international competitors. The same is true of Singapore Airlines. Its aim from the start wasn't to better their local competitors—it set out to offer the world's best service, backed by world-class marketing and advertising execution. Both companies retained the services of the best designers, marketing, and advertising agencies available anywhere on the globe.

The reasons weren't to be found solely in pride, nor in extravagance. Rather, building a brand that can hold its own on the world stage is sound competitive strategy for the simple reason that, sooner or later, it will have to compete with world-class brands. If your brand comes off second best from its first major competitive encounter with a world-class brand, then it will remain with the stigma "damaged goods." Contrast this with a competitive battle based on price: If the price you set proves to be too high, or too low, it can be readily adjusted. But if you spend money building a brand, put it into battle, and find that consumers rank it as inferior, then it's difficult to recover. If you decide in a second round to upgrade your brand, customers are likely to respond "but haven't I seen that before?"

Even if you could succeed in capturing the market with a brand that's not world-class, you would always be exposed to local Asian customers deserting you when global brands became more widely available or when they became richer. As the competitive landscape changed, you would be faced with either building a new, world-class brand from scratch or attempting the fraught task of trying to upgrade your brand against established consumer prejudice. If you are going to accept the brand-building challenge, you should adopt international standards as your benchmark right from the word "go."

Choose Either a Distinctively Asian or a Global Image

The third lesson from Asian brand pioneers is the need to decide clearly either to emphasize the "Asian-ness" of your brand or to camouflage it by choosing to create a global ("stateless") brand. Either strategy can be effective, depending on the nature of the product or service and the potential sources of your competitive advantage. What won't work is to be stuck in the middle between these two choices.

Singapore Airlines, Shangri-la, and Lee Kum Kee are examples of brands that have succeeded by emphasizing and leveraging their Asian heritage. Singapore Air and Shangri-la bolster their brand image by leveraging off Asian traditions of hospitality and calm. Banyan Tree built a strong brand around its "sanctuary for the senses" promise, leveraging "health spa" signature services based on traditional Asian massage and images of Asian serenity and mediation.

Acer, by contrast, took the opposite approach. With the help of an Australian branding services company, it chose the name *Acer* (from the Latin "maple") for its wide global acceptability. Added advantages came from the *ace* within the name, connoting "leading edge, winning, quick and decisive." A conscious effort was taken to downplay its links with Taiwan, which, at that time, was a byword for cheap goods of dubious quality. Similarly, in 1983, when Toyota's chairman Elji Toyoda decided to challenge the luxury car market in the United States, the company chose to create a new global brand, Lexus, to distance it from the mid-range Toyotas and reflect a more global image. This strategy has proved very successful as Lexus has consistently ranked among the top-selling luxury car ranges in the United States since the early 1990s.[13]

Perhaps the most extreme example of downplaying Asian heritage is the successful Hong Kong clothing company Giordano—a name chosen to position the brand in the heart of European couture, while benefiting from largely Asian cost structures. Inside its stores, Giordano continues to associate itself with a Western fashion image, by creating sub-brands for its lines such as "Simply Stretch" for a line produced with 3 percent lycra and "Simply Tank" for a funky line of "combat" casuals.

Clearly there is no right or wrong answer to the role of "Asian-ness" in brand building. What successful Asian brand pioneers demonstrate, however, is the need to choose. By the mid-1990s, LG, then known as Lucky Goldstar, found itself stuck midway between Asian-ness and global acceptability. Its name was identifiably Asian—reflecting its founding entrepreneur's feeling for astrology and luck to point the way to wealth. Beyond that, however, it failed to leverage positive Asian images in the services of the brand. Yet, at the same time, Lucky Goldstar was considered inappropriate for an increasingly high-technology, global company with a wide range of interests from flat panel displays to consumer electronics and biotechnologies.[14] In 1995, the company changed its name to LG.

These three lessons from Asian branding pioneers: promise only what you can deliver; aspire to build a world-class brand; and choose either a distinctively Asian or a global image, offer a starting point for tackling the brand-building challenge ahead. But for Asian companies, as latecomers to the branding game, two further questions are paramount: How can the traditional, decades-long brand-building cycle be shortcut? and How can the enormous costs of building a global brand (potentially running into billions of dollars if mass media advertising is used as the main tool) be contained?

Strategies for Building Asian Brands

To tackle the challenge of building brands rapidly and at low cost will require innovative strategies that depart from the well-worn path trodden by multinational brand builders in Asia and elsewhere. The chances of success will also be higher if the heritage of Asian business strengths and existing perceptions of Asian culture in consumers' minds can be leveraged. We now turn to the issues involved in finding the right combinations of these elements to craft effective strategies for building Asian brands.

Shortcutting the Brand-Building Cycle

There are three main ways a company can shortcut the traditional brand-building cycle and dramatically speed up the process. The first is to build the new brand by associating it with a powerful image that is already well established in consumers' minds. The second is to acquire an underutilized existing brand and use it much more intensively. The third is to gain access to a brand through alliance.

Building a Brand by Association

Building a brand by association amounts to finding an appropriate image that customers already have in their minds and then inserting your brand into that picture. Forget the time-consuming process of creating a new ideal and convincing customers to adopt it. Like the cuckoo, you drop your offering into an existing scene and let the positive associations enhance the way it is viewed by potential customers.

Consider the case of British India, the Malaysian-owned fashion brand that, in the space of less than three years, was able to take its place alongside luxury brands like Gucci and Ferragamo in shopping malls across Asia, the United States, and Europe. It earns a price premium by delivering "colonial chic."[15] But rather than painstakingly building a new image of colonial chic in the minds of customers, Pat Liew, the company's founder, decided to take a different route. Liew recognized that many consumers, both in the West and in Asia, still had a nostalgic idealism about the days of the British Raj. For them it conjured up perceptions of a privileged lifestyle in a less hurried era, while connoting tropical informality and warmth. If it were possible to successfully associate the new brand with this bygone era, these existing perceptions could be leveraged. Once the connection was established, consumers' nostalgia and romantic imaginations would create an automatic halo effect.

Forging that association wasn't easy. It started with the choice of name: British India. The company created fashion designs based on revival and reinterpretation of garments worn in the days of the Raj using modern fabrics and manufacturing techniques. Displays and marketing materials were designed to spark associations with a bygone romantic ideal.

This brand-building strategy attracted early criticism and doubters. Liew was told, for example, that "in Singapore, India was associated with contract workers and poor quality, while in Dubai there was concern about colonial imagery and a request for a name change." But Liew's insistence on using British India illustrates the advantages of leveraging existing associations in consumers' minds. The company didn't have to accept the time-consuming (and expensive) task of building a new image from scratch. Instead, by choosing the right name and brand execution, it borrowed an existing image and basked in the glow of an ideal customers already had in their heads. In this way, it was able to shortcut the usual brand-building process.

As we look to the next round of competition, Asia's service traditions and cultural heritage offer a rich vein of existing perceptions that might be leveraged for brand building by association. Royal Selangor has become the world's most famous brand of pewter goods (and the largest producer and distributor globally) by association with "craftsmanship passed down through generations" and highlighting Malaysia's long traditions in the use of tin (the main constituent of pewter)—captured through its tag line "Malaysia's gift to the world."[16] Selangor had a strong history to draw on: It was established by Chinese pewtersmith Yong Koon in 1885, soon after he arrived in Malaysia.[17] But what allowed Selangor to pull ahead of its competitors was its decision to focus on building a strong brand that could leverage this heritage and authenticity. The brand emphasized that its products were the real, handcrafted articles. This image was backed by the title "Royal," added to the brand name after a royal warrant was bestowed on the company by a Malaysian sultan in 1992.

In leveraging its Asian "heritage" credentials, however, Selangor was able to combine them with innovation and modernity. The company has a strong record of new product introductions and use of contemporary designs created by reinterpreting products from its past. It has also been innovative in funding distribution channels to "expand accessibility of our products" as the current managing director, Yong Poh Kon, a grandson of the founder, puts it.[18] This has included establishing seventy branded shops and hundreds of branded counters inside department stores, spanning twenty-five countries.

This strategy of building a strong brand by taking associations with Asian heritage and traditional culture and combining this with modern technologies and systems has proven successful for other companies as well. Shangri-la, consistently ranked top hotel brand in Asia, for example, also has firm roots in Asian heritage—in this case Asian service culture. Its guiding philosophy, "Asian hospitality from caring people," is built around five core values of Asian service: respect, humility, courtesy, sincerity, and helpfulness.[19] Communication of these values starts with its brand name: *Shangri-La*, chosen by owner Robert Kwok to associate his hotels with the mystical Tibetan mountain paradise described by English novelist James Hilton in his classic book *Lost Horizon*, where the inhabitants were perfectly mannered and its serenity was the essence of perfection. It permeates Shangri-la's advertising and marketing materials. But again, the traditional Asian service on which the brand is built is delivered using state-of-the-art planning and human resource management systems, including a performance-related compensation structure adapted from U.S. models.[20]

Clearly, however, building a brand by association won't work for every company, especially where the choice is for global acceptability instead of an emphasis on Asian distinctiveness. An alternative is to acquire an existing, perhaps foreign, brand.

The Acquisition Route

Malaysia United Industries (MUI) sought to speed up access to a strong brand when, in April 1998, it acquired 40 percent of the ailing British clothing and fabric designer and retailer Laura Ashley. The price tag for this stake was $72.5 million for a company that had notched up four consecutive years of heavy trading losses. But what MUI was looking for wasn't so much a healthy business but an underutilized brand. The Laura Ashley brand seemed to fit the bill: It was widely recognized and appreciated as an icon of classic English country-house designs, and awareness of the brand far outstripped the size of the company's existing sales revenues. Within the ailing company, therefore, MUI felt it could obtain a healthy but grossly underleveraged brand. Its aim was to connect this brand asset to an efficient Asian supply chain, creating and capturing higher value-added in the process.

Exploiting the potential of the brand it acquired, however, has proved slow and difficult. Problems with Laura Ashley's tortuous and inefficient supply chain and the ill-judged expansion of its retail network under the former management turned out to be deep-seated. MUI shifted production to Malaysia, refurbished all of the stores, and expanded the online and mail-order business. By 2000 it appeared to have turned the business around, reporting a modest profit. But in early 2003, MUI was forced to close most of Laura Ashley's European stores and arranged a rights issue to inject a further $15 million of cash into the business.[21] Nonetheless, MUI has gained access to well-known brand at a speed and a cost well below the hundreds of millions of dollars over years of investment it is estimated would have been required to build a similar quality brand from a zero base.

The Hong Kong–based cruise company, Star Cruises, meanwhile, has used acquisition to help expand its brand into new markets. In March 2000 the young Asian-based cruise company acquired the larger, well-established Norwegian Cruise Lines (NCL), boosting it to the world's fourth largest cruise operator with seventeen ships. NCL had established markets in North and South America, Alaska, the Caribbean, Europe, the Mediterranean, and Antarctica—a strong brand and loyal customer base. Star has successfully used this new brand as a vehicle to exploit its innovative cruising formats into the NCL brand, including "freestyle" cruising, which replaces Europe's more traditional shipboard culture with more casual and flexible resort-style cruises. Introducing this new concept probably would have faced considerable hurdles in Europe—an established market where customers are unwilling to a risk precious vacation days by booking with an unknown brand. Access to NCL, an established brand, helped Star overcome these barriers.

The jury is still out, however, on using acquisitions to shortcut long brand-building cycles. In 1993, for example, Royal Selangor bought the British silversmith, Comyns, with the aim of bolstering the prestige image of its products. Almost a decade later, commentators were suggesting the acquisition had yet to pay real dividends.[22]

Leveraging the Strength of Someone Else's Brand

A third potential route to shortcutting the brand-building process is to access an existing brand from a partner company. Rather than creating a new brand by association with an image that is already established in potential customers' minds, a more direct (and therefore more certain) route may be to use a brand that they are already familiar with. This can be achieved either by negotiating a license to use the brand from its owner or by forming an alliance that gives the brand owner a share of the revenue or profits you generate. Looking to enter Korea, for example, the U.K.'s number one supermarket chain, Tesco, faced the problem of lack of brand awareness among local consumers. Its solution was to partner with one of Korea's best-known brands: Samsung, to create the Samsung Homeplus hypermarket chain. Despite its widely diversified business empire, Samsung had virtually no experience of food retailing. But Samsung was considered by Koreans as a high-quality and reliable company. Through its alliance, Tesco was able to effectively borrow its joint-venture partner's brand, avoiding the necessity of building a brand afresh in the face of a Korean public often skeptical toward foreign entrants in a business that combines the culturally specific elements of food and retailing. This partnership, which combines the reassurance of a local brand with an international retailing format, has proved very successful. Since its establishment in 1999, Tesco has opened thirteen Samsung Homeplus stores, with a further forty-two earmarked by 2005, and has been voted the most popular hypermarket chain in Korea.

The key to successfully borrowing an existing brand, of course, is to ensure that its established brand image and values are compatible with those you want to project. The most relevant are probably the least available: those of direct competitors. The trick, therefore, is to find an established brand in a noncompeting sector with characteristics that are relevant to enhance the perception of your product or service in the minds of potential customers. As the Tesco–Samsung alliance illustrates, choosing the right candidate brands is often a subtle art that requires a keen understanding of buying behavior. It was not immediately obvious, for example, that an electronics and industrial conglomerate like Samsung had much to offer a food retailer. But given the need for reassurance about quality and reliability in the Korean context, the Samsung stamp of approval was a powerful influence on willingness to purchase, even when transferred from a very different product line.

For a latecomer to the branding game, speed is an important element. Building a brand by association, acquiring an existing brand that is underutilized, or accessing an existing brand through an alliance all provide potential shortcuts to the long conventional cycle of brand creation. But the question of cost is often equally significant.

Reducing the Costs of Brand Building

Many Asian companies find themselves at a cost disadvantage in brand building compared with established international competitors. This is because their global rivals are already at the stage of amortizing decades of past branding investments or they have the ability to spread fixed costs of marketing across an existing global revenue base that few Asian companies can match. To overcome this handicap, it will be essential to find ways to improve the ratio of brand impact over cost; in short, to build brands more cheaply than is the established norm.

From the outset, Asian companies need to parlay their heritage of tight cost control in manufacturing and operations into the new arena of building brands. Several other strategies can then be used to reinforce this underlying strength. These include leveraging public relations (PR), choosing marketing channels that offer lower unit cost and extended viewer engagement compared with the more obvious route of TV campaigns, and actively leveraging word-of-mouth recommendation.

Leveraging Public Relations

Building a brand through PR has two big advantages over the use of conventional advertising. First, it's generally much cheaper per thousand target customers reached. Second, PR messages can be more authoritative than direct advertising because they often are seen as coming from an independent, more objective source. Even indirect PR can have a powerful impact. For example, when bad weather caused Richard Branson to abort his Virgin Global Challenger balloon flight over China, the fact that officials initially denied him permission to land turned the problem into a high-profile media event. At a stroke, Virgin's brand was introduced to more Chinese than years of TV advertising could have achieved.

Some Asian companies have successfully used PR to reduce the cost of brand building. A prime example is Acer, today one of the most widely known brands in Asia. From the early days of the company, it gained PR for its brand by ensuring that the world's press were aware that this then-little-known Taiwanese company had beaten IBM in getting the Intel 386 chip into a personal computer (PC) available in the market. Acer's chairman, Stan Shih, has followed this up with a sustained and formidable PR campaign run from his personal office, taking every opportunity to publicize Acer through interviews in magazines, newspapers, and journals and by high-profile public speaking. Likewise the up-and-coming Chinese appliance manufacturer, Haier, has used PR to leverage awareness of its brand with senior management frequently giving interviews and making public statements that appear in the world's press.

The cost-effective creation of the Banyan Tree brand, meanwhile, was achieved partly through a concerted effort to provide travel journalists with easy-to-use press packs and interesting editorial copy to publish in their magazines. The cost of this PR was relatively low compared with advertising, while the credibility of editorials in magazines was vastly higher than an advertising pitch. Banyan Tree's Edwin Yeow has also remarked that editorial coverage was more effective in conveying the "holistic Banyan Tree experience."[23]

Banyan Tree further leveraged PR to build its brand by entering its properties in competition for all major travel industry awards and by taking its entry into these competitions seriously, with the right backup from senior management. As early as 1997, barely two years after its launch, Banyan Tree started its winning streak of a series of highly coveted international awards and accolades given by the travel industry and various publications for its resorts and spas. These awards proved invaluable in independently reinforcing the quality of its brand.

Among the normally secretive Chinese business fraternity, companies such as Acer, Banyan Tree, and Haier have found it relatively easy to leverage PR because the world's media lack material and comment from managers in China and throughout much of Asia.

Choosing Marketing Channels with a High Impact-to-Cost Ratio

When first embarking on a brand-building campaign, many managers automatically think of a TV advertising budget as the primary marketing channel. The total costs of building a brand through TV advertising can be daunting, and it's not necessarily the highest impact per dollar of spending. As old marketing hands know well, it's not only how many people you reach, but the quality of the target audience in terms of their purchasing power and potential interest in the product and service, as well as the time you have your brand in front of them. TV, as a mass medium, often scores low on both audience quality and the time for which they are exposed to the message.

Acer is again a good example of a company that was quick to see the value of exploring alternative marketing channels beyond TV. For more than a decade, it has put its Acer name on the luggage trolleys at Asia's airports: both the "heavy luggage" trolleys and the small carts used inside Asia's massive airport terminals after check-in to shift hand luggage and duty-free purchases.

Compared with the mass of Asian TV viewers, people traveling through airports include a high concentration of potential customers for Acer's PCs: both business buyers and more affluent consumers who can afford to travel by air for leisure. The terminal carts therefore score highly as a channel to reach the target audience. Just as important, think about how long these potential customers are exposed to Acer's message. It takes five to ten minutes to walk from the check-in or arrivals hall to the gate in sprawling modern airports. So potential customers have the Acer name and tagline prominently displayed in front of them for a period equivalent to between ten and twenty TV slots of thirty seconds! The impact-to-cost ratio of this "airport cart" channel has, not surprisingly, proved high.

Some Asian companies are increasingly recognizing the value of sponsoring events that fit with the desired image of their product or service. Taiwan's bicycle brand, Giant, for example, has become the world's largest sponsor of professional bicycle racing.[24] Samsung, meanwhile, took out leases on some of the world's most prominent electronic billboard locations—like Piccadilly Circus in London and Times Square in New York.

At Banyan Tree, meanwhile, the impact-to-cost ratio was maximized by centralizing marketing efforts. Contrary to the industry norm of having general managers overseeing the marketing and sales activities of their respective hotels, Banyan Tree's marketing and sales function, consisting of about twenty-five staff, was centralized at its Singapore corporate headquarters. Yeow explained: "General managers at the resort level usually come and go in a few years, and we believe that they should focus on delivering positive guest experience. To ensure consistency and continuity in brand building, we feel that it is better to centralize our long-term marketing strategy."[25]

The centralized marketing budget consisted of 7 percent of the total revenue of each resort. Marketing expenditure was split between 60 percent for trade and 40 percent for consumer. Banyan Tree emphasized the wholesaler network as a key marketing channel, restricting the number of wholesalers it worked with to three to five in each country—a policy that rewarded committed wholesalers with a degree of exclusivity.

Banyan Tree engaged a top-flight advertising agency to kick-start the brand over the first two years. But after gaining initial recognition in the industry, it cut back on advertising to keep costs down and relied more on public relations and direct-marketing programs. Banyan Tree advertised mainly in prominent travel magazines such as *Condé Nast Traveler* and *Premier Hotels & Resorts*. Collaboration with magazines for model shots was another way for the resorts to gain exposure. An example was with a popular Korean bridal magazine. Its target market fitted well with Banyan Tree's target customers, honeymooners. Banyan Tree also participated in specific, event-related advertising and engaged extensively in collaborative advertisements with business partners all over the world, such as airline magazines and Citibank's Credit Cards Division, to offer special deals.

The implication of these examples is clear: Creative thinking about the best marketing channels to use can be key to dramatically improving the cost-efficiency of building a brand.

Actively Leveraging Word of Mouth

Brand building is obviously cheaper if you can get others to do it for you, through word of mouth. Personal recommendation from satisfied users is also much more effective than a supplier's advertising claims, which are often discounted as puffery by the recipient.

Word-of-mouth promotion does not have to rely purely on serendipity; it can be facilitated and encouraged by a subtle, well-orchestrated campaign. Take the example of what is now Thailand's second biggest mobile phone company, DTAC (formerly Total Access Communication). In July 2000 its CEO, Boonchai Bencharongkul, was spotted standing knee-deep in the mud of a rice paddy in Saraburi, a hundred miles north of Bangkok, demonstrating his new low-cost mobile handsets. He had made these flying visits to talk to farmers for months. It may seem like a strange way of marketing. But the aim was to set off a chain reaction that would sweep through Thailand's 43 million farmers as they told their friends that, instead of waiting years for a land-line telephone in their homes, they could now have an affordable telephone service instantly, clipped to their belts. To help things along, the company added a *D* to its old name so that every time it was relayed from person to person, it would sound like a recommendation—the word *dee* means "good" in Thai. The strategy paid off: Once word started to get around, DTAC was signing up 30,000 new customers every day.[26]

Passenger testimonials, meanwhile, have helped Bangkok Airways quadruple its passenger numbers in the eight years to 2002 while simultaneously growing profits. Rather than challenge the incumbent, Thai Airlines, with a low-cost operation from inconvenient airports, Bangkok Airways adopted the opposite strategy: It is a full-fare, all-frills airline that flies tourists directly between major tourist sites. Its routes connect the historic sites of Angkor Wat in Cambodia, Hue in Vietnam, Luang Prabang in Laos, and Sukhothai and Bangkok in Thailand. But it's not only the convenience of easy connections between these major attractions that gets tourists talking to their friends. In its hub at Sukhothai,

Bangkok Airways has built its own open-air departure pavilion where all passengers can help themselves to free drinks and snacks, read magazines, surf the Internet, visit the on-site ceramics museum, or simply gaze out at the immaculate gardens that surround this innovative terminal. This service experience isn't advertised. Instead, by taking traditional Thai hospitality even one step further than passengers expect, it stimulates word-of-mouth brand building because most people find it remarkable.[27]

Word of mouth also played an important role for Creative Technology's Sound Blaster range. Back in 1989, the innovative Singapore company released its first Sound Blaster audio card into a market filled with generic computer peripherals. At the time, the demand for audio cards was restricted to a relatively niche market. Creative realized that if it could promote Sound Blaster to a core group within that niche, word of mouth would do the rest. Creative sent its product to editors at the major IT- and PC-related press around the world. Within months, rave reviews and word of mouth within the IT community had propelled Sound Blaster to the number one selling audio card, and by the time the PC revolution had taken hold, the Sound Blaster brand was not only the global de facto industry standard but had become synonymous with audio cards.

Shaping brand-building strategies that shortcut conventional timescales and reduce the total costs involved will be essential to allowing Asian companies to catch up and overtake established Western brands in the quest to capture higher value-added in the next round of competition. But can this focus on building a single, pan-Asian brand proposition work? What are the implications of Asian diversity for branding as we look toward competition in the future?

Branding for Asia's Diversity

As we argued in chapter 1, powerful forces driving Asian integration are now at work; national fiefdoms are coming under increasing threat. On the other hand it is premature to assume that a single, uniform brand will fit the needs of Asia's diverse customer base in most industries.

Here the experience of the pan-Asian satellite TV network, STAR TV—now part of Rupert Murdoch's global News Corporation—is instructive. It quickly discovered that while some categories, like STAR

Movies, which broadcasts mainly Hollywood films, could maintain the pan-Asian approach, much of the content needed to be localized to particular markets. Thus the MTV music video channel, for example, had to be increasingly customized to local markets with "Canto Pop" in Cantonese, separate from the Korean or Mandarin-Chinese repertoire. India, meanwhile, developed its own unique content across most of the channels through a joint venture with Zee TV that used the southwestern footprint of the satellite.[28]

Finding the right balance between pan-Asian branding and local adaptation, therefore, will be key. This requires choices about both the extent of variation in product specification and marketing message, as well as the interaction between the two. The four main alternative strategies are summarized in figure 5-3.

Getting the Right Mix of Product and Brand Uniformity

Because of the historical power of national fiefdoms, both product specifications and brands have tended to vary across Asian markets in the past. Even seemingly ubiquitous brands such as Maxwell House coffee, for example, actually show marked variations across Asia. In markets like Singapore or Hong Kong, Maxwell House is positioned and

FIGURE 5-3

Product-Marketing Strategies for Asian Diversity

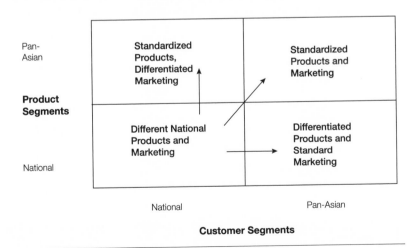

marketed as a middle-to-low-end product whose appeal lies largely in convenience. In other countries with little or no tradition of instant coffee, such as Indonesia, it is marketed as a modern and sophisticated product with an upmarket price tag. In China, it is sold as an exotic foreign brand in individual sachets combining instant coffee, creamer, and sugar, in deference to the fact that milk and granulated sugar are not staples and therefore aren't readily available in the average Chinese kitchen. Maxwell House thus sits in the bottom left quadrant of figure 5-3.

At the other extreme, a few products have succeeded in Asia with identical branding across the region and minimal difference in product specification. Coca-Cola is a good example: The brand positioning and packaging is virtually identical across the region, as is the taste, with slight variations in sweetness due to the bottlers' discretion when adding sugar syrup to the Coke concentrate (positioning it in the top right quadrant of figure 5-3). Another example was the magazine *Asiaweek*, which presented itself to readers as "the Asian authority" distributing exactly the same edition across the region.[29]

Looking to the future, however, pressures to reap economies of pan-Asian integration while still responding to deep-seated economic and cultural differences are likely to make strategies based on either product or brand uniformity (but not both) increasingly attractive.

Common Branding, Localized Products

One option is to drive for pan-Asian brand uniformity, while adjusting to local tastes by varying the product specifications (the bottom right quadrant of figure 5-3). This strategy has been adopted by Unilever, for example, in its ice cream business. Its Walls ice cream has a ubiquitous red-and-yellow-heart packaging and fresh, hygienic image right across Asia. But the product inside the wrapper varies markedly. Rather than standard chocolate or vanilla, corn-flavored Walls is provided in Thailand, "green bean thread" in Malaysia, and "red bean" flavor in China. Unilever therefore reaps the economies of scale available from pan-Asian branding, including potential to advertise on pan-Asian satellite TV stations and to sponsor Asia-wide sporting events. Underneath this brand umbrella, however, localized product specifications limit the economies available in production, purchasing, and management of a pan-Asian supply chain.

Uniform Products, Localized Branding

A final alternative in responding to Asia's diversity is to supply an identical product across Asia, but to allow the branding marketing approach to vary by location (the top left quadrant of figure 5-3). Philip Morris's Marlboro cigarette is an identical product across Asia, including its trademark packaging. But the marketing used to build Marlboro's brand image varies from the lone cowboy image used by the company throughout much of the world. In Malaysia, where a sense of community is core to peoples' thinking, a marketing campaign based on four herdsmen has proved to be more effective. In Hong Kong meanwhile, a society that emphasizes material success, the lone cowboy is depicted arriving at his ranch in a helicopter.[30]

These choices need careful consideration as part of a solid brand-building strategy. Moving too fast to standardize brand position and product specification will result in customer desertion. At the same time, maintaining differences in product and brand that are less and less relevant in the face of market integration means a company misses out on opportunities to reap scale economies and cut costs through rationalization.[31] If competitors successfully move to a more integrated strategy, meanwhile, the laggards will find their cost positions undermined.

As Asian companies begin to get serious about building powerful Asian brands and find rapid and cost-effective ways to do so, Western multinationals operating in Asia will also need to respond.

Western Brands in the Next Round

Western brands have long had the upper hand in an Asian environment where branding took a back seat in local companies. That situation is changing as Asian competitors ramp up their branding efforts. The shrewd deployment of strategies to speed up the brand-building process and do it at much lower cost means that the outcome of this new competitive battle is by no means certain. Complacent Western multinationals risk being outmaneuvered by Asian companies with a newfound focus on turning their local knowledge and Asian heritage and service culture into powerful brands.

For a preview of the potential strength of Asian companies when they focus on brand management, look no further than the experience of Esprit. Established in California in 1970, Esprit was split into two companies in 1997: a U.S. arm, Esprit de Corp., and a second company, Esprit Holdings, with the Asian and European assets, run from Hong Kong by Michael Ying Lee Yuan. Over the next five years, the Hong Kong company developed Esprit into a powerful lifestyle brand covering cosmetics, eyewear, costume jewelry, watches, bedding, shoes, accessories, and fragrances, as well as its core clothing lines. It created a branded chain of 1,700 dedicated shops and 6,300 concessions in department stores, including Esprit Megastores, and a flourishing licensing business based around the brand. The U.S. twin under an independent management, meanwhile, struggled to develop the brand. In 2002 the Asian company eventually purchased its by-then sickly U.S. sister.

This potential challenge to the historic dominance of Western-owned brands in the Asian market should act as wake-up call to Western multinationals as we move into the next round of Asian competition. Three responses are called for.

Using Branding to Reestablish Differentiation

First, Western multinationals operating in Asia need to refocus on the role of branding: to reestablish differentiation from local competitors who will increasingly seek to break out of the standardized, mass-market segments and capture higher value-added. This need for a renewed emphasis on branding isn't confined to luxury goods where brands have traditionally been critical. Even familiar household products will need to rediscover the power of branding in the next round of competition. Take the case of Taikoo sugar, owned by Hong Kong's Swire Pacific. In late 2001 Taikoo began a rejuvenation of the brand with a new logo and packaging, TV commercials, and a point-of-sale program to improve what the company call its "shelf vision" in supermarkets. All of these initiatives were designed to reinforce the message that sugar is not just a commodity and to make Taikoo the brand of choice for an increasing number of consumers. It now has a range of twenty different branded varieties including "Sugar and Spice" grinders with chocolate and cinnamon flavors to enable consumers to add an exotic touch to coffee, cereals, and desserts.[32]

Improving Impact-to-Cost Ratio for Brand Spending

Second, Western multinationals need to recognize that the race to achieve a higher impact-to-cost ratio for brand spending than competitors will become an increasingly important dimension of Asian competition in the future. As more and more Asian companies apply their cost-management capabilities in the arena of marketing and begin to deploy innovative strategies to build brands more cheaply and quickly than conventional approaches allow, Western multinationals will need to rethink their own approaches to brand investment. Rather than simply sticking to well-worn routines for maintaining and strengthening their brands, new channels will need to be considered, including greater use of PR, finding ways to stimulate word-of-mouth marketing, leveraging brand associations, and acquiring underutilized Asian brands.

Reaping Cross-Border Marketing Synergies

The third and perhaps most far-reaching implication of the new battle for brand strength emerging in Asia is for Western multinationals to make better use of the pan-Asian reach many enjoy to reap greater cross-border marketing synergies. Because of the historical fragmentation of Asia into separate national markets, many multinationals have approached brand development in the region on a market-by-market basis. This strategy, however, prevents them from exploiting a potentially significant advantage: the chance to reap cross-border scale economies in brand building that are denied to Asian competitors who typically lack the same international reach.[33] Reaping the economies from cross-border integration of marketing initiatives isn't easy. It often requires the rationalization of localized brand variations, agreement on the use of common marketing materials or a single format rendered in multiple languages, use of shared media and pan-Asian channels or sponsorships, and the coordination of new product launches. But experience has shown that the biggest barrier lies in the mind-sets of managers of multinationals' Asian subsidiaries.

Take the example of Unilever, a company that has taken significant steps to reap cross-border marketing economies in Asia while preserving its ability to adapt to local market differences. To achieve this feat, its managers had to begin thinking differently about consumer segmentation. For example, as Ralph Kugler, chairman and CEO of Unilever Thai Holdings, put it, it should be recognized that "discrete Chinese communities can have more in common between them than, for instance, their neighbours on a Kuala Lumpur street do. Hence, the Chinese TV series, *Pao Boon Jin* ("Made in Taiwan"), is popular throughout the region."[34]

New structures also had to be established, such as pan-Asian "champion groups" for each of its product groups through which managers from each Asian subsidiary could work together to make joint decisions about marketing and product lines. Key to the success of these groups was that each had a "sponsoring chairman" drawn from a different country than the "champion unit" that had responsibility for implementation of the group's activities (usually the subsidiary with the greatest depth of capabilities in the product). This mechanism helped preserve a balance between powerful national subsidiaries and promoted country buy-in to cross-border marketing initiatives.[35]

Rising to Asia's New Branding Challenges

In Asia's next round of competition, therefore, it is clear that both Asian companies and Western multinationals face new branding challenges. For Asian companies, the key will be to build strong brands that help them capture a share of the increased value-added that future innovation and new ways to leverage Asian service traditions and cultures promise to create. This will require a number of barriers that have historically stood in the way of Asian brand-building to be overcome, including widespread misperceptions about Asian consumers' responses to brands, the heritage of a trading mind-set, and the broad diversification that characterizes the business portfolios of many Asian corporates. Innovative strategies that enable Asian companies to shortcut the conventional, decades-long brand-building process and to do so at substantially lower cost, will be essential. Here the use of brand building by association, targeted acquisitions of underutilized brands, alliances, new ways to leverage PR, channels with a high impact-to-cost ratio, and word-of-mouth marketing all have a role to play. Going forward, there are also important lessons to be drawn from the experience of Asia's brand pioneers: Promise only what you can deliver; aspire to world-class branding; and choose to be either distinctively Asian or globally acceptable rather than falling between these two stools.

For Western multinationals operating in Asia, a renewed focus on branding is called for if differentiation is to be maintained, and the cost-effectiveness of existing marketing and brand maintenance expenditures need to be fundamentally reevaluated in response to Asia's changing environment.

In rising to these brand-building challenges, both groups must wrestle with the issues thrown up by inherent Asian diversity on one hand, and strong pressures for greater integration between Asian markets on the other. Subtle combinations of product and marketing uniformity and local variation will be required, along with a redefinition of market segments in an Asia where the commonalities across pan-Asian segments need to be weighed against national differences. The capacity to reap cross-border synergies in branding will become an important competitive weapon.

But cross-border brand building is just one aspect of a larger issue that more and more companies in Asia will face in the next round of competition as market integration continues and the barriers protecting national fiefdoms break down: the internationalization challenge. What does a successful internationalization strategy look like? What capabilities does my company need to operate successfully across borders? How will my organization structure and processes need to change to reap the benefits of internationalization? These questions are the subject of chapter 6.

Chapter 6

Creating a New Breed of Asian Multinationals

From unlikely beginnings as a poorly capitalized Taiwanese start-up in 1976, Acer fashioned a multinational organization with subsidiaries in forty-three countries, becoming one of the top ten information technology (IT) companies in the world. Petroliam Nasional Berhad (Petronas), Malaysia's national oil company, has built a formidable portfolio of overseas assets, such that 75 percent of its revenues come from outside Malaysia. Recall, meanwhile, that Charoen Pokphand (CP) has agribusiness subsidiaries spread across twenty countries, including Thailand, India, Indonesia, Malaysia, Taiwan, Turkey, and Vietnam, and 110 operations in China alone. These companies are unlike traditional Asian exporters whose internationalization amounts to little more than a set of overseas sales offices. They have also gone much further than those (including a number of well-known Japanese corporates) that have simply relocated manufacturing to low-cost sites while leaving every other core business function like R&D, marketing, and finance firmly back at home base. Instead, companies like Acer, Petronas, and CP have built full-fledged multinational businesses where virtually every aspect of their activities spans international borders.

But such Asian companies that are truly multinational are still a rarity. Asian companies have tended to be international traders rather than international investors. Even where they have accumulated significant assets overseas, most have run their financial empires more like a portfolio of independent investments than as an integrated multinational business. Western multinationals, by contrast, have built extensive networks of national subsidiaries across the Asian region. But these country units have generally not been as tightly integrated as their units in North America and Europe.

These strategies were viable while Asia remained divided into a collection of national fiefdoms. Being multinational wasn't necessary in an Asian playing field where competitors in each national market could shelter behind a wall of barriers ranging from overt restrictions on investment by foreigners to differences in regulation and high costs of transport and communication. As we saw in chapter 1, however, the next round of Asian competition will see these former national fiefdoms under relentless attack. They will be broken apart by a combination of the mounting pressure to release cross-border economies and political imperatives to discipline domestic industries and reinvigorate growth by making Asian industries more competitive by opening the gates to consolidation.

The demise of national fiefdoms will demand that Asian companies that aspire to be among the winners in the next round of competition embrace the challenge of building a new breed of Asian multinational— an organization capable of exploiting regional and global economies of scale and moving capabilities, systems, and knowledge across borders in ways that play to the strengths of Asia's heritage. Fortunately, this challenge is also accompanied by a unique opportunity: the chance for Asian companies to use internationalization as a way to learn and acquire new capabilities, not just to reap economies from exploiting their existing products, services, and know-how. Being latecomers to internationalization can, therefore, be turned into an advantage if Asian companies are able to use the opportunity to leverage international diversity, rather than reluctantly adapting to it (as did most of the multinationals that have gone before).

For Western multinationals already operating in Asia, meanwhile, the demise of national fiefdoms will demand tighter integration between their Asian subsidiaries both as a means of lowering costs and leveraging best practice and local innovation.

In this chapter we examine the opportunities and the difficulties involved and how both Asian companies and Western multinationals can best go about meeting the new challenges of internationalization that winning in Asia's next round of competition will present. We begin by explaining why full-fledged internationalization is becoming an imperative for future success in Asia.

The Internationalization Imperative

A number of powerful forces are coalescing to create new pressures for the internationalization of Asian companies. These include (1) gradual but persistent moves to dismantle many of the barriers to cross-border trade and investment that have historically separated Asian markets, (2) national policies designed to promote homegrown multinationals, (3) the pressure for Asian companies to match the international economies being achieved by their multinational competitors, and (4) the limits to growth imposed by the need to arrest, and in many cases unwind, the Asian heritage of opportunistic diversification.

Falling Barriers to Cross-Border Trade and Investment

Following the Asian financial crisis of 1997, the International Monetary Fund (IMF) and other international bodies exerted intense pressure on the governments of many Asian countries to gradually open up their markets to international competition. Singapore has probably implemented the most far-reaching and rapid changes in this direction, but similar liberalization processes have been initiated in Thailand, Korea, Taiwan, and even Indonesia and Malaysia. These have included the liberalization of restrictions on inward foreign direct investment and cross-border acquisitions as well as moves to reduce intra-Asian trade barriers. On January 1, 2003 the Asian Free Trade Area (AFTA) came into force among six members of the Association of South East Asian Nations (ASEAN)—albeit with some exceptions and "transition arrangements" (such as Malaysia's schedule to reduce tariffs on imported vehicles down to 20 percent by 2005 and the Philippines' partial exemption on tariffs on imported petrochemicals). Singapore already has a free trade agreement in place with Japan, and is also negotiating similar arrangements with India, Thailand, and the Philippines. Bilateral negotiations to reduce trade barriers are under way between the United States and ASEAN nations. Serious discussions are also under way about the integration of the so-called "ASEAN + 3" economies—China, Japan, and South Korea along with the ASEAN bloc.

In the scramble to attract foreign investment in the slower growth years that have followed the 1997 crisis, meanwhile, many Asian governments have been forced to relax restrictions on foreign direct investment into their countries. Korea, for example, has relaxed restrictions on hostile takeovers by foreign companies and opened up twenty-one industries where foreign investment was previously barred. Indonesia now allows wholly owned foreign subsidiaries in wholesale and retail trade as well as in all manufacturing sectors. Even Thailand, where some statements by Prime Minister Thaksin Shinawatra have included nationalist rhetoric, increased limits on foreign ownership of financial services companies and lifted former requirements for foreign investors to locate in designated regions of the country.

China's entry into the World Trade Organization (WTO), meanwhile, is forcing its complex network of barriers to trade and investment to be gradually dismantled. It has promised, for example, to reduce tariffs on industrial products from an average of 24.6 percent in 2001 to 9.4 percent by 2005, to allow foreign banks to do business in local currency by 2004, to relax the current ban on foreign ownership of telecommunications providers to a ceiling of 49 percent, and to remove long-standing regulations that exclude foreign companies from wholesaling and import/export trade. While the implementation may face a degree of foot-dragging (as evident in the new regulations that restrict foreign banks to opening one new branch in China per year and require each branch to be separately capitalized at $72 million), the long-term trend toward greater integration of China with the Asian and global economy is clear and probably irreversible.

As the barriers to trade and foreign investment fall throughout Asia, cross-border competition will inevitably increase. The strategy of sheltering behind walls of national protection will become less and less tenable; Asian companies that traditionally controlled their national fief-doms will face competition from imports and, even more important, from foreign investors who set up shop locally—right on the local baron's front lawn.

National Policies to Promote Homegrown Multinationals

A number of Asian governments have adopted policies to encourage the development of homegrown multinationals by promoting the internationalization of their leading companies. These range from direct influence over the strategies of companies they control, through incentives such as subsidized loans for overseas investments, to industrial policies that fostered intense home-based competition in particular industries, encouraging firms to look to alternative markets. Historically, such government policies were an important driver of international expansion by Japanese and Korean companies that created many of the well-known Asian multinationals that exist today, such as Hitachi, Matsushita, Mitsubishi, and Toshiba of Japan and Hyundai, LG, and Samsung of Korea.[1] Today the Malaysian, Singaporean, and Chinese governments are following policies to promote a new wave of internationalization by companies headquartered in their countries.

Petronas is a successful example of this policy at work. The momentum for its international expansion had its roots in Malaysian Prime Minister Mahathir's mission to make Malaysia a champion of developing countries and an exporter of both capital and expertise to the third world. Following Mahathir's strong support for Nelson Mandala's presidency in 1994, the new South African government is said to have tacitly backed Petronas in its 1995 bid to acquire a 30 percent stake in South Africa's biggest refiner and petroleum marketing company, Engen.[2] Success in this deal gave Petronas control of almost 30 percent of South Africa's retail fuel market and 17 percent of its refining capacity. By 2003, Engen contributed almost 20 percent of the Malaysian company's total revenues. But it also proved an important platform from which to launch further international expansions. This included deals for exploration and production in Sudan, including a 1,500-kilometer pipeline that enabled Sudan to become a net oil exporter by 1999. This venture was undertaken in partnership with China National Oil Corporation and Sudapet, Sudan's national oil company.

Petronas went on to develop significant business in fifteen countries, in part by pursuing a strategy of focusing on countries where some of its main international rivals are either greeted with suspicion or barred from entering. These include operations in Iran, Algeria, Turkmenistan, Pakistan, and China. In total, more than three quarters of Petronas's $20 billion in revenues now come form outside Malaysia.

Key to the government's promotion of Petronas's overseas expansion was the fact that Malaysia's own oil reserves were dwindling. But many other sectors of the Malaysian economy have an analogous problem: a small home market. As a result, many other Malaysian companies with strong links to the government have also been encouraged to expand internationally either through setting up "greenfield" operations over-seas (as in the case of Sime Darby) or through acquiring particular assets or capabilities (such as the acquisition of Laura Ashley by Malaysia United Industries detailed in chapter 5).

Singapore's government has also actively promoted the internation-alization of companies headquartered in Singapore, most directly through its influence on government linked companies (GLCs; de-scribed in chapter 2). This began with the publication in 1993 of Singa-pore's "master plan," dubbed "The Next Lap," which included the idea of leveraging Singapore's existing competencies in the global market through the growth of Singaporean multinationals as an important plank of development.[3] The reasons are obvious: (1) Singapore's home market is tiny, so if its companies are to grow, they must expand overseas and (2) since the population the island can support is limited, increased gross domestic product (GDP) will have to come from exploiting the skills of Singaporeans internationally. More recently, the international-ization message has taken the form of direct calls by senior members of the government for GLCs to expand their reach across the Asian region. Significant offshore investments by GLCs like SingTel, DBS bank, the engineering company SemCorp, and Singapore Technologies can all be seen, in part, as a response to this policy agenda.[4]

Finally, China began in the late 1980s to expand the role of its "inter-national trust and investment corporations"—of which China Interna-tional Trade and Investment Corporation (CITIC; discussed in chapter 2) is the best known—with the dual aim of securing supplies of key raw materials and accessing technology and know-how from overseas.

Between 1985 and 1990, the number of foreign affiliates of Chinese companies, as well as China's investment abroad, increased more than three-fold.[5] In the next phase, the Chinese government provided various incentives to assist its exporters to develop sales and distribution subsidiaries in overseas markets to support exports. With China's accession to the WTO and the resulting emphasis on its integration into the global economy, a new phase has begun in which the Chinese government for reasons of global competitiveness, as well as national pride, wants to see the emergence of strong multinationals headquartered in China.

The fact that these countries, along with other Asian governments, are pursuing policies that promote the emergence of homegrown multinationals for reasons of national development means that the private risk-reward trade-offs for individual firms are being skewed in favor of internationalization. This internationalization will, in turn, lead to more cross-border competition. Even those companies outside the direct influence of government, therefore, will need to respond by joining the new, more international competitive game.

Matching the Advantages of Western Multinationals

It is not only the need to respond to the creation of Asian multinationals promoted by their governments, however, that will force an increasing number of Asian companies to become more international. An equally important imperative for internationalization will be the need to match the improved cross-border economies Western multinationals will be able to achieve as barriers to the flow of goods and services across Asia are dismantled.

Where trade and cross-border investment barriers had already been removed, multinational companies such as Shell, GE Capital, and Citibank have quickly moved to dominate their chosen market segments across Asia. Citibank's success in building a pan-Asian business in credit card services is a good example. Citibank had been operating branch banking in Asia for more than a decade, over which it developed subsidiaries in fifteen Asian countries. Its breakthrough came, however, when deregulation and improved communications technologies allowed it to launch an integrated, pan-Asian credit card business based on creating a new service platform—the Asia-Pacific Consumer Card. Citibank targeted its card services at Asian professionals who valued the ability to use the card seamlessly as they traveled and valued the association with a well-recognized global bank. Rival Asian banks, almost all of which lacked a substantial network outside their home countries, were unable to match Citibank's cross-border advantages: an unparalleled ability to spread fixed costs, the scope to mount cost-effective pan-Asian marketing campaigns, and the chance to transfer expertise and learning across countries using a common service platform.

As Western multinationals are able to take advantage of their international reach in the way Citibank did, Asian companies will themselves be forced to further internationalize in order to remain competitive.

The End of Growth Through Opportunistic Diversification

As we argued in chapter 1, opportunistic diversification into a large number of different industries was the main way many Asian companies grew in the past. This strategy had the obvious attraction of permitting them to leverage preferred local access to capital, raw material supplies, distribution, licenses, and relationships many enjoyed in their local markets. But the 1997 crisis and tougher competitive environment that followed revealed the weakness of this strategy: Capabilities and resources were spread too thinly over too many unrelated businesses. Asian companies, such as Renong in Malaysia, Daewoo in Korea, Siam Cement in Thailand, and the Salim Group in Indonesia, that grew by opportunistic diversification lacked the depth of knowledge and managerial capabilities to compete with more focused players across such a wide variety of businesses.

But moving to a more focused portfolio means a smaller business unless growth can be found from other sources. The end of opportunistic diversification as a viable strategy will therefore force Asian companies to turn their attention to opportunities for growth by geographic diversification through cross-border expansion of their core businesses where they enjoy a depth of specialist capabilities. Shifting to a more focused strategy inevitably leads to the quest for greater internationalization among Asian firms.

The Drive to Internationalize

These four forces—falling barriers to trade and investment, national policies to promote the emergence of homegrown multinationals, the need to match the cross-border advantages available to Western multinationals, and the end of opportunistic diversification as a viable source of growth—will force Asian companies to squarely face the challenge of internationalization in the next round of competition.

There is evidence that this is already happening. As early as by 1999, data on foreign sales and investment by 426 Asian companies showed a marked increase in their pace of internationalization in the wake of the 1997 financial crisis. Among Singaporean companies, for example, foreign sales as a percentage of total sales had increased from 34 percent to 44 percent between the pre- and postcrisis levels. Overseas assets as a proportion of total assets, meanwhile, grew even more steeply—from 19 percent to 31 percent. Among Malaysian companies, the proportion of foreign sales rose from 19 percent to 28 percent, while increased investment overseas drove the share of foreign assets up from 13 percent to 18 percent.[6]

In Singapore, this internationalization drive was led by large companies acquiring foreign assets. SIA, for example, purchased 49 percent of London-based Virgin Atlantic Airways; Singapore Telecom acquired Optus in Australia and a stake in Indonesia's largest mobile phone operator, Telkomsel; Neptune Orient Lines bought into U.S. logistics operator APL; and DBS (formerly Development Bank of Singapore) invested in both Thailand and Hong Kong with the ambition of becoming one of the region's leading banks. Firms of all sizes from Malaysia, meanwhile, increased their percentage of foreign assets and sales. In Hong Kong, the increase in internationalization was more modest and led by its smaller companies.

The extent of this new wave of internationalization also varied across industry. The manufacturing sector, where levels of foreign sales and assets were already increasing precrisis, internationalized still further in the aftermath. Companies in some industries that were historically national, such as real estate and the "process industries" (e.g., chemicals) also began to make significant moves overseas after the crisis. The relatively high level of foreign sales and assets in sectors like commercial and services and fast-moving consumer goods (FMCG) was maintained but showed little sign of increasing further, with the exception of smaller firms, who reacted by internationalizing their sales. Meanwhile, the low level of foreign sales and assets in the financial services sector persisted, with a few exceptions such as banks like DBS and Standard Chartered.

Overall, however, there can be no question that the 1997 Asian financial crisis stimulated a drive to internationalize both sales and assets among a wide cross-section of Asian companies. Perhaps just as important, it also began to alter Asian corporate mentalities about the role of internationalization in their future strategies. The other forces of change in the competitive environment that we outlined earlier in this chapter have reinforced this need for a fundamental reassessment. The author's own, albeit anecdotal, experience with the senior management of Asian companies suggests that internationalization is now firmly on the Asian corporate agenda in more and more companies. Given the significance of a demise of traditional national fiefdoms, however, it needs to come even further to the fore.

Yet it is one thing to recognize the potential of internationalization as a tool, if not a necessity, to compete in the next round; it is quite another to successfully address this new challenge. The heritage of Asian corporations, added to the fact that, with the exception of Japan, they are latecomers to the internationalization game compared with their European and American counterparts, brings special challenges. These challenges, and how they might be overcome, are the subject of the next sections. Fortunately there are also potential opportunities to bypass the long, traditional road to becoming true multinationals.

Overcoming the Handicaps Imposed by Asia's Business Heritage

Asian companies face a number of internationalization challenges that are peculiar to their heritage, or at least more severe than faced by companies elsewhere in the world. Some of the baggage that we identified in chapter 2 that stands in the way of successful internationalization includes overcentralization of decision making, underinvestment in intangible assets, and the fact that a long period of sheltering behind national barriers has resulted in many companies relying on sources of competitive advantage that are unique to their home-country location and lacking the capabilities required to build and run successful international organizations. These handicaps are aggravated by the pursuit of strategies that frequently focus on establishing local presence ("planting the flag") rather than building an integrated overseas network.

Breaking Free of the "Plant-the-Flag" Mind-set

Traditional models of internationalization have tended to be based on taking products or services and systems companies perfected at home and replicating these offerings in new, national markets.[7] To achieve sales growth, companies following this approach begin by selling in "nearby" countries (where cultural and economic closeness was more important than geographic distance). This makes it possible to enter new markets without significantly changing either the specifications of the offering or the operations, processes, and systems that were used to deliver it. Such firms, therefore, start internationalizing by establishing sales, distribution, and service offices overseas. As the local sales grow, they typically add new activities to their offshore subsidiaries, creating minireplicas of their home-base organizations.

Following this internationalization strategy often leads to widely dispersed networks of international subsidiaries linked back to headquarters, but relatively independent of each other. Internationalization becomes a matter of "planting the flag" in promising new markets.

Asian companies that have adopted this traditional internationalization strategy have frequently suffered from its limitations. Companies like Samsung automobiles and Daewoo Motor ended up with subsidiaries scattered from Poland to Uzbekistan, each operation isolated from its sisters.[8] In its first phase of internationalization (1993–1997), the Filipino fast-food company, Jollibee, established twenty-three stores, scattered across ten countries. Lacking the critical mass to gain customers' attention in each of these isolated markets, and with little scope for sharing local fixed costs among stores, each was operating at half the estimated minimum efficient scale.[9] When the Singaporean bank, DBS, acquired Thai Danu bank in Thailand, meanwhile, it initially established little in the way of structure to integrate its new subsidiary either with the headquarters or with the banks in which it held a stake elsewhere. It posted only two permanent employees from Singapore into Thai Danu. Despite their best efforts, there was no way they could get on top of the problems that had hit Thai Danu during the 1997 crisis, let alone make significant progress toward integrating it into the DBS network.[10]

While Asian corporates continue to adhere to this outdated plant-the-flag model of internationalization they will be unable to build a successful new breed of Asian multinationals. Leading-edge multinationals from the United States and Europe are, today, reaping significant network economies by interlinking their subsidiaries in a tightly connected web. Such a web may be designed to exploit the synergies between subsidiaries (as recommended by Christopher Bartlett and Sumantra Ghoshal in their blueprint for creating "transnational" corporations) or to unlock new potential for innovation by mobilizing dispersed, locally imprisoned knowledge by building "metanational" structures.[11] Unless they get beyond the idea that internationalization means little more than establishing a local presence and start building an international web designed to exploit these network economies, Asian companies will be unable to compete with their multinational rivals from other parts of the world.

Breaking out of this plant-the-flag mind-set, however, is only the first step Asian companies will need to take toward building tomorrow's Asian multinationals. To successfully meet this challenge, the other handicaps that stem from Asian companies' heritage (mentioned above) must either be neutralized or parlayed into new types of advantage. The first of these handicaps is their chronic underinvestment in intangible assets.

Investing in Intangible Assets

As we saw in chapter 2, many Asian companies have prospered based largely on what can be termed "resource-based" advantages: access to low-cost raw materials and labor, preferential access to capital, and government licenses obtained through local relationships. The Salim Group and Asian Pulp and Paper in Indonesia or Renong and TRI in Malaysia would be good examples. These companies often came to dominate their home markets.

These resource-based advantages, however, are largely immobile. A company that thrives because of low raw material costs or access to a government license can potentially export its product competitively. But a company that relies on resource-based advantages will have little to add to an overseas market as a foreign direct investor.

The more enlightened of Asian companies, such as Astra of Indonesia or San Miguel of the Philippines, built efficient local assembly plants, powerful distribution networks, and, in some cases, strong local brands to reinforce their underlying resource-based advantages.[12] These types of advantages that rest on physical assets can be replicated in a foreign location. But to the extent that a company is no better than its local or other foreign competitors in building assets like plants, distribution networks, and brands in an overseas market, it will lack any competitive advantage as a foreign investor.

Foreign direct investors mostly win when they have "system-based" advantages that leverage intangible assets like quality systems, marketing competence, technology, and know-how that are proprietary. These are the kinds of competitive advantages that can be transferred to markets where these systems are lacking. Leading multinationals such as Unilever, Procter & Gamble, British Petroleum, and IBM have prospered by reaping the advantages of their ability to transfer these intangible assets across borders. The problem for most Asian companies is that they generally haven't invested enough in these intangible assets to give themselves a strong platform of systems, brands, and technologies that they can use to outcompete the incumbents when they enter an overseas market.

There are exceptions. As we mentioned in chapter 1, the Thai group Charoen Pokphand (CP), for example, has successfully grown throughout Asia by transferring its integrated agribusiness system across borders. The system includes a bundle of seed and breeding technologies, supply chain integration and logistics systems, performance measurement and record-keeping templates, training, and productivity improvement tools. By transferring this system to a new country, beginning with recruiting, training, and supplying farmers who become high-productivity producers for CP, the company is able to establish an agribusiness supply chain in the countries it enters that reaches productivity levels that traditional techniques and competitors are unable to match. Its system-based advantages give CP a clear way to add value as a foreign direct investor. Banyan Tree, the resort company discussed in chapter 5, successfully transferred its resort development, management, and marketing systems to re-create its "sanctuary for the senses" resorts in Thailand, Indonesia, and the Maldives.

If other Asian companies are to be in a position to internationalize successfully, they too will need to invest in these kinds of intangible assets. Like CP and Banyan Tree, they will then have something unique that can be transferred into the foreign markets they enter. In the next round of competition in Asia, bringing the cash to build capacity in a foreign market simply won't be enough to compete with either locals who have an automatic inside track or Western multinationals that are capable of leveraging their systems, brands, and technologies across an integrated Asian network.

Building International Capabilities

Another important factor impeding the internationalization of Asian companies is the significant gap that often exists between their existing capabilities and the skill base necessary for effective expansion across borders. When DBS acquired Thai Danu bank in Thailand, for example, it had only a handful of staff with extensive overseas experience. Its systems for managing overseas units were designed for the relatively simple exchanges between the headquarters and a branch of the bank, not for the complex interaction between Singaporean divisions and a significant overseas entity like Thai Danu, which at the time had over ninety branches of its own. In its well-oiled Singaporean machine, meanwhile, specialist capabilities were most important. By contrast, in controlling and integrating an overseas subsidiary, the skills of an "all-rounder" with entrepreneurial flair were most critical. These capability gaps cost DBS dearly in the initial aftermath of the acquisition as the Asian financial crisis of 1997 worsened. Subsequently the bank recognized that if it were to successfully build and manage an Asian regional bank it would have to systematically fill the capability gaps that were impeding its international expansion with a mix of selective hiring, training, and job rotation to build experience.

Likewise, when the Taiwanese computer giant, Acer, set out to build a global position in the branded, personal computer business, its CEO, Stan Shih, observed: "This is the weak point of Taiwanese companies— they are not able to exploit their technical capability to the level where it reaches their market potential. . . . Global expansion and decentralization demand many qualities from managers—business sense, understanding of corporate mission, the ability to control operations, adapt to local conditions, and adjust to change. It is difficult to develop such people, especially to meet the needs of overseas operations."[13]

The message is clear: Internationalization is not a game for amateurs or pure opportunists; success demands that companies invest in building, hiring, or acquiring a cadre of management and staff with the necessary experience and skills first to establish or acquire viable operations overseas and then to run the resulting international network. Because of the heritage of diversification across industries rather than national borders, many Asian companies have yet to put these capabilities in place.

Restructuring Overcentralized Organizations

A final handicap that many Asian companies must overcome before they can internationalize successfully is the fact that decision making in their organizations is typically highly centralized. As we saw in chapter 2, although today's Asian corporates have evolved from diverse roots, almost all share a common heritage of centralization. This has many benefits: It facilitates frequent, face-to-face interaction (the ultimate in "high-bandwidth" communication), promotes chance encounters, and helps engender the development of teams where people are both "in tune" and "in synch" with each other. What centralization doesn't do, however, is make it easy to run a far-flung international network successfully.

Of course this is not a problem unique to Asian companies; many of today's successful Western multinationals faced the same challenge. It is particularly acute for Asian companies, however, because they have traditionally relied on close personal ties between individuals (often from the same family group), high levels of shared understanding, and subtle, highly personal interactions in which decision factors and criteria are implicit to manage their companies. Organizations with a much greater reliance on explicit rules, procedures, and memos in the management process, by contrast, generally find it easier to cope with the "tyranny of distance" that frequently accompanies internationalization. With more of their management processes explicit and codified, they can make more use of information and communications technologies to bridge distances and time zones. The management processes and style of many Asian companies, by contrast, tend to aggravate the tyranny of distance and limit the scope for effective information and communications technology solutions.

Some Asian companies have addressed this problem by dispatching family members or trusted lieutenants to manage their overseas subsidiaries, thereby ensuring that key managers have a shared understanding of the organization and management process and are likely to be in tune with others in the group. Obviously, however, for most large companies this provides only a limited and temporary solution. Asian companies' international expansion is therefore likely to be impeded by the nature of their management processes compared to competitors that have grown up in a different management tradition.

This impediment to internationalization can be observed even among Korean companies like Samsung who have been in the vanguard of recent overseas expansion by Asian companies. When setting up a plant in Berlin, for example, Samsung had at one point more than two hundred of its engineers or the engineers of its partners stationed there to transfer the knowledge from Korea to Germany.[14] Afterward it invested heavily in programs to socialize German workers and supervisors into the culture of the company and to integrate them into the tacit knowledge base of Samsung. On the one hand, this could be seen as evidence of an enormous commitment from Samsung to its Berlin plant. But it also demonstrates its inability to transfer culture and know-how in a more cost-effective way.

These problems are aggravated by the "functional" structures Asian companies have typically adopted. In the past this kind of organization structure made sense because the challenge of most Asian companies was to build world-class capabilities in the key functions that drive competitiveness in the home country: operations, marketing, sales, quality, finance, and so on. The best way to build strength in these areas is to adopt a strong functional organization where each group is clearly focused on achieving excellence in its specialized, functional activity. This approach was strongly embraced by Japanese, Korean, and Singaporean companies, although less so by corporations from other Asian countries, especially those managed by the overseas Chinese (recall our analysis in chapter 2).

Once the priority shifts to international expansion, however, these functional structures act as a handicap. They encourage companies to go down the self-defeating path of trying to replicate the full set of different functions, each with the right depth of capabilities, in a new, overseas subsidiary. This simply doesn't work because the total investment requirements to replicate miniversions of the home-based organization around the world are crippling. Worse still, functional organizations tend to place most of the emphasis on excelling in their core activities by replicating the way they do things at home. They are therefore generally poorly attuned to adapting to the peculiar needs of foreign operations that are as yet too small to justify changing their standard processes and systems.

To overcome the barriers to internationalization their existing structures impose, Asian companies will need to divide their people into smaller teams or business units, each charged with responsibility for its own bottom line. The role of the remaining central support functions will then need to be redefined as specialist service providers that sell their skills to a large number of internal customers. Successful internationalizers like Petronas have used just such an approach. It seems to have worked even in the demanding task of integrating ventures in secondary oil- and gas-producing countries (such as South Africa or Turkmenistan) into its international network.

If more Asian companies are to overcome these barriers to internationalization and build a successful new breed of Asian multinational, however, they will need a strategy for systematically overcoming the handicaps they face. Our next topic, therefore, is: What might such as strategy might look like?

Building a New Breed of Asian Multinationals

In creating a new breed of successful, "Asian-style" multinationals, it makes sense to use the existing strengths of Asian corporate heritage as a platform on which to build. Three aspects of this heritage that we identified in chapter 2 seem particularly promising as building blocks: skill in building and managing networks of alliances, capability for rapid learning, and adaptability.

Leveraging Alliance Networks

The successful blueprint for tomorrow's Asian multinationals might look more like an international network of alliances than a global juggernaut that clones its home-based organization around the world. The use of alliances to underpin international expansion can help to overcome barriers to entry and provide a way to compensate for gaps in capabilities and experience to operate in foreign markets. Forming alliances can also speed up the rate at which a company can extend its international reach, compared with trying to build equivalent capabilities in-house—an important benefit for Asian companies that are frequently latercomers to the internationalization game in their industries.[15]

The alliance established by Chinese home appliance maker Haier with Japan's Sanyo is a good example. Haier was looking for a way to break into the notoriously close-knit distribution channels that hamper easy access to the Japanese market. Sanyo had an inside track into Japan's network of dealers, but as a potential alliance partner, what could Haier offer it in exchange? Haier recognized that its most valuable asset in Sanyo's eyes was the integrated distribution and service network it had built up across China—a market where distribution is normally fragmented and hard to manage. The following alliance deal resulted: Haier would open its Chinese distribution network to Sanyo's products in exchange for the same access to Sanyo's established network in Japan. This was an important step in Haier's internationalization, not only because it provided access to potential Japanese consumers but also because it provided a window into one of the world's lead markets, with arguably the most demanding and sophisticated buyers anywhere on the globe.

Another good example of the use of alliances to accelerate internationalization is the innovative deals that Taiwan's Uni-President Enterprises Corporation (UPEC) has made with multinationals that are already in China. UPEC is a $7 billion conglomerate that grew as its ancestor, President Foods, diversified into new business. Its food business still notches sales of over $2 billion per annum and operates an extensive international network that now includes operations in China, Hong Kong, Indonesia, the Philippines, Thailand, and Vietnam. It also owns San Francisco–based Famous Amos Chocolate Chip Cookie Corporation and Wyndham Baking Company, Inc., the third largest cookie company in the United States.

In its first phase of international expansion from 1991, UPEC had set up a number of joint ventures with state-owned enterprises in China. Over time, these ventures have had mixed results. One problem has been that while UPEC has a long-term and grand development plan for mainland China and would like to reinvest all its profits back into its local operations to enhance its market position, many of its local partners have been eager for quick returns and want to use the cash generated to pay off their debt, rather than for reinvestment. This divergence of goals became a roadblock to UPEC's expansion plans and inhibited its attempts to build a strong market position.[16] UPEC therefore decided to try a new tack to extend its reach into China: forming alliances with global companies already operating there.

The philosophy underlying these alliances includes the belief that the issues that it faces are common to any foreign company doing business in China and the recognition that no company in the world today has sufficient resources to exploit the full potential of the Chinese market. It therefore decided to approach other multinational companies to mutually develop business and share costs. UPEC identified distribution as a particularly fertile area for co-operation. It has been extremely flexible about designing the right kind of alliance structure on a case-by-case basis. It has formed different co-marketing, distribution, and cost-sharing alliances with six out of the thirty-two outlets in China run by the French retailer Carrefour; with Japan's Nissin Foods in cooking oils, Kikkoman in soy sauce, and Kirin in beer; and with America's Cargill in grain. In May 2003, UPEC announced a strategic alliance with Nissin Foods, one of the world's largest instant noodle producers, to mutually develop the instant noodle business in Greater China (mainland China and Taiwan).

Singapore's SingPost also believes alliances are the most effective route to becoming international. In 2000 its CEO, William Tan, says he realized that his multinational customers required a service provider with global reach and that "in order to provide that service we must globalize; the only way to do this is to form alliances with other like-minded postal companies."[17] Acting on this view, SingPost formed a joint venture with the corporatized British Post Office and the Dutch postal and courier group TNT Post. The three operators agreed to transfer their international business operations into the new joint venture company whose target customers include multinational direct-marketing firms, publishers, e-commerce merchants, and financial institutions. Overnight this gave SingPost a substantial share in a $750 million company with global reach.

Rather than following the usual international path involving escalating commitments from a representative office, through sales units and manufacturing to full-fledged subsidiaries, therefore, Asian firms can use these kinds of alliance strategies to speed up the process of extending their international reach. Taking the alliance route plays to the traditional strengths of corporate Asia in competing through networks of relationships. This strategy also has the benefit of providing opportunities for rapid learning by drawing on a partner's existing knowledge base.

Mobilizing Global Learning

As latecomers to the internationalization game, one of the key challenges for Asian companies is how to catch up with their more-experienced multinational competitors by building their knowledge quickly. One answer lies in building a sophisticated capability to access and mobilize learning from around the world.

To see what is involved, consider the case of the telecommunications operator SingTel. Facing deregulation and new entrants into its home market, as far back as 1992 SingTel had set a target of earning 15 to 20 percent of revenue from overseas operations within five years. When Lee Hsien Yang took over as CEO in 1995, he revised it to 20 percent by 1998 and 50 percent by 2004.

SingTel's first step toward internationalization involved buying a series of minority stakes, mainly in local telecommunications operators and cable companies in Europe. Most of these failed to evolve into much more than rather passive financial investments and did little to help SingTel develop into a true multinational business. In 1997, therefore, Lee decided to restart SingTel's internationalization drive in a new direction: with a focus on Asia and involving substantial investments in up-and-coming Asian carriers in which SingTel could be actively involved in management and international learning.

The result was a network of interests including Globe Telecom in the Philippines, AIS in Thailand, Bharti in India, and 100 percent of Australia's number two carrier, Optus. Determined to access and mobilize international learning across this new network, SingTel reevaluated the way it shared knowledge with and between its regional associates—the key channels were seats on the respective boards, attendance at board meetings, and subsequent reports from each company. Beyond these routine monitoring functions, activities had been on an ad hoc basis. SingTel found that the benefits quickly dissipated because they were project-based and team members returned immediately to their local roles within each company. To build an international company, this approach would have to change.

What eventually replaced the formerly ad hoc, limited integration between SingTel's international units was a set of structures and processes specifically designed to generate value by mobilizing the knowledge available across the group. This began with a change in mindset. As Lum Hon Fye, who was appointed head of SingTel's new regional mobile unit (RMU) put it: "We have done a lot more work regionally, as a group, than has ever been done in SingTel before. A dedicated unit helps of course but when I say there is a lot of focus, I do not mean only the RMU itself—the RMU is merely a catalyst—what is important is that the entire organization gets involved—many more people in the line today are involved in regional work and projects than there have ever been—so even middle managers are getting involved whereas previously, it was only the highest levels."[18] Consciousness of the fact that SingTel was now an international company steadily began to sink in.

The establishment of a series of ongoing regional working groups followed in four key areas where SingTel believed there were potential synergies from mobilizing knowledge internationally. These included:

- *Human resources.* Plans were made for exposing high potential talent to different markets so that individuals destined for higher responsibilities within SingTel had at least one career posting with an overseas unit.

- *Benchmarking and knowledge management.* All of the units adopted common indicators, such as average revenue per user (ARPU) and minutes of use (MOU), to allow the development of a Web-based regional knowledge management system to encourage benchmarking and the exchange of best practices and to keep employees of the extended group updated on key developments across the region.

- *Product development.* All units agreed to share their product road maps and to make decisions as to which unit would take the lead on which new products. This turned out to be especially valuable in the area of content acquisition, allowing SingTel group, for example, to benefit from Globe Telecom's strong track record in tying up with different types of content partners in the Philippines.

- *Technology and equipment purchasing.* The international units were able to pool their know-how and resources in negotiations with suppliers for 2.5 generation and 3G equipment, causing "suppliers to sit up and pay attention to SingTel's new status in the region," with consequent improvements in the prices and service they offered.

The benefits of establishing these structures and processes to access and mobilize knowledge internationally were both immediate and practical. Lucas Chow, SingTel's head of mobile services, for example, found a solution to an enduring problem he had back home in Singapore. He recalled: "We knew that paging is a declining business, and I was scratching my head as to how I was going to rescue the decline and milk this cash cow as long as I could. It happened in one of the review meetings I had with AIS in Thailand—they had looked beyond the company and all the issues they had and had actually taken the mobile service and bundled it with the paging service and offered it to paging subscribers to try to slow down the decline."[19] Chow thought this was an excellent idea and immediately introduced a similar offer in Singapore, a move that proved successful in enhancing its revenue streams.

Approaching internationalization from the perspective of acquiring new capabilities and mobilizing pockets of knowledge scattered around the world, as SingTel has done, harnesses Asian companies' historical strengths in learning from the world in a new way: going beyond licensing overseas technologies and products to create in-house structures and processes that can mobilize international learning. The opportunity for Asian companies to redefine the primary upside of becoming more international in terms of expanded opportunities for learning from the world, not just projecting a home-based formula into new markets, therefore, is a potentially powerful strategy for addressing the challenge they face as latecomers to the global game.

Exploiting Adaptability

Adaptability is the final aspect of Asian heritage that can be leveraged for advantage as Asian companies meet the internationalization challenge they face. In chapter 2 we identified the fact that, where they had ventured abroad, Asian companies had generally proved adept at adapting to subtle local differences in consumer behavior, competition, and government objectives, even when this required strategies that Western observers viewed as unorthodox. In the next round of competition, this adaptability will need to be exploited in an extended range of international environments while still maintaining sufficient integration between international units to reap the cross-border synergies available.

The experience of Japan's leading brand of soy sauce, Kikkoman, has key lessons for how to achieve this balance between adaptation and integration. The Kikkoman Corporation traces its origins back to the early seventeenth century to soy sauce production enterprises located in Noda, Japan. By 1917 it was already the largest maker of soy sauce in Japan. It registered Kikkoman International Inc. in San Francisco in 1957, and by the late 1970s it began expanding its international operations to include subsidiaries in Europe and Asia.

Sales in the United States, however, were limited mainly to immigrants from Japan, Americans of Japanese descent, and other ethnic Asians. To break out of this niche segment, it would be necessary to develop ways to integrate soy sauce into mainstream American food culture. Test kitchens were built in Kikkoman International headquarters in San Francisco, and home economists and culinary experts were recruited to create recipes that called for soy sauce. The resulting recipes were printed in booklets attached to the necks of soy sauce bottles, giving the average U.S. consumer a wealth of ideas on how to use soy sauce as a meat marinade for grilling and to flavor ground meat in hamburgers, casseroles, and a variety of other American dishes. Kikkoman marketed its product under the slogan "All Purpose Seasoning," which was displayed prominently on its bottles, and packaged the product in containers sized for U.S. supermarket shelves.

Kikkoman repeated the process of subtly adapting its offering to local market conditions as it expanded into other countries. In Australia, Kikkoman adapted its marketing to position its product within the strong "barbecue" culture. But because Australians are also significant consumers of seafood, it extended the "delicious on meat" concept that had proved successful in the United States to incorporate ideas for use of the sauce in the preparation of seafood dishes. After researching the European market, Kikkoman decided to launch its product in western Germany because, as Yuzaburo Mogi, the company's CEO explained, "countries with a Latin heritage, such as France, Italy and Spain, were strongly proud of their food cultures, and seemed less receptive to foreign foods. Germans, however, were more receptive to foreign foods if the taste was agreeable."[20]

When Kikkoman opened a production plant in Walworth, Wisconsin, in 1971, it pursued a policy of hiring local people not only for production jobs but also for management positions. The company decided early on to adopt U.S.-style management practices. An American was hired as the first personnel manager, and the U.S. flag crowned the building's entrance. Necessary technicians and management personnel from Japan were kept to a minimum and obtained housing in different parts of Walworth to avoid the creation of a "Japanese village" in the town. Even today, after thirty years of the plant's operation, of the 140 employees currently working in the plant, only seven are from Japan.

Kikkoman demonstrates the kind of adaptation that Asian companies are well equipped to adopt—much more subtle and extensive than many Western multinationals that see their mission as "bringing a successful formula perfected in America or Europe to the world" are willing or able to achieve. Kikkoman defined the potential scope of their adaptation broadly, encompassing product positioning, marketing, and management practices. They were constantly willing to experiment and learn in order to get the best fit between their offering and the local environment, while still retaining the core of what differentiated their product (in Kikkoman's case, the fact that it was naturally brewed rather than being chemically produced by combining hydrolyzed vegetable protein with salt, water, corn syrup, and artificial coloring). This capability for subtle and continuous adaptation across a broad front, while holding firm on core values, is something Asian companies should exploit to the full in meeting the challenge of internationalization.

It should, however, be clear from these examples of how Asian companies can deploy the strengths of their heritage in the service of internationalization that creating a successful Asian-style multinational cannot be achieved in a one-off leap. Instead, what is required is a sustained, step-by-step campaign, akin to climbing a staircase.

Climbing the Internationalization Staircase

The most important steps in this "staircase to internationalization" are depicted in figure 6-1. While each step is broadly self-contained and in sequence, reality is never as neat as this exposition. Steps will to some extent overlap, and preparations for a future step may sometimes run in parallel with its predecessors. At the same time, it is important to recognize that the task of internationalization is analogous to climbing a staircase: Each step represents a quantum change that must then be consolidated before moving on. Significant internationalization is seldom achieved from linear, incremental change. It is no more possible, for example, to be halfway into a foreign market or half-prepared with the capability to integrate an overseas operation than it is to be half pregnant. Internationalization also tends to be resource-intensive over a prolonged period, so that prioritization and focus on those aspects that will lay the foundation for future stages is imperative.

The first step involves defining a viable internationalization strategy, answering the questions: What added value do I bring to the foreign market? and What market positioning does that imply? Recall Kikkoman's clarity in answering these questions. Its value-added was well defined: A naturally brewed soy sauce is made simply from soybeans, wheat, salt, and water in a process that takes several months, resulting in a product with a rich, complex flavor with a savory, almost meatlike, taste and a delicate aroma, compared with the chemical concoctions produced by many of its competitors. Its strategy for positioning this product was to experiment with subtle adaptations until it achieved a unique fit with local market behavior and local customer culture.

But, as we saw in the previous section, rather than developing a strategy that encompasses clear value-added and market positioning, many Asian companies in the recent wave of international expansion have tried to adopt the inadequate strategy of merely "planting the flag," rather than working out how to bring a unique competitive advantage to the foreign market.

The second step begins with identifying capability gaps that will impede your company from operating effectively outside its home environment, be they in people, systems, or management style. For example, one of the keys to success at SingTel was a realistic assessment of the gaps in its internationalization capabilities. The goal is then to fill these gaps through a systemic process designed to maximize learning relative to the resources and time expended to augment the capability base with external resources like new hires or through alliances.

Despite the obvious need to build these internationalization capabilities before making major investments overseas, many companies have tried to skip this step either consciously or through neglect, as we saw, for

FIGURE 6-1

The Internationalization Staircase

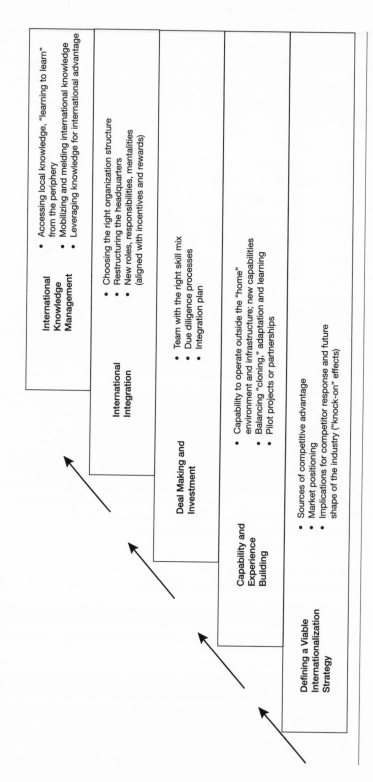

example, with DBS. While it may be possible to accelerate a company's movement through the steps, skipping steps is generally not a viable option.

Once a solid platform of capabilities is in place, the third step involves augmenting local presence and context-specific capabilities through investment, acquisitions (recall SingTel), or alliances (the strategy adopted by Haier and UPEC). This step is necessary to overcome the hurdle of depending solely on home-based advantages. To ensure that these kinds of deals add value, however, a new set of capabilities must be put in place including the capacity to undertake international due diligence, to transact deals, and to formulate a viable integration plan. To achieve this, a mix of internal capability building and effective leverage of external advisers and local hires may be necessary.

The fourth step involves remaking the overcentralized structures that abound in today's Asian companies and restructuring functional organizations to create a set of smaller business units and corporate departments that accept their role as providing services rather than exerting control. This requires restructuring the headquarters organization, not simply trying to integrate new, overseas subsidiaries into unchanged home-base structures. Incentive and rewards, management development, and career planning also need to be aligned with international performance objectives, otherwise a dominant home-country will solely concentrate on local performance and leave the management of overseas operations to "sink or swim."

In the final step, once a strong overseas presence has been established, foreign subsidiaries can begin to switch their role from "learners" to "teachers" as well. To achieve this transition, a two-way flow of knowledge between home and overseas must be established. The headquarters needs to develop the mind-set and channels to allow it to learn from its overseas operations—as we saw with SingTel. Foreign units can act as a powerful source of new ideas, technological probes, and innovations about how customers in a different environment might use the product or service in new ways that open up greater opportunity. This requires a new set of capabilities to be built that can access and mobilize knowledge scattered around the international operations and to leverage this for international advantage.

Climbing this internationalization staircase presents formidable challenges. As more and more Asian companies accept the imperative of internationalization and build the capabilities to make it happen, however, they will narrow the gap with the Western multinationals operating in Asia today or with those wishing to compete for a share of Asia's growth in the future. This, in turn, will challenge Western multinationals to raise their game in Asia as well.

New Challenges for Western Multinationals

Many of the Western multinationals operating in Asia have a head start when it comes to achieving the potential benefits of cross-border integration. They already have an international reach that spans the region through established subsidiaries and experience of how to adapt to local conditions. But arguably the presence many multinationals have established in Asia is more suited to prospering in yesterday's competitive environment rather than being well attuned to winning in the next round—especially against the new breed of Asian multinationals that seems likely to evolve as Asian companies rise to the challenge of internationalization.

When compared with the demands of Asia's changing competitive environment, the limitations of Western multinationals' existing bases in Asia typically lie in three areas: the "long, thin arm" problem, lack of cross-border integration within Asia, and the belief that it is sufficient to "think global and act local." If Western multinationals are to avoid losing ground to locals in the next round of Asian competition, these limitations will need to be addressed.

Overcoming the "Long, Thin Arm" Problem

Because many Western multinationals originally came to Asia in search of lower-cost locations for their manufacturing or service operations, their units in Asia are primarily manufacturing plants or operations centers. Others came in search of growth markets, so that sales and service units formed the core of their Asian operations. In both cases, the Asian subsidiary began as an extension of a global function—such as manufacturing or sales—within the multinational.

Such a subsidiary necessarily had strong links with the multinational's global headquarters. However, the links were essentially one-way: from the parent to the subsidiary in Asia. The role of the Asian units was to execute functions directed from headquarters or to apply a business formula already perfected back at home base. Just as the fingers on a hand execute commands from the brain, Asian subsidiaries acted like the end of a long arm of the corporate center. The arm was also "thin" in the sense that the breadth and complexity of knowledge that flowed along it was constrained.

This evolution has resulted in Asian units that have only limited influence on the strategies, design, or development of their own functions and activities and, equally important, only limited interactions with sister subsidiaries, outside the headquarters, within the multinational organization. Clearly there are exceptions: Hewlett-Packard (HP), for example, has given one of its Singapore units the global responsibility for its ink-jet printer line, including design, management of the global supply chain, and international marketing. This unit's links into the HP global network have had to become extensive and capable of facilitating constant, two-way flows of complex knowledge. But this situation is rare; the Asians units of Western multinationals seldom have a charter that allows them to develop a breadth and depth of activities and capabilities equivalent to major subsidiaries elsewhere in the world (the number of multinationals with centers of excellence in Asia for major product lines, for example, is still few).

Unless this situation changes dramatically, the local subsidiaries of multinationals are likely to see today's competitive advantage eroded as more and more Asian companies broaden the range of capabilities in which they are world-class to include innovation, brand building, and supply chain management.

More Cross-Border Integration

The second deficiency of many Western multinationals in Asia compared with the demands of the next round of competition is that they have designed their operations around national subsidiaries that have only limited integration with their Asian sister units. This was a sensible strategy in an Asia divided into national fiefdoms, separated by barriers to the flow of trade, investment, and communication. But as the walls around these national fiefdoms steadily collapse, Western multinationals will need to reassess the competitiveness of their existing structures in the context of a much more economically integrated Asia. The achievement of cross-border synergies will move from being the icing on the cake to becoming core to survival.

Paradoxically, therefore, Western multinationals also face their own form of the internationalization imperative in Asia's next round of competition. Unlike many of their Asian cousins, they generally don't need to extend their reach across Asia by building new subsidiaries. But they do need to much better integrate the subsidiaries they have. Arguably, reforming an existing organizational structure is sometimes even more of a challenge than building one from scratch; old dogs, after all, don't always easily learn new tricks.

Take the case of the Anglo-Dutch multinational, Unilever. Seeing the relentless growth of cross-border competition and Asian competitors starting to leap over national boundaries by opening units in new countries, Unilever decided to reexamine the scope for improving its cost base and leveraging best practices by better integrating its many subsidiaries across Asia. Despite its long history and significant market shares in Asia, Unilever identified a long list of unexploited synergies to be gained from better integrating and coordinating its subsidiaries operating in the same business "across the water" within Asia. These included opportunities for joint purchasing, dedicating plants in some countries as the regional supply base for particular product lines, shared product development, common branding, and shared marketing campaigns. To achieve these synergies without undermining its continued ability to respond to local market conditions, however, Unilever had to move incrementally toward integration over a period of years. This involved setting up a set of regional coordination groups in which power was carefully balanced among the chairpersons, the units responsible for supplying services (such as product development) to their sister units, and representatives of the units acting as internal customers. These groups were gradually given more responsibilities and resources as they gained experience and the country managers became more comfortable operating with more cross-border integration and dependence on the pan-Asian network for the performance of key activities within their business.[21]

What Unilever found, therefore, was that while the benefits of greater cross-border integration in terms of lower costs and improved margins were both significant and relatively easy to identify, actually achieving them in practice required a complex multistage process through which existing structures and mind-sets could be reshaped. This is despite the fact that Unilever, like many Western multinationals, already had decades of experience in adapting its global business formula to local Asian markets, and its managers were expert at "thinking global and acting local." The harsh reality is that in the next round of competition, this set of skills, alone, is unlikely to be sufficient to succeed.

Beyond Thinking Global, Acting Local

In the Asian competitive environment of tomorrow, it won't be enough for the managers of Western multinationals to be able to think global, act local. The reason is that being expert at taking a global business formula and adapting it to a local market largely ignores the opportunity to take learning from a local Asian market and apply it to reshaping the company's strategy across Asia (or for that matter, the world).

Thinking global, acting local often means that best practices and innovations generated in the course of adapting a global business formula to a local market remain imprisoned locally: They don't get propagated across Asia and the world. While this remains the case, Western multinationals in Asia won't be able to fully exploit the learning they are accumulating inside their Asian operations. The long-term consequence of this failure will be an inability to keep pace with their Asian cousins as they become increasingly capable of taking what they learn in one Asian country and deploying that learning elsewhere. In short, while Asia remains a recipient and implementer of best practice within Western multinationals rather than a strong contributor to global improvement and innovation, their competitive advantage will erode relative to Asian rivals capable of milking what they learn in Asia for all it is worth.

To prevent this erosion in their competitive advantage, managers of Western multinationals in Asia will need to learn to go beyond adapting a global business formula locally and begin to think local and act global as well.[22] In other words, they will have to become much better at identifying how the uniquely Asian aspects of their local operations can contribute to their company's global strength. Asia will have to move from being an implementer to become a contributor and, in some cases, a strategic leader within Western multinationals if they are to win in the next round.[23]

Asian Globalization

The demise of national fiefdoms in the face of falling barriers to cross-border trade and investment, national policies to create homegrown multinationals, the need to match the advantages of Western multinationals, and the end of growth through opportunistic diversification mean that as we enter the next round of competition it is becoming imperative that Asian companies internationalize. With some notable exceptions, too few Asian corporates have built full-fledged multinational companies where virtually every aspect of the business spans national borders to form an integrated international network. In Asia's changing environment, many more will have to grasp this challenge.

But as latecomers to the internationalization game, Asian companies are unlikely to win by mimicking the strategies followed by the Western companies that went before them on the path to globalization. They need to play to the strengths of their Asian heritage to create a new breed of Asian multinational whose competitive advantage is drawn, in part, from its distinctiveness from today's global giants from the Americas and Europe.

In this chapter, we have sketched out some of the strategies that might distinguish tomorrow's successful, Asian-style multinational, including (1) much greater use of alliances as a way to internationalize, (2) using international expansion to acquire new capabilities and to mobilize pockets of knowledge scattered around the world rather than plastering the world with a business formula perfected back at home base, and (3) an emphasis on subtle adaptation that harnesses the power of local diversity rather than trying to bulldoze it out of the way.

Before they can build a new breed of Asian multinational, however, Asian companies will need to begin by breaking free of the widespread conception of internationalization as a process of planting the corporate flag in new countries. The winners will be companies that recognize that "climbing a staircase"—building new international capabilities in a systematic way, step-by-step—is a much more appropriate analogy. The first step is to be clear about the distinctive value-added a company can bring to its target markets when it ventures overseas. What follows must be a sustained campaign to build the experience base, structures, and capabilities necessary to run an international organization. Those who fail to make this investment and try to rely, instead, purely on deal-making skills (Hong Kong's PCCW comes to mind), risk seeing their internationalization ambitions collapse as its weak foundations give way.[24]

As Asian companies continue to move down the internationalization road, Western multinationals operating in Asia will face their own internationalization imperative. This may seem a paradoxical claim: Surely the global players established in Asia have already demonstrated their international credentials? But the reality is that what many Western multinationals have built in Asia are structures designed to win yesterday's competitive battles. To succeed in the next round, their Asian subsidiaries will need to evolve beyond being "long, thin arms" of the parent, with a much broader and deeper set of local capabilities. Western multinationals in Asia will also need to refashion their existing set of subsidiaries, each focused on a national market, into a much more integrated Asian network. Finally, Western multinationals will need to go beyond "thinking global, acting local" to become much better at fully exploiting the learning they are accumulating inside their Asian operations. This means upgrading the role of Asia to a full contributor and, in some product lines, a strategic leader within their global networks rather than relegating it to the role of implementer of the global formula in local markets.

Addressing these internationalization challenges won't be easy for either group. But beyond the immediate potential for lower costs, better margins, and a stronger flow of innovation, the internationalization of Asian business holds out the prospect of an even more important, long-term prize: new opportunities to reshape Asia's competitive playing field. These opportunities are the subject of chapter 7.

Chapter 7

Consolidating the
Asian Playing Field

Compared with the world's other major economic regions, Asia's industry remains fragmented. The structure of Asia's retail sector is a good
example: In the United States, there are around six retailers for every
hundred households; in Asia the figure ranges from seven in Singapore
to over twelve in China and Japan. A few large retail chains have started
to emerge, such as CP's Tesco-Lotus in Thailand and UPEC's chain of
3,304 7-Eleven stores in Taiwan and 173 stores in the Philippines, along
with French-based Carrefour's hypermarket operations that span Asia.
But fragmentation is still endemic. In large, emerging Asian markets,
among which China is the most prominent, this kind of fragmentation is
repeated across industry after industry. China's top four brewers, for
example, control just 10 percent of the total market, while the United
States has four big beer producers that together account for 83 percent
market share. In China's home appliance business, meanwhile, some
consolidation has taken place, but the top four suppliers still account for

only around 60 percent of the market, compared with the big four in America who control 95 percent.

Local variations in infrastructure and consumer preferences, of course, play a role in determining the level of market concentration that is economically efficient in different environments. Not every market will come to be dominated by a few, large players. But it is difficult to avoid the conclusion that Asia's industry fragmentation, measured both within national markets and across the region as a whole, owes more to history than it does to economics.

Every now and then a window of opportunity opens up that allows forward-thinking, bold companies to fundamentally reshape the playing field itself by driving industry consolidation and, in the process, to improve the potential for making sustainable profits. In the United States and Europe, we have seen waves of consolidation transform industry after industry over the past twenty to thirty years. As we enter the new millennium, that same window of opportunity to reshape the playing field is beginning to open for more and more Asian industries as diverse as banking, telecommunications, and cement.

This window for industry consolidation is opening now for two main reasons. First, because, as we have seen throughout this book, the changing competitive environment in Asia—driven by the delayed impact of the 1997 Asian financial crisis, more intense competition from China, and the elimination of protected national fiefdoms—is putting increasingly intense pressure on Asian companies to become more efficient and more focused about where they invest their resources in the future. This means that more and more companies will be forced, however reluctantly, to dispose of businesses where they lack the scale and the prospect of building sufficient depth of capabilities to compete in the next round.[1] This will create a new supply of businesses for consolidators to mop up, which wasn't there in the past.

Second, the barriers that have stood in the way of industry consolidation are coming down. Asian governments have been forced to relax restrictions on the takeover of companies within their borders, especially by foreign companies. Across Asia, governments need foreign investment to help clean up corporate assets that clog the asset restructuring corporations they created immediately after the crisis and restart growth by promoting acquisitions that will create more efficient and internationally competitive industry structures. The stigma in the minds of many Asian managers that equated being acquired with failure is starting to change as acquisitions are coming to be seen much more as part of the normal process of business evolution. And throughout much of Asia, even the Asian public is becoming more used to the idea of takeovers, including the purchase of local assets by foreigners. A survey in 2000 found that some 83 percent of mangers thought that Asian firms should be considering acquisitions, including cross-border deals. Surveying the general public, the same pollsters found that 63 percent of people were "not concerned" about companies in their country "falling into foreign hands through mergers," and only 7.1 percent were "very concerned."[2] As a result of these developments, the feasibility of strategies designed to drive industry consolidation is increasing.

But setting out to drive consolidation and reshape an industry is an ambitious goal that is fraught with danger. Embarking with a flawed vision of what kind of playing field might be engineered, doing the wrong deals, or misjudged timing can lead to very expensive mistakes and even threaten a company's survival.

In this chapter we examine the potential, and the pitfalls, of trying to reshape the Asian playing field by using "strategic assembly" to drive industry consolidation. What sort of advantages should be sought? Where are the danger zones? We also discuss how to identify a window of opportunity to drive industry consolidation. Next we tackle the organizational challenges posed by the need both to successfully execute multiple acquisitions and to restructure and integrate them into a unified competitive force. Finally, we address the issue of maintaining momentum once the consolidation phase has run its course.

As with many of the other strategies discussed in this book, we will argue that the winners in the next round will be those who manage to cherry-pick world best practice in how to go about the task of driving industry consolidation and to combine this with approaches that leverage the strengths of Asia's business heritage. We argue that Asian strengths in identifying future choke points in the industry activity chain, adaptability, capability to learn from the acquired company, and the use of minority stakes and alliances can all be leveraged to increase the chances of success.

Strategic Assembly As a Route to
Industry Consolidation

At its most basic, *strategic assembly* is the idea of undertaking a series of acquisitions, each one forming another piece of the jigsaw that will become a large, integrated network of operations.[3] But successful strategic assembly is seldom just about "becoming number one" in a market, or even leapfrogging competitors to move into the top tier of players. That is only part of the story. An equally important outcome of strategic assembly is its impact on the future shape of the playing field: It can be used to drive industry consolidation—especially if it triggers a knock-on effect among competitors that begin assembling their own portfolio of acquired companies for fear of being left behind. The future structure of the industry, which rivals are left, and the way they compete, can all be transformed. The long-term implications for profitability are obviously profound.

In Europe and the United States, this cycle has been successively played out in many industries. The Swedish appliance maker Electrolux, for example, assembled dozens of acquisitions over the 1980s, transforming the structure of the white-goods industry. Henkel has led consolidation in the formerly fragmented business of adhesives, starting with the U.S. maker of superglue, Loctite, and following up with a continual stream of acquisitions. Indeed, across all its market segments, Henkel has made more than two hundred acquisitions over the past five years, reshaping the playing field in many areas where it competes.

Similar strategies are beginning to emerge in Asia. One of the most striking instances has been in the Southeast Asian cement market, long a fragmented, localized business. Starting after the 1997 financial crisis, three global players—LaFarge, Cemex, and Holderbank (now Holcim)—between them assembled controlling stakes in over twenty Asian cement companies. Today their networks account for more than 60 percent of the total cement capacity in the region. The competitive playing field has been transformed as a result. The use of strategic assembly to drive industry consolidation has begun in Asian banking with the Hong Kong and Shanghai Banking Corporation (HSCB), Standard Chartered, and DBS each buying up a series of local banks across Asia. The future is likely to be dominated by new kinds of competition between these regional banking networks. Likewise, in the telecommunications market, successive acquisitions by Vodaphone, SingTel, SK Telecom, and NTT DoCoMo are reshaping the competitive playing field.

Despite a slowdown caused by the 2001 U.S. recession, the fact that consolidation of Asian industry is gathering pace is evident in the aggregate data shown in figure 7-1. Since the 1997 crisis, there has been a dramatic rise in the number of M&A deals involving Asian companies, both in terms of the number of transactions and their value. And while mergers and acquisitions announced in Asia fell around 13 percent to an estimated $123 billion in 2002, this reduction reflected a fall in equity values rather than a slowdown in the underlying rate of M&A activity.[4]

Even more interesting, however, is that the bulk of this growth in M&A has been between Asian companies—a reflection of the fact that M&A is being used by Asian players to rationalize their corporate portfolios and drive industry consolidation, not primarily either to dispose of businesses to U.S. or European buyers or to acquire new assets on distant continents. More and more leading Asian companies are moving in the direction of strategic assembly and a determination to drive consolidation in their industries.

Before embarking on strategic assembly, however, five critical ingredients for success need to be put in place:

1. A well-developed set of scenarios that capture the goals of strategic assembly. What is the competitive playing field likely to look like when the phase of rapid-fire acquisitions, including a likely "chain reaction" among competitors, comes to an end?
2. A clear rationale for why a window of opportunity for industry consolidation has opened up.
3. An effective acquisition screen to assess the suitability of acquisition candidates.
4. The internal capabilities to manage a disciplined acquisition process.
5. A road map for integration and an effective process to make it happen.

In the rest of this chapter, we look at how these ingredients can be marshaled in a way that gives strategic assembly—a pivotal element in winning the next round of Asian competition—the maximum chances of success.

FIGURE 7-1

M & A Trends in Asia

VALUE OF DEALS

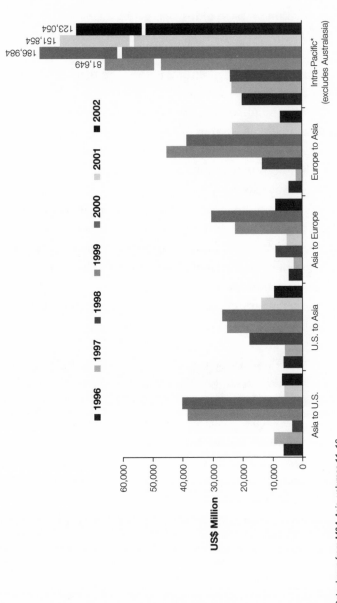

Source: Data drawn from *M&A Asia*, volumes 11–16.

has turned out to be a playing field of titans, all with similarly efficient cost structures, slugging it out in cutthroat competition.

This example drives home a fundamental lesson: Before embarking on a strategy to reshape the competitive playing field, develop scenarios for the sort of industry structure that might reasonably result and what the distinctive competitive advantage will be in this new environment. These scenarios help clarify the target outcome and the risks faced by the consolidation strategy. Kodak's success in reshaping China's photo film industry is a good example of how successful restructuring toward a target scenario might be pulled off.

Targeting the Future Shape of an Industry

When Eastman Kodak negotiated a deal with the Chinese government in 1998 to take over three large, state-owned enterprises in the photographic industry (Shantou Era Photo Materials, Xiamen Fuda Photographic Materials, and Wuxi Aermei Film & Chemicals Corporation) and integrated them into a holding company with Kodak's existing operations, its aim was to assemble the future leading player in the Chinese market. In return, the Beijing government agreed to close down two other domestic film plants.[5] But Kodak also knew that Fuji of Japan and the largest Chinese-owned player, Lucky Film Corporation, would remain important competitors and, in the wake of Kodak's moves, would probably try to make a series of acquisitions themselves.

Knowing that it would need to compete in a tripartite game with two other large players, Kodak therefore looked beyond its immediate scale advantage. It expected that competition on the postconsolidation playing field would shift from price to quality, brand strength, and convenience. As a result, Kodak set aside a further budget of $700 million to rapidly expand its network of franchised retail outlets and local processors, introduce new technology, and invest in building brand loyalty. To cement its first-mover advantage, it negotiated an exclusion on other foreign companies' acquiring state-owned assets in the photographic industry for a further four years.[6]

Kodak subsequently continued its strategy of strategic assembly, which led it to acquire five of the seven largest state-owned photographic film companies.[7] It began opening new "Kodak Express" branded shops at the rate of three a day, passing a total of 8,300 by early 2003. Its market share of the roll-film market is estimated to exceed 60 percent at attractive margins.

The reshaped playing field has been transformed from a fragmented, state-owned industry to competition between three leading players, primarily on quality, brand, and convenience. Fuji launched a program to upgrade its 3,000 outlets to offer digital services, and Lucky announced plans to open 2,700 new, specialized shops. The bases of competition were transformed, shifting the focus away from price discounts. And the consolidation initiated by Kodak may yet continue; Fuji and Lucky began talks on various forms of strategic alliance in early 2003.

As a precondition for successful strategic assembly, it is obviously critical to consider the likely outcome in terms of market structure, the relative strengths of remaining competitors, and the competitive focus (e.g., price, brand, technology, convenience) that will emerge. It is equally important to think through which part of the chain of activities to try and consolidate. The case of satellite TV broadcasting in Asia shows the importance of focusing on the right part of the value chain when developing feasible scenarios for reshaping an industry.

Focusing on the Right Stage in the Value Chain

When Hutchison Whampoa of Hong Kong launched STAR TV in 1991, there was only a single satellite, AsiaSat1, with available transponder capacity capable of beaming TV signals across the Asia region from Japan to India. Companies ranging from the newscaster BBC World to movie supplier Home Box Office and music video company MTV were eager to extend their audience reach by supplying content to the new, pan-Asian service.[8] Programs were therefore available to STAR at competitive royalty charges.

Just five years later there were more than a dozen satellites beaming TV programs down to Asian viewers. Competition for popular content among competing TV channels drove royalty levels up. Profits in Asian satellite broadcasting were squeezed razor thin. Some strategists argued that the answer was for a few leading players to drive consolidation through strategic assembly. But the question was, where in the chain could profitable consolidation be achieved?

The production of TV programs was divided between huge movie houses like MGM Films and Universal Studios, major TV networks like NBC or Nippon Hoso Kyokai (NHK), and a myriad of small, independent program producers around the world. Given this global market structure, a strategy of strategic assembly was impractical. An alternative was to acquire satellite broadcasters in Asia, but this strategy too faced severe problems. While consolidation was possible in specialized segments, like business news, where CNBC and Asia Business News had merged to form a dominant player, more general consolidation was hampered because many of the satellite broadcasters were owned by large, overseas TV networks or backed by governments. Moreover, given the possibility of piggybacking off the excess capacity of telecommunications satellites, consolidation gains could easily be set back by the entry of new competitors (including telecommunications companies seeking to broaden their service offering).

When Rupert Murdoch's News Corporation bought STAR TV in 1993, it sought instead to execute the assembly strategy in the part of the chain where it believed consolidation could be made to stick: in the cable redistribution of satellite broadcasts that serve the large urban centers of Asian cities. In the high-rise apartment blocks of cities like Taipei, Hong Kong, or Singapore, it's impractical for each household to have its own satellite dish. Instead, cable companies wire up the building and supply it from a single satellite dish mounted on the roof. Once this wiring is installed, it becomes a "natural monopoly" that it generally doesn't pay to duplicate. Unlike program production or satellite broadcasting, therefore, cable redistribution offers a potentially fertile ground for gaining more control over the TV broadcasting value chain and improving profitability by driving consolidation. It has been a long haul, but there are signs that News Corporation's strategy is starting to pay dividends, whereas attempts to reshape the playing field by acquiring satellite broadcasters or program makers would have been doomed to fail.

As the STAR TV story illustrates, focusing on the right link in the value chain is key to successful strategic assembly. Effort needs to be concentrated on a part of the value chain that can act as a proverbial "mountain pass," or choke point along the chain of activities.[9] As we saw in chapter 2, in the boom years Asian companies were adept at finding these choke points when the aim was to control the supply of key components or services that would become scarce as demand expanded. As we move into the next round of competition, these same skills need to be redirected toward identifying points in the chain where fragmentation and excess capacity can be consolidated to create new choke points in an era where overcapacity, rather than shortage, is the norm.

Getting Clarity About the Window of Opportunity for Industry Consolidation

Having painted some realistic scenarios about what a reshaped playing field might look like and decided where in the chain of activities to focus your drive for industry consolidation, the next key issue is that of timing. Go too early and the costs of persuading unwilling sellers and carving a path through regulatory barriers are likely to be prohibitive.

Take the example of pioneers like DBS bank or Standard Chartered Bank as they sought to build regional networks across Asia through acquisition, beginning the process of consolidation and rationalization in Asian banking. Back in the mid-1990s, these attempts were continually frustrated by government regulations designed to maintain control of banking in the hands of nationals and by buoyant markets where incumbents felt little pressure to merge. This position began to change after the 1997 financial crisis when many Asian banks were on their knees and needed to be recapitalized. But restrictions on foreign ownership were slow to change; governments were reluctant to allow their banks to be acquired by foreigners. It was not until 2001 that the window for reshaping the Asian playing field really began to open. In Hong Kong, for example, the numerous family controlled banks with just 1 to 2 percent market share, which had long held out for independence, began to sell, and even mid-sized players like Dao Heng Bank Group accepted takeover bids (in Dao Heng's case from Singapore's DBS). By 2002 consolidation began to gather pace in Taiwan, where fifty-two banks had been vying to serve a market of just 23 million people. In Malaysia, the fifty-three banks and finance companies that crowded the market in 1997 have been consolidated into ten "anchor" banking groups.[10]

While there are dangers and costs in trying to drive industry consolidation before conditions are right, joining the consolidation fray too late also carries considerable risks. Once a process of industry consolidation is initiated by a few major players, it often gathers pace quickly, setting in train a chain reaction. Recall the experience in Southeast Asia's cement industry. Early moves by Cemex of Mexico sparked a series of rapid-fire acquisitions by La Farge, Holcim, and Blue Circle (itself later acquired by La Farge). In just three years, twenty-six acquisitions were made by these companies, giving them controlling interests in well over half the local capacity.

This type of chain reaction is common because buyers who wait too long to enter the game risk finding that the best acquisition targets have already been sold to competitors. On the other side of the equation, the pressure on potential sellers often increases as they come under pressure form larger, merged rivals that begin to improve their cost-competitiveness by exploiting economies of scale and eliminating duplication of fixed costs. Industry consolidation may also mean that spot markets on which to buy and sell product shrink and export opportunities dry up, as formerly independent companies withdraw from the open market and transact more and more business internally with the new parent or sister companies within their corporate group. In the case of cement, for example, export trading was rapidly replaced by intracompany transactions, leaving independent cement producers more and more isolated. These developments, in turn, increasingly forced the remaining independent players to consider selling out.

So, if getting the timing right is essential for strategic assembly to succeed, what are the indicators managers might use to decide if a window of opportunity for industry consolidation is opening? There are a number of telltale signs:

- Potential new sources of scale advantage

- Signs of strategy decay among small and medium-sized incumbents

- Shifts in the regulatory regime

New Sources of Scale Advantage

As we have already cautioned, industry consolidation is not a foregone conclusion. No law of nature says that all industries will be inhabited by a few large players. In many industries, a fragmented structure of small suppliers can thrive based on advantages like strong personal relationships, detailed local knowledge, flexibility, low overheads, more staff autonomy, and the kind of responsive, customized service that large companies often find it difficult to reliably deliver from a massive, corporate machine. So before pushing ahead with a strategy designed to drive consolidation, managers need a convincing answer to the question: "What has changed that makes a large-scale operation potentially *more* competitive than it was in the past?" In short, the first indicator that a window of opportunity is opening to drive industry consolidation is the emergence of new sources of scale advantage.

New sources of scale advantage can arise because of a change in technology that increases the minimum efficient scale of operations or drives up the minimum investment stakes required to stay in the game. Over the past ten years, for example, the minimum efficient scale of a semiconductor wafer fabrication plant has moved from a facility costing $300 million to a large and better-equipped plant costing over $1.5 billion. This has been a major force driving consolidation at the fabrication part of the semiconductor supply chain. Likewise, the introduction of new, "computational chemistry" and biometrics technologies has raised the scale intensity of pharmaceutical research, leading to consolidation in drug development.

In other cases, the emergence of new types of scale advantage will depend on the confluence of changing customer behavior and new technology. Changing lifestyles and increased car ownership, for example, have led to a shift in shopping patterns, which has opened the way for the emergence of so-called hypermarkets. But before hypermarkets could become viable, improvements in transport and communication infrastructure were required, along with investments in integrated IT systems for managing inventory and the logistics necessary to enable global sourcing. Once in place, this complementary infrastructure paved the way for new sources of scale advantage in retailing that favored large retail chains over "mom and pop" stores, medium-sized retailers, and even national champions in the retailing business. Similarly, new sources of scale advantage in banking required the willingness of customers to transact through call centers and computers instead of local branches. The growing popularity (or at least acceptance) of these new distribution and service channels, combined with the scale advantages and high fixed costs of setting up call centers and e-banking, has begun to open the door to consolidation in banking.

But beware of wishful thinking: The availability of new, large-scale technologies is not a sufficient indicator that industry consolidation will be profitable. Look no further than the pan-Asian TV stations, the ultimate in scale economies and spreading of fixed costs, which have struggled to compete with smaller broadcasters offering locally tailored programming. The burden of proof is to be able to show convincingly that industry consolidation will deliver a higher level of product or service quality to customers and/or achieve at least a comparable offering at a more competitive cost.

The potential for consolidation to contribute directly to customer satisfaction by rendering it economic to supply a wider range of products or services than could be supported by a smaller-scale operation also needs to be factored in. As we saw in chapter 5, the ability to provide Asian consumers with more variety and greater customization will be key in the next round of competition. Strategic assembly generates increased scale in any national market or allows the accumulation of pockets of demand in different countries (or both). It can therefore play a critical role in allowing a company to offer a wider and more customized offering at competitive prices by enabling fixed costs to be amortized and otherwise subscale variants to be supplied in economic volumes.

Signs of Strategy Decay Among Small and Medium-sized Incumbents

A second set of indicators are signs of strategy decay among smaller and medium-sized incumbents. They might even include signs of decline among the number four, five, or six largest players in some markets.

Especially in Asia, where many of the companies in fragmented industries remain family owned or controlled, incumbents can be slow to acknowledge that the time for consolidation is ripe. In some cases they actively seek to thwart it. It is important, therefore, to get beyond the rhetoric to the reality so as to understand: How well are the incumbents positioned to prosper in the future and why?

This can require considerable detective work because declining profitability, mounting losses, or falling market share probably won't be evident until after industry consolidation starts to happen and intense competition from new, larger players actually begins to bite. By this time, any first-mover advantages to be gained by pioneering industry consolidation may well be lost. Just as we saw in chapter 5, therefore, what we need are prospective indicators of declining performance: signs of strategy decay that preface trouble ahead.

Indicators of strategy decay among incumbents might include:

- Desertion by more sophisticated or forward-looking customers; revenue stagnation

- Defections of dynamic staff and disputes between management and owners over future strategic direction

- Failure to invest in new technology

- Downward rerating of shares so that price/earnings (P/E) ratios are falling despite stable or even growing profits

Detecting strategy decay is more an art than a science, as we saw in chapter 4. Detailed and in-depth understanding of incumbents is required to understand whether a market is ripe for consolidation, not just an assessment of broad trends. But given the critical importance of getting the timing right, investment in careful analysis will be repaid many times over in terms of reducing the risks associated with strategic assembly.

Shifts in the Regulatory Regime

A shift in the regulatory regime is perhaps the most unequivocal indicator that a window for industry consolidation is opening. In the recent past, regulatory changes in Asia have often directly or indirectly removed legal barriers to industry consolidation or even included government initiatives designed to force consolidation. Following the 1997 Asian financial crisis, for example, governments from Thailand to Korea and Indonesia relaxed rules on the acquisition of local companies by foreign-based multinationals across a wide variety of industries. Primarily designed to restart the much-needed inflow of foreign investment after the crisis, these regulatory changes indirectly opened the way for strategic assembly and industry consolidation.

The dramatic consolidation of the Southeast Asian cement industry, referred to above, was possible only because changes in foreign investment regulations opened the door to foreign acquisitions. Taiwan, meanwhile, introduced a series of measures directly aimed at encouraging consolidation of its banking sector, including tax incentives, changes in accounting rules, and legislation that allowed companies to use shares, instead of cash, to make acquisitions. Recall that in the consolidation of Malaysia's banking and finance industry, policies were even more proactive. Working through an arm of the central bank, the government originally announced that it wanted to see the industry consolidate into six banking groups. When the process stalled, a number of "forced marriages" were arranged, under the threat of licenses being withdrawn.

Changes in regulation can signal the opportunity for leading firms to drive industry consolidation, but obviously opportunity and desirability are not the same thing. Regulatory changes act as an indicator of when a window for industry consolidation has opened up, not whether it will be profitable to utilize it. Indicators that new sources of scale advantage are emerging and that strategies of incumbents are beginning to decay also need to turn from red to green before it makes sense to proceed with strategies to drive industry consolidation.

Once you have decided that the timing is right for industry consolidation and thought through viable scenarios for what the future competitive playing field might look like when the market settles down, there comes the inevitable confrontation between your strategic plan and the reality of available acquisition targets. The final outcome is necessarily a compromise between these two: your ideal sequence of deals and those that are practicable given the willingness or vulnerability of sellers. The outcome of strategic assembly almost always reflects a mix of strategy and opportunism.

Assuming the basic strategy of consolidation is valid, whether the resulting acquisitions are economically sound fundamentally depends on three factors:

- The effectiveness of your screening process

- The effectiveness of your acquisition process

- The effectiveness of your integration process

Developing an Effective Acquisition Screen

Given the objective of strategic assembly is to build a leading position in a market by successive acquisitions, it might appear that almost any candidate that could potentially add market share and scale would suffice. But, there are at least three core dimensions on which potential target companies should be screened: existing strategy, health, and culture.

The first criterion for screening should be the existing strategy of the target. Some companies depend on sources of competitive advantage that are specific to their existing positioning and/or ownership. An entrepreneurial founder, for example, with strong personal relationships with customers, staff, and suppliers may be key to a target company's success; or a target's sales may depend on nationalistic loyalty to a locally owned brand; another target's profitability may rely on niche positioning. Acquiring and integrating a company with these kinds of highly specific, and therefore fragile, advantages in the quest for scale and consolidation presents a high risk that its strengths will be unintentionally destroyed in the process. The more the existing strategy of the target needs to be revectored as part of strategic assembly, the less suitable such a candidate will be. Targets that require a U-turn in strategy before they fit the goals of the consolidator must be screened out. If the intent is to acquire a portfolio of companies, then each potential target also needs to be screened for possible impediments to their future integration with others in the target group.

Second, is the health of the target. Nothing wrong with buying up target companies in poor shape: They are likely to come considerably cheaper than their healthier rivals. But buying a company in poor health—one that is losing money and has dissatisfied customers, demoralized staff, or operational or quality problems—assumes that you, as the acquirer, have the capacity to turn that company around. Turnarounds are notoriously difficult for the inexperienced, can distract management, and delay the time when the benefits of integration can be achieved. Acquiring a series of companies in poor health can result in continual fire-fighting that clouds focus on the strategy of assembling and integrating multiple companies to achieve economies of scale. Given these risks, the point is this: Your acquisition screen should be set to discard those potential targets that have health problems beyond the capability of your own management to correct rapidly (bearing in mind that your management may be further stretched by the need to manage the integration of multiple companies simultaneously).

Take the example of China's Haier, which has evolved from operating a single refrigerator factory in Qingdao, China, to become the dominant supplier of white goods in China, including refrigerators, freezers, and washing machines, through a succession of eighteen acquisitions.[11]

Screening out targets that Haier's management feels it cannot successfully turn around is an important part of the company's consolidation strategy. Zhang Ruimin, Haier's CEO, describes this process as "hunting the stunned fish, not the dead ones."[12]

On the flip side of the health coin, there can be a persuasive argument for buying strong companies on the basis that it is better to have available "best-of-breed" companies as part of your portfolio rather than letting them become part of a competitor. Your acquisition screen therefore needs to take into account the risk that your competitor will be strengthened if it is able to buy up companies in good health.

Third, is the culture of the target company. Strategic assembly that involves combining a multiplicity of different cultures has the possible advantage that it is easier to justify the need for a new, overarching culture as a unifying force. On the other hand, cultural differences between the acquired parties complicate the process of integration. The difficult and time-consuming nature of cultural change may well justify cultural compatibility with your core operation and among targets as an important screening criterion.[13]

Properly qualifying a set of potential targets is the strategic challenge. Successful strategic assembly then depends on the quality of your acquisition and integration processes.

Building a Disciplined, but "Asian," Acquisition Process

Detailed studies of successful strategic assemblers, such as Henkel, Electrolux, and British Petroleum, show that the ease of integration and even the long-run results depend heavily on the nature of the acquisition process, both before and during each deal.[14] Rather than simply importing approaches that have proved successful in the United States or Europe, however, this means developing a process that plays to Asian strengths and is well adapted to the local context. The successful merger between United Overseas Bank and Overseas Union Bank in Singapore demonstrates the importance of adopting an "Asianized" approach.

A decade ago Singapore had ten domestic banks. By 2003 they had been consolidated into just three. The inevitability of consolidation was in little doubt, but how it played out depended as much on the process the protagonists adopted as on the economic fundamentals at work. As part of its strategy of becoming a major regional player, the acquisitive

DBS bank cast itself in the role of primary driver of consolidation in its Singapore home base as well as abroad. The process it adopted was direct and clear: It advised the Singapore Stock Exchange that it was launching a hostile bid for Overseas Union Bank (OUB).

But this approach meant that Lien Ying Chow, the nonagenarian who had built OUB from scratch into one of Singapore's leading banks and was still its major shareholder, received the details of the bid by fax. He was reportedly "very, very upset."[15] Hours later he received a telephone call from an old rival, the seventy-two-year-old Wee Cho Yaw, founder of United Overseas Bank (UOB), inquiring about Lien's health and indicating that he would value the opportunity to come over for a chat.

Wee's UOB reportedly proposed a deal in which all of the directors of Lien's OUB would be invited to join the board of a merged entity and the jobs of the senior executives of both banks would be protected. At the same time, hard-nosed plans were devised for improved efficiency and rapid integration of the two banks. A merger was agreed on and subsequently consummated.

The lessons of this story are more complex than they might initially appear. They don't argue for a consolidation strategy based on the time-honored Asian practice of dealing with your friends. In fact, as members of two different Chinese clans in Singapore (one Hokkien and the other Teo Chew), Wee and Lien were not particularly close. Rather it is testimony to the value of combining world best practice in acquisition process while respecting Asian ways of doing business and the need to preserve "face" (the social standing of the individual). As part of the industry's consolidation drive, the merger between UOB and OUB made sound economic sense: Both banks brought a profitable and largely complementary customer base to form a combined entity at least three-quarters the size of Singapore's largest bank, DBS. But the process had to find the right line between preserving this economic integrity while incorporating Asian cultural fineness.

Other key elements in fashioning a successful hybrid acquisition process—one that combines Asian and Western elements—include:

- *Casting the due diligence net widely.* It is important to look beyond traditional financial due diligence that focuses on the balance sheet, stocks, and physical assets to include an assessment of the quality of a target company's intangible assets such as its management processes, human capital, culture, and customer relationships. Such a broader assessment not only informs management about where its exposures are postacquisition and what needs to be done to integrate the company but also provides an improved view of how much the company is really worth.

In its first major acquisition, that of Thai Danu bank, DBS bank of Singapore, for example, rightly focused on an assessment of the quality of the target's loan book. But by restricting its due diligence largely to a financial assessment, it failed to recognize the weakness in Thai Danu's credit control systems and the fact that many of its branches were losing money. DBS later discovered that the high degree of autonomy the previous owners had given to branch management, combined with poorly integrated IT systems, made it impossible to know if an individual in default at one branch also had taken out loans at one or more of the other ninety-six branches! This contributed to a tidal wave of nonperforming loans and subsequent heavy write-offs. In its subsequent acquisitions, DBS ensured it cast its due diligence net widely.[16]

• *Capturing and leveraging experience from previous acquisitions.* One of the clearest findings of research into acquisitions is that companies that capture and leverage what they have learned from past acquisitions significantly improve the probability of successfully managing the next one. The rapid-fire sequence of acquisitions that often underpins strategic assembly provides a golden opportunity to accumulate and apply learning. But all too often in large companies, the individuals involved are moved on to other jobs within the company and the learning is lost. Part of the solution to this missed opportunity is to codify the learning in a corporate acquisition guide, a discipline successfully adopted by experienced acquirers like Henkel, Electrolux, and British Petroleum. However, written manuals can capture only a fraction of the richness of practical experience. Ensuring that at least some members of today's acquisition team are redeployed as the "seed corn" for tomorrow's acquisition teams is therefore essential.

• *Assembling and managing an effective task force.* Just as it is critical to ensure a degree of continuity in successive acquisition teams so that past experience can be passed on, it is equally important to assemble a team with the right complement of skills. People with experience and internal credibility in each of the main functional areas from marketing to operations and human resources, as well as finance specialists, should be involvedto ensure both the broad due diligence discussed above and full consideration of the opportunities and potential problems with the acquisition. It is also essential to include one or more individuals who will play a significant management role in the target after the acquisition. If the acquisition is completed by a team of specialists who then pass the newly acquired firm on to others to manage like the proverbial hot potato, many of the important integration issues are almost sure to be ignored in the run-up to taking control of the new company. Nasty surprises for both sides are apt to result because the implicit, psychological contract that emerges during the acquisition process will be devoid of shared understanding about what will happen post acquisition.

When Haier took over the state-owned Huangshan TV factory in the city of Hefei in Anhui Province, for example, the Haier integration team found that the Huangshan managers had no notion of the market disciplines Haier's ownership would bring and the need to adjust to consumer tastes in product features and quality. Said one Haier manager, "they assumed they could just go on selling what they produced and when I told them Haier checked 100 percent of its products, they were shocked and told me they only needed to check about 1 percent or 2 percent."[17] Failure to unearth issues like this risks integration getting off on the wrong foot, causing suspicion and potentially stalling the process for months. These risks can be reduced by including some of the key line managers who will work with the target during the postacquisition integration.

- *Making appropriate use of specialist advisers.* Historically, many Asian companies have been loath to make proper use of professional advisers, preferring to do deals based on personal relationships and being skeptical of the value added by expensive teams of accountants, lawyers, and investment bankers. But the judicious use of professional advisers does have an important role to play: Their specialist skills and experience can save money at the end of the day. As DBS discovered when it decided to eschew advisers (apart from the limited involvement of an accounting firm in its due diligence) in its first major acquisition—that of Thai Danu—lack of access to professional advisers can lead to expensive mistakes. The DBS stance was justified on the basis of its longstanding relationship with Thai Danu as a 1 percent shareholder with a seat on the board. This "relationship" turned out to have provided little insight into the real nature of the company it was buying, yet it encouraged the DBS to try to shortcut accepted acquisition processes. DBS learned from this experience and made effective use of professional advisers in support of its subsequent acquisitions.

In addition to providing an experienced second opinion and adding greater discipline to the acquisition process, advisers can be used as a foil that enables difficult issues to be raised or on unpalatable stance to be justified. This is an important third-party role in Asia's relationship-oriented culture in which face is important.

At the same time, using outside advisers should not lull an acquirer into a false sense of security that "the experts will take care of it." Advisers need to be used as part of a team; draw on their specialist skills, but don't assume that they know your business as well as you do or that you can abrogate responsibility for management judgment to third parties.

- *Avoiding premature lock-in.* Acquisitions can develop a momentum of their own, especially when strategic assembly calls for a rapid-fire stream of acquisitions in the quest to drive industry consolidation. Those involved can get caught up in "the thrill of the chase" and lose objectivity, especially during the negotiation phase. A successful technique is to set up two teams: one composed of those who are directly involved in the acquisition process and a second whose role is to act as both sounding board and devil's advocate—ensuring that the right questions about the potential acquisition are raised and discussed and that ambiguous motives are clarified. Two key questions that this second, "shadow," team needs to keep asking are: "If we don't do this acquisition, what is our alternative?" (since negotiating without a fallback position is highly dangerous) and "Why is a better alternative target impossible?" (in other words, how much are we compromising our ideal?).

In addition to providing a source of cool perspective, the shadow team can also act as a catalyst to restart the process when negotiations around an otherwise sound acquisition stall.

Clearly the right acquisition process will vary from one situation to another. But two tests of its quality always need to be applied:

- Does the acquisition process result in deals that fit the purpose of strategic assembly at reasonable prices?

- Does the acquisition process contribute to smooth and rapid integration rather than generating unrealistic expectations and aggravating contentious integration issues or sweeping them under the carpet?

Managing Successful Integration

While the acquisition process is important in setting up the conditions for successful strategic assembly, the old adage that "value creation takes place only after the acquisition" (everything beforehand only expends resources or carves up existing value) remains paramount. The key factors improving the odds of the successful and rapid integration usually demanded by a strategy of strategic assembly include:

- *Decisively clearing the decks for integration.* When Kodak acquired each new Chinese state-owned company, for example, it typically faced overmanning, environmental exposures from chemical waste, losses draining away cash, and obsolete equipment. Integration could not proceed until these issues were addressed. Within the first six months, Kodak reduced the staffing in its first two acquisitions from 5,978 to 1,771, retrained the remaining staff, introduced environmental safeguards, stemmed the losses, and closed one plant and began reequipping the others. Only then were the acquired companies ready to be integrated under Kodak's brand and into its supply and distribution chains. Failure to act quickly and decisively to get the acquired company into viable shape, even in the face of imperfect information, introduces potentially costly delays into the integration process.

- *Communicating the new vision.* Strategic assembly has clear goals of reaping increased economies of scale, rationalizing duplication, improving and possibly broadening the product offering, and driving industry consolidation. This vision needs to be widely communicated both externally and internally to give purpose to the integration process and demonstrate the future benefits of what is often painful rationalization and culture change. Key to Haier's integration strategy, for example, has been the communication of broad goals, like its aim to become the largest player in the market segments for which it competes, while simultaneously communicating specific performance targets to its newly acquired employees in areas such as quality. Each time it makes an acquisition, Haier's management famously recounts stories like CEO Zhang's early decision to smash all "defective" refrigerators—even if the paint was merely scratched—to illustrate the company's belief that there are only two categories of output: "good quality" and "rubbish."[18]

- *Developing and executing a blueprint for rationalization.* Successful integration requires a detailed campaign that lays out priorities, a transitional structure (including an integration "champion" and specific task forces to tackle the main integration areas), and a critical path chart (much like the plan required for a construction project or new product launch). After the slow beginning to integration of its Thai Danu acquisition and hampered by the lack of a clear integration blueprint, for example, DBS moved decisively to set up "project supersonic." At the core of the project were detailed plans for tackling nonperforming loans and for integrating Thai Danu's credit control and performance measurement systems with those of DBS, backed by a senior team (one of the first cross-functional team projects in DBS) drawn from Finance & Tax, Credit Administration, and Institutional Banking. The team was led by an ex–J.P. Morgan executive, Chng Lay Chew, who had joined DBS to head the Planning, Analysis & Control group in Institutional Banking. This was later developed into a Regional Integration Centre (RIC), established in Bangkok to coordinate and integrate the group's acquisitions in the region under an experienced DBS executive, Chong Kie Cheong. With six months of intense integration activity behind him, Chong reflected: "One of the reasons that we have been able to achieve so much since setting up the RIC here in Bangkok is that integration issues appear much clearer when you are on the ground.

Sitting in DBS Towers in Singapore, the problems were all academic. Once we moved here and began to live, eat, and breathe DBS Thai Danu Bank, the requirements became obvious."[19]

• *Harnessing diversity.* The first phase of integration is usually dominated by problem solving, rationalization, and transfer of best practice from the parent to the acquired company. But by bringing together a number of companies with different histories and potentially diverse business cultures, strategic assembly is likely to provide access to a rich pool of different types of knowledge and practices. A second phase of integration, and an additional layer of advantage, can be gained by mobilizing and melding this diversity to generate innovation.[20] This requires a major shift in management mind-set from a drive for greater consistency and conformance in phase one of the integration to a drive to harness diversity in phase two. Even in the first phase, however, managers need to have an eye on the possible future value of the target's distinctive know-how or ways of doing things, so that these assets are not destroyed by the integration bulldozer.

SingTel's experience in strategic assembly provides a good example of the benefits both of increased scale and consolidation *and* of harnessing the diversity of knowledge and experience that a series of acquisitions presents. A series of acquisitions and minority stakes in Australia (where it bought the number two player, Optus), India, Indonesia, the Philippines, and Thailand had transformed the company from a national champion leader into a significant regional player with over 12 million subscribers. This allowed it to access the benefits of scale across a range of activities—from greater purchasing clout with equipment suppliers like Nokia, to ability to better spread the fixed costs of developing improved billing systems, through to increased interest from music and video publishers such as Sony and MGM that SingTel needed to persuade to develop content for its third-generation (3G) services.

But equally important were the benefits gained by harnessing diversity. SingTel discovered, for example, that its Filipino associate, Globe Telecom, had a strong track record in tying up with partners that provided content from popular films like *Bridget Jones* and *X-Men* for their SMS platform. It was agreed that further deals by Globe would now be negotiated for the entire group, as opposed to merely the Philippine market. Its Thai associate, AIS, meanwhile, had considerable experience in dealing with the problem of a decline in the user base for paging services and had successfully dealt with the issue by bundling their mobile and paging services together—an innovation that was subsequently replicated by SingTel back in its home market. The company was also able to leverage the combination of strong engineering skills within SingTel with Optus's strong capabilities in marketing and the design of innovative customer offerings by setting up centers of excellence for these activities with regional mandates, based in Singapore and Australia, respectively.[21]

To reap the kinds of benefits SingTel was able to extract from its role in industry consolidation, however, is more than a matter of applying world best practice in integration management. The key to its success was to combine these sophisticated techniques with two time-honored strengths of Asian business heritage: the mind-set to learn from, rather than simply try to control, its new partners and the capability to achieve a high level of integration by using a network of minority stakes that had to be approached more as alliances than takeovers.

Maintaining Momentum

The period of rapid-fire acquisitions or alliance building that characterizes successful strategic assembly can act like an adrenaline rush, each new acquisition extending the promise of industry dominance and making it easier to attract resources and new investment as it increases the size and reported earnings of your company. At some point, however, as one U.S. senator aptly put it, "things that cannot go on forever do eventually come to a stop."[22] This point may come when attractive targets for acquisition become scarce or when customers or regulators start to react against what they see as an undue concentration of economic power. The result is what Philippe Haspeslagh and David Jemison call the "stalling dynamic"—a deceleration that can be painful and, if not properly handled, also costly.[23]

What is required is a shift from the logic of assembly to a new logic that emphasizes ongoing management and continued innovation. The challenges we discussed in chapter 4 now come to the top of the agenda, along with the need to devise organization structures that can continue to streamline operations and manage coordination, possibly across borders, of the types analyzed in chapter 6. This means turning attention toward building the capabilities, structures, and processes to smoothly manage the much larger and more complex company that emerges from strategic assembly. It also means having the foresight, during the assembly phase, to protect the kinds of uniqueness and diversity within the acquired companies that are likely to be valuable in contributing to innovation in the future, rather than paving your trail of acquisitions with a homogeneous formula that will prove a barrier to future innovation. Finally, it means continually reminding yourself and your fellow management teams that strategic assembly and industry consolidation are means to an end, not the end itself. The potential prize is to reshape the Asian playing field into a more fertile ground on which to grow profits and value in the future.

Chapter 8

Winning Strategies for Asia's New Reality

Our starting point for this book was the sea change taking place in the Asian competitive environment in the new millennium. Asian companies are finally breaking the bonds imposed by the 1997 financial crisis and coming to terms with the end of asset speculation and rent collection as primary sources of profits. The engine of growth is shifting from exports to Asian market demand. China's rapid development is redrawing the Asian playing field. National fiefdoms are coming under increasing threat from cross-border competition. Together these forces are signaling the emergence of a fundamentally new competitive game—and there will be no going back.

We argued that, in the wake of this changing economic landscape, it will take a different kind of company to succeed in Asia's next round of competition. The winners will be companies that manage to rise to five challenges thrown up by the new environment:

- Making a step-change in total productivity

- Building new capabilities for innovation

- Creating strong Asian brands

- Extending and integrating their international networks

- Reshaping the Asian playing field by driving industry consolidation

But in a world where it is also increasingly important to be "different, not just better," success won't come from trying to mimic the approaches already adopted by companies in the United States and Europe. Instead, winning in Asia's next competitive round will require Asian companies to rediscover some of their traditional strengths and to jettison unnecessary baggage from the past—to create, in combination with the best business practices learned from around the world, a new breed of Asian multinational company. For Western multinationals operating in Asia, it will mean remaking their local operations to compete with stiffer rivalry from the new-style Asian competitors that are likely to emerge and to better exploit their own distinctive capabilities.[1]

The bulk of our analysis has been devoted to exploring these challenges and opportunities, examining what companies will need to do to succeed and assessing their preparedness for the competitive battles ahead. In this final chapter we draw together these threads, proposing a framework to help managers craft a viable strategy for Asia's new reality.

Clearly there is no single recipe for winning in Asia in the new millennium. There are many potential routes to success. Any strategy with a chance of succeeding in the new reality will have to address the key challenges discussed in this book. That will mean making some basic choices that many managers in Asia have shied away from for too long. There are also a number of important principles that will improve any company's chances of revitalizing its strategy for the rigors of Asian competition in the next round. Foremost among these is the principle of playing to your distinctive strengths—be they an Asian corporate heritage or global experience—while being open to absorb and adapt world best practice.

Strategic Choices in the New Asia

Choosing your competitive battlefield—where to compete—is the first decision any corporate strategist must make. In the new reality of Asia, this decision demands that managers stake out their territory on two key dimensions: (1) value-added versus cost and (2) local versus pan-Asian or global. Figure 8-1 lays out the options.

In contrast to the heady boom years of the 1990s, competitive advantage in tomorrow's Asia will have to be based on some mix of four core ingredients: improved productivity, local brand and service, innovation, and internationalization that is designed to reshape the Asian playing field and reap cross-border synergies. Different companies will combine these ingredients in different winning recipes. Success by focusing on a single ingredient, however, will be rare. Trying to make quantum leaps on every front simultaneously, on the other hand, risks loss of focus and substantially reduces the chances of success.

The trick for winning in Asia in the new millennium is to choose the right locus on the playing field depicted in figure 8-1 and, over time, the right trajectory of initiatives to successfully move your company around in this space. There are some strategies, like attacking low productivity in activities that fall outside the core operations and building local brands backed by the capacity to deliver an excellent customer experience, that can be implemented without wholesale restructuring of the

FIGURE 8-1

Strategic Choices for Winning in the New Asia

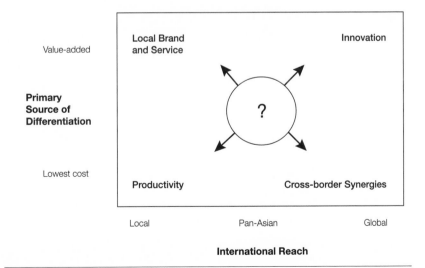

existing organization. Such initiatives do not depend on building an integrated international network capable of reaping cross-border synergies.

To go beyond these strategies and move toward the righthand side of figure 8-1, however, will require companies in Asia to adopt new approaches to international expansion and the integration of units overseas. In order to reap the benefits of innovation, for example, an international network capable of spreading the costs of developing new products and services will be key. In the longer term, therefore, internationalization and the associated reshaping of the Asian competitive playing field will be a prerequisite to moving onto the next, higher plane of profit potential.

It is important to recognize this potentially powerful interdependency between moving to higher value-added and expanding international reach. Attempts to become a world-class innovator from Asia without the international network both to source new knowledge and to rapidly amortize the cost of innovations over a large sales base may be doomed from the start. Even where the intent is to focus on maintaining a position as lowest-cost supplier, this strategy is likely to prove increasingly difficult to sustain by those that lack the reach or integrated network to reap cross-border synergies. As we saw in chapters 6 and 7, these potential synergies may operate at the pan-Asian or the global level depending on the nature of the activities that can be integrated and whether the key competitors are Asian or global players.

In some industries there is a question over whether a focused, national champion can even survive as the competitive landscape is reshaped around them by others with international reach. In other industries it will be possible to develop sustainable positions by focusing on some mix of productivity improvement and local brand building and service excellence (the left side of figure 8-1).

Choosing a Viable Positioning

Choosing a viable positioning on the competitive playing field depicted in figure 8-1 obviously requires a detailed analysis of your specific industry and company situation. The relative importance of local brand building, service, and productivity improvement will depend on the competitive situation in your specific market and the capabilities and resources available to your company. But in assessing whether a locally focused strategy will be viable relative to strategies based on internationalization, there are a set of indicators that can help in determining whether a particular positioning is viable for your company. These are summarized in table 8-1.

TABLE 8-1

The Viability of Local Focus Versus International Reach

Market characteristic	Locally focused strategies viable	International reach required
Customer behavior	• Customer behavior and demand varies mainly by different pan-Asian or global segments (e.g., teenage fashion, or environmentally aware).	• Customer behavior and demand varies mainly by local differences (e.g., driven by local culture and heritage, regulations, or climatic conditions).
	• Customers are local or, if multinationals, buying decisions are taken independently by local management.	• Customers are multinationals that require a consistent or integrated service across borders.
	• Most customers only buy locally.	• Customers are mobile.
	• Local customers tend to be demanding and sophisticated compared with elsewhere in Asia or globally.	• Customers are much more demanding and sophisticated elsewhere in Asia or globally compared with locally.
Innovation	• Most innovation is incremental, or breakthroughs are possible with a few creative people and limited resources.	• Most innovation requires high-fixed-cost R&D and significant investment sustained over many years.
Marketing	• Marketing tends to be mainly "push," based on initiatives that must be implemented by local distributors or at many points of sale.	• Marketing tends to be mainly "pull," based on mass advertising (such as TV) where there are potential scale economies in brand building.
Scale economies	• The minimum efficient scale can be achieved with a moderate share of a local or national market.	• The minimum efficient scale operation is large relative to any local market.
Competitors	• Primary competitors are local or national champions.	• Primary competitors are increasingly pan-Asian or global.

By rating your market environment on each of the dimensions outlined in table 8-1, you can decide on the importance of internationalization to your company's future strategy. If your assessment is weighted toward the righthand column of table 8-1, moves to extend your international reach will be essential.

Prioritization and Sequencing Your Strategy

Once a long-term, target positioning has been identified, getting there may involve a series of incremental steps to build the capabilities necessary to support it. Some companies, for example, will be in a position to move directly to the top right corner of figure 8-1. Others will lack the required launching pad for this strategy in terms of competitive cost base, brands, or service quality.

Productivity Focus

Given Asia's widespread productivity gap, a major push toward improved productivity, especially in the distribution, sales, and administrative areas we discussed in chapter 3, will have to be an important early focus for many companies in Asia. Until reliable processes and capabilities required to make a step-change in productivity in these areas are built, few Asian companies will be ready for a renewed push beyond exporting to become full-fledged multinationals. Even among those who choose to focus on their domestic market, the burden of low productivity will continue to sap their competitive strength unless decisively tackled. And poor productivity will continue to drain companies of the surplus necessary to invest in high-quality service or strong local branding.

For foreign multinationals operating in Asia, meanwhile, low productivity beyond the factory gate or high-efficiency service center will constrain their ability to take advantage of the future potential of Asia as a key market rather than as a source of supply. For many foreign multinationals too, an early focus on neglected areas of productivity will be required.

As we saw in chapter 3, the mix of initiatives that is required to achieve the necessary step-change in productivity will vary by industry, country, and company across Asia. But the priority areas for attack will be functionalism, pipeline fog, squandered lead time, wage illusion, and the traders' curse. In tackling these black-spots, investment and technology will play a role. But even more important is a change in mind-set: the recognition that productivity in "soft" overhead areas and in parts of the supply chain pipeline traditionally left to others is where the real scope for productivity improvement in Asia today lies. Equally, it will be necessary to accept that the rewards will come not from shiny new equipment or the latest expensive software but from relentless and detailed enhancement of "the way things are done."

For some companies in Asia, importing technology and innovative product and services designs and being able to deliver them to a local market more cost-effectively than their competition, both local and multinational, will be a viable strategy. But this narrow focus will come under increasing pressure as competitors either reshape the Asian playing field by driving consolidation and internationalization or adding brand, service quality, and homegrown innovation on top of newly productive supply chains. Many companies will have to significantly expand their strategic horizons beyond the productivity game.

Before a company shifts its strategic focus to other areas like innovation, branding, or internationalization, however, it will be essential to build systems and processes that not only lock in productivity gains but also act to ensure continuous productivity improvement that drives down the cost base year after year.

Innovation

In chapter 4 we argued that Asian firms that choose to make innovation an important part of their competitive strategy must begin by deciding whether to pursue breakthrough innovation, extension innovation, or improvement. They will then need to launch a set of innovation initiatives to expand the strategic options open to their businesses. This portfolio of options on the future needs to cover the main changes in consumer preferences and behavior, as well as the major technological changes that might emerge as the uncertain future unfolds. A robust set of processes and capabilities must be built to manage the innovation pipeline through which ideas move from experimentation and launch as ventures to be scaled up into fully contributing businesses.

Innovation lies in the upper right corner of figure 8-1, reflecting the fact that innovation strategies in Asia will increasingly be bound up with internationalization initiatives. To be effective as a strategy for winning in the next round of Asian competition, innovation will need to be viewed as an international activity. Innovations that are solely exploited in a local market are unlikely to recoup fixed development and launch costs. Innovation that draws only on the pool of knowledge available locally, meanwhile, will seldom be able to compete with innovation strategies that draw on the larger and richer pool of knowledge scattered around the globe. Reliance solely on local resources is unlikely to result in the world-class innovation necessary to compete in an increasingly open and globalized market. This means developing the capability to "learn from the world" knowledge that can be the raw material of innovation, rather than simply licensing or imitating innovative products or services developed by others or proven technologies that are no different from those competitors are using. To achieve these ambitious goals and meet the challenge of innovation, targeted acquisitions and new-style alliances in which Asian companies are active players in the innovation process, rather than passive recipients, will play a potentially important role.

Multinationals, meanwhile, will need to exploit their innovations into Asia more fully and more rapidly. They will be forced to match their Asian competitors' innovation efforts in order to better keep up with changes in fashion, and the new technologies and processes emerging from tomorrow's more innovation-focused Asia.

Brand Building and Service Quality

It might be tempting to see Asia's brand-building challenge in terms of global brand wars like that between Coke and Pepsi. But the reality, even in the case of so-called global brands, is that brand equity is usually built by sustaining thousands of small, frontline initiatives over a long period—"one market" or even "one customer" at a time. As we saw in chapter 5, brands are also more about capturing potential value created by excellent service or quality products. Successful brands are almost always backed by real differentiation, not just puffery. Finally, as we have already noted, consumer behavior and effective marketing strategies still vary markedly between cultures and countries across the Asian region.

These considerations suggest that if Asian companies are to rise to the brand-building challenge, they must focus on sustained brand-building initiatives tailored to specific markets and individual consumer experiences rather than on grandiose schemes for instant global or pan-Asian branding. They need to underpin these initiatives with a capability to deliver an improved product or service experience "on the ground" to each individual customer. Multinationals, too, need to strengthen the equity of their brands in Asia market by market and customer by customer, before looking to achieve economies of regional or global branding. The branding and service quality components of the strategic playing field therefore sit in the upper-right corner of figure 8-1.

As we saw in chapter 5, this must begin with a change in mind-set about the role of brands in capturing extra value-added in profits. As latecomers to the brand-building game, they will also require innovative approaches both to shrinking the normal time scale it takes to build a strong brand and to improving the cost economics of brand building. Many multinational companies whose brands are still relatively unknown in Asia will face similar challenges: having a "global" brand gives them a potential head start, but it doesn't eliminate the need for the hard work and sustained investment required to build brand equity in a new region.

Cross-Border Synergies and Consolidation

In chapter 6, we highlighted the fact that internationalization of Asian companies in a way that could effectively reap cross-border synergies required a sustained set of initiatives akin to "climbing the internationalization staircase." These included defining a viable internationalization strategy (one that went well beyond "planting the flag" in overseas locations), filling capability gaps and building specific new capabilities required to support internationalization, deal making on foreign investments and acquisitions, creating an integrated international organization, and developing effective mechanisms for international knowledge management.

But the prize for building more international Asian companies is much larger than cross-border cost synergies alone. In chapter 7 we argued that, as we enter the new millennium, a window of opportunity to reshape the playing field is beginning to open for more and more Asian industries as diverse as banking, telecommunications, and cement. Those companies that successfully take advantage of this unique juncture in the cycle of Asian business development will change their profit-making potential for decades to come. Others will be left stranded as the tide of restructuring passes them by. To drive the restructuring of the Asian playing field, companies will require new capabilities to execute a strategy of "strategic assembly." Here, skills in quickly identifying, assessing, and executing overseas acquisitions and then reshaping these into a fully integrated business will become critical.

The challenges of executing some mix of these four core strategies—dramatic productivity improvement, cost-effective innovation, local brand building backed by service excellence, and achieving the cross-border synergies and industry consolidation necessary to reshape the Asian playing field—are formidable. Most companies will therefore need to prioritize their initiatives, building each one as a solid platform from which to launch the next. Just as the final positioning will vary by industry and company, so will their optimal sequence of priorities. Based on our observations above, however, a typical sequence is that shown in figure 8-2.

Following such a sequence would involve an initial focus on productivity improvement, followed by a push to "add value" through local

FIGURE 8-2

A Typical Sequence of Priorities for Winning in the New Asia

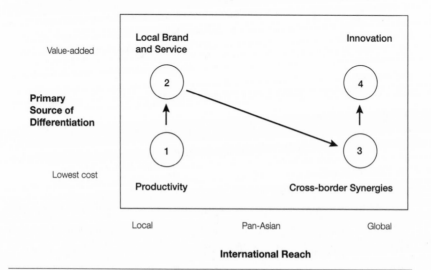

branding and service and the systems that underpin them. This second stage will help extend and deepen your stock of intangible assets, like brands and systems. These assets can then be used as a distinctive platform from which to launch an assault on international markets. Having extended your international reach, and in the process built an improved network for "learning from the world," a renewed focus on innovation makes sense. And of course, since the competition never stands still, a company may need to be continually moving through this cycle.

Leveraging Your Existing Competitive Advantages

The opportunity to leverage your existing strengths will also be an important consideration in choosing a winning strategy for the new millennium. This will require Asian companies to rediscover some of the strengths of their unique heritage and to leverage these foundations to create new sources of competitive advantage that distinguish them from global rivals from the West. Rather than mimicking traditional multinationals from the United States and Europe, Asian companies will win by combining their traditional strengths with an ability to cherry-pick and integrate the best technologies and ideas they can cull from around the world to create a new and distinctive breed of Asian corporation.

Western multinationals operating in Asia, meanwhile, will need to fundamentally challenge the strategies that won them a share of Asia's rapid growth over the last two decades. These strategies will need to be revised and renewed to deal with the very different competitive environment, including stiff rivalry from the new and stronger breed of local Asian competitors that will emerge. Rather than cloning their global strategies or reluctantly adapting them to Asia, Western multinationals will need new approaches to the market that allow them to more accurately pinpoint, and then to fully exploit, their own distinctive strengths.

Leveraging the Unique Strengths of an Asian Heritage

The strongest Asian competitors are already rising to the challenges presented in this book in ways that leverage their unique advantages and local knowledge. This process has the potential to rewrite the orthodox, Western rules of management about everything from innovation to internationalization. The opportunities to differentiate by leveraging Asian business heritage that we identified in chapter 2 fall into four categories: competing through cooperation, redefining innovation, leveraging Asian culture and service traditions, and betting on speed and flexibility.

Competing Through Cooperation

One of the main strengths of Asian companies is their skill in building and managing networks of alliances with those offering complementary resources and capabilities, suppliers, governments, and even competitors—in short, competing through cooperation. In the past this capability was directed toward reducing risk, maintaining family or personal control, and currying preferential treatment. But this heritage has latent potential to be redeployed to help meet the challenges in the next round by:

- *Engineering a new type of supply chain, based on networks*—creating a new alternative to the linear, "production line" concept of supply by harnessing Asian strengths in assembling and managing alliances (as did Li & Fung).

- *Internationalization through forming and managing alliances and deploying an "Asian way" in acquisitions*—buying and integrating capabilities, rather than simply buying "size" (demonstrated by the success of Hong Leong in hotels and Petronas in oil).

- *Driving industry consolidation through "staged acquisitions"*—using alliances and minority stakes to develop a better understanding of potential partners and to build relationships as a prelude to full merger, rather than through hostile takeovers (as with SingTel in telecommunications).

- *Borrowing partners' existing brands*—as a way to shortcut long, traditional brand-building cycles (as in the Samsung-Tesco alliance).

- *Using alliances to access world best practice*—extending the net to capture new and improved ideas, complex technologies, and market knowledge from around the globe that can't be accessed through digital technologies or fact-finding missions (a route used by Shiseido and Proton).

Competing through cooperation, therefore, clearly has widespread potential as an Asian strength that can be applied in new ways.

Redefining Innovation

Throughout this book we have seen evidence of Asian companies innovating in ways that go far beyond the narrow view of innovation as Nobel prize–winning research. These innovations range from Charoen Pokphand's concept of an efficient, high-technology supply chain for foodstuffs tuned to Asian conditions to Acer's novel ways of building a global brand rapidly and at low cost. In the next round of competition, there will be even greater opportunities to win by redefining innovation in ways that play to traditional Asian strengths in creative commercialization of new technologies and ideas for new business models. These include:

- *Redefining the innovation agenda to include the right mix of breakthrough, extension, and improvement*—to create a viable "portfolio of options on the future" that spreads risk and gives proper recognition to the role of commercialization, not just invention.

- *Adopting "learning from the world" as the blueprint for innovation*—by mobilizing and integrating the best technologies and market knowledge available both at home and globally (as did Acer, Creative Technologies, Legend, and Merlion Pharmaceutical) rather than adopting the innovation metaphor of isolated inventors in a proverbial garage.

- *Going beyond R&D to question orthodoxies and unlock innovation in every activity across the business*—such as rapidly and cheaply building brands by using innovative, nontraditional methods by leveraging off existing customer perceptions (as with Malaysian-owned British India leveraging off "colonial chic"), through acquisition (as with Star Cruises' acquisition of Norwegian Cruise Lines and Malaysia United Industries' acquisition of Laura Ashley), leveraging PR (Banyan Tree), and high impact-to-cost ratio channels (Acer's airport trolleys).

Redefinition of innovation to create a new, Asian-style approach that is distinctive from the Silicon Valley, lone-ranger formula points the way forward.

Leveraging Asian Culture and Service Traditions

Asia's ancient cultures and traditions provide the raw material for Asian companies to develop distinctive service approaches, processes, and brands that set them apart from U.S. or European competitors. Potential strategies here include:

- *Leveraging Asian traditions in service operations*—in every area that touches the customer, as we saw with Haier in white-goods distribution and sales and with Shangri-la in hotel management.

- *Marshaling Asian culture to provide core brand values*—as we saw with Banyan Tree and Singapore Airlines.

- *Deploying world-class systems in support of traditional Asian relationship management*—by using state-of-the-art software and systems working in the background to inform dealings with customers and suppliers and to broaden channels of communication rather than depersonalizing them.

It will pay to ask how traditional Asian culture and service ideals can be harnessed as future sources of differentiation rather than surrendering this potential advantage to compete on the same terms as Western multinationals.

Betting on Speed and Flexibility

Speed, flexibility, and first-mover opportunism are capabilities that many Asian companies accumulated through their heritage of "rice-trader" deal making that suited yesterday's competitive environment. But these same qualities also have a key role in the next round of competition if they can be repurposed to:

- *Commercialize productivity improvement technologies ahead of global competitors*—by redirecting Asian companies' traditional eye for first-mover advantage and their capabilities in rapidly commercializing new technologies toward solving the problem of poor productivity outside manufacturing.

- *Leapfrog the legacy systems that can hold back international competitors*—taking advantage of the "clean slate" for introduction of new technology outside manufacturing and basic service operations in Asia, as we saw with Charoen Pokphand in agribusiness.

- *Manage risk through rapid experimentation and learning*—refocusing Asian companies' traditional strengths in learning and adaptation of existing technologies toward the new challenge of pushing out existing frontiers by rapid experimentation and incremental learning rather than by bold, high-risk moves.

To execute winning strategies in the new millennium, more Asian companies will need to systematically identify and leverage these types of strengths, making a virtue of their Asian heritage and creating a new type of company. As we have seen throughout this book, they will also have to jettison some of the baggage of their past: overcentralization of decision making; a love-affair with asset accumulation; opportunistic diversification, and consequent lack of focus; underinvestment in intangible assets like brands and systems; and attempts to go on sheltering behind national fortresses in the face of growing cross-border competition.

Leveraging the Strengths of Multinational Experience

As foreign multinationals come under increasing competitive pressure from these local Asian companies, they too will need to revisit the potential strengths that come from the experience that their Asian competitors generally lack. To understand the core assets that can be leveraged to compete in Asia in the new millennium, three tests need to be applied:

1. *Nonsubstitutability.* The asset needs to be "nonsubstitutable"—in the sense that Asian competitors can't effectively offer an equivalent product or service to the customer without it. No use trying to leverage expertise in building and running a large network of insurance agents if up-and-coming Asian competitors can substitute them with a branded offering distributed by telephone or Internet.
2. *Nontradability.* The asset needs to be "nontradable," so that Asian competitors can't simply buy or license it at a competitive price. As we have seen repeatedly in this book, most materials,

equipment, and standardized and codified technologies can be purchased and integrated by strong Asian competitors. The asset has to be something that is either protected by patent or can be obtained only through experience and "learning by doing."

3. *Nonimitability.* The asset needs to be difficult to imitate, so that it will take years for Asian competitors to accumulate and master. No use having great know-how if it can be rapidly gained through experience by Asian competitors that, as we saw in chapter 2, often believe that "it's not what you know, but how fast you can learn."

Some of the unique experience that many foreign multinationals enjoy that satisfy these criteria, but have not yet been fully exploited in Asia, include:

- *Experience in building and managing tightly integrated networks of overseas operations.* To exploit this potential asset means multinationals operating in Asian need to become much more serious about pan-Asian and global integration, leaving behind yesterday's scatter of isolated national subsidiaries and facing up to country barons who resist loss of independence.

- *Existing experience in the deployment of advanced technology in customer relationship management, logistics, and administration.* The old adage that "Asia's different" should no longer be used as an excuse for inefficient supply and service chains. As Asia's productivity gap begins to close in the next round of competition, foreign multinationals will need to more fully and rapidly exploit their experience in implementing and integrating advanced technology in order to stay ahead.

- *A renewed focus on effective brand building.* In the next round of competition, multinationals won't be able to take their brand premium for granted. In a 2002 survey of elite consumers in China, for example, over 50 percent of those surveyed said they preferred Chinese brands to foreign ones.[2] As we saw in chapter 5, many activities involved in brand building can benefit from overseas expertise and experience. But to exploit this potential advantage multinationals will have to increase their investment in brands in

Asia. Better localization of branding, marketing, and service will also be required.

- *Leveraging their overseas experience in innovation by combining it with growing Asian capabilities and distinctive approaches by localizing more innovation in Asia.* Foreign multinationals can make the most of their innovation advantages by restructuring their processes to learn from Asia and to benefit from the availability of high quality researchers and engineers at lower cost. In the new millennium the innovation game in Asia is much more than exporting technology and systems from home. It is also about using Asia as a vibrant source of new ideas, technologies and approaches.

To leverage their distinctive experience in these areas, many multinationals will need to substantially restructure their Asian operations and build new, local capabilities that are lacking in their Asian subsidiaries today. They will also need to change the mind-set about the role of Asia both at headquarters and among sister subsidiaries elsewhere in the world. It won't be enough to see Asia as a low-cost base for manufacturing or standardized services operations or as a market for mature product offerings. Instead, Asian operations will need to be viewed as full partners in the multinational's global network, and Asia will need to be recognized as an increasingly sophisticated market and source of innovation, not just the recipient of technology proved elsewhere.

Joining Forces: The Next Frontier?

Throughout much of the discussion and analysis in this book, winning in Asia in the new millennium has been expressed in terms of a competitive battle between an increasingly powerful set of local Asian companies and foreign multinationals, as well as among Asian companies themselves. But the need for every company to substantially "raise its game" in the new Asia suggests an alternative route to success: Asian companies and foreign multinationals joining forces to forge new combinations of the distinctive strengths and experience of Asian companies with those of foreign multinationals.

This will require fundamentally new types of partnership between Asian and foreign companies that differ markedly from the old-style joint ventures where the Asian party brought local connections and experience and the foreign partner brought technologies, products, processes, and cash. As we saw in chapter 6, Asian companies will form more partnerships with small and medium-sized companies from around the world to gain access to specialist, proprietary technologies that they can integrate into their established operations. But there is also potential for new types of partnerships between Asian companies and large, established multinationals—partnerships that combine the distinctive strengths on a more equal basis and recruit Asian players to international consortia to improve their competitive strength in a global battle between different alliance groups. Examples include the recruitment of Singapore Airlines into the Star Alliance (led by Lufthansa and United Airlines) and the recent linkages between major players in telecommunications and NTT DoCoMo.

In finding a winning strategy for the next millennium, such alliances may represent the new frontier. Take the case of Chinese companies. In the 1990s, joint ventures were out, and more and more companies decided to go with wholly owned foreign entities. But the local Chinese companies did not stand still. In many traditional industries (from white goods to beer), they became dominant competitors. Today they dominate PCs and are gaining ground fast in mobile phone handsets and telecommunication switches.

Today, Galanz is number one in the world in microwaves, with 40 percent of the global market; China International Marine Containers has captured almost 50 percent of the global refrigerated container market; and Haier, TCL, and Legend dominate the Chinese markets in white goods, TVs, and PCs, respectively. They are all starting to eat into the export market and to invest in subsidiaries to sell and service their products overseas. By 2002 the Haier brand, for example, had won almost 50 percent of the U.S. market for small refrigerators—sub-180-liter units that could serve as minibars in hotel rooms or that students could squeeze into dorm rooms. China's Pearl River Piano brand, meanwhile, now controls 10 percent of the U.S. market in that very Western of instruments, based on its highly automated production facility in Guangzhou—today the world's largest piano-making plant.[3]

Initially, foreign companies ignored them. Then they competed aggressively with them. Now multinationals have begun to take a different tack: Recruit the Chinese company as part of a global alliance network. Examples abound: SAIC of Shanghai (China's largest auto maker) in alliance and cross-shareholding with General Motors and Daewoo, Tsing Tao beer with Anheuser-Busch, Haier with Sanyo, China's TCL with Panasonic, and Toshiba with Phillips in consumer electronics.

There should be no doubt that it will take a different kind of company to succeed Asia's next round of competition. Unquestionably this will require determined efforts among both Asian companies and multinationals operating in Asia to raise their game in the five key areas we have identified: productivity, branding, innovation, cross-border integration, and industry consolidation. But maybe the fastest and most effective way to create the new kind of company the next round of competition in Asia demands is to join forces between East and West.

Whatever route your company chooses to take into Asia's future, the new reality of competition in Asia is unavoidable: Amid renewed opportunity, there will be a sharper divide between the winners and losers. Only one question remains: In which group will your company end up?

Notes

Preface

    1. J. C. Abegglan, *Sea Change*, New York: Free Press, 1994.

Chapter One

    1. P. J. Williamson and K. Wilson, "CP Group: From Seeds to Kitchen of the World," Case no. 06/2002-4994 (Fontainebleau: INSEAD, 2002).

    2. G. Redding, "The Smaller Economies of Pacific Asia and Their Business Systems," in *Oxford Handbook of International Business*, ed. A. Rugman and T. Brewer (Oxford: Oxford University Press, 2001).

    3. P. J. Williamson, "Corporate Responses to Asia's Economic Crisis: Myth, Reality, and the Challenges Ahead," working paper no. 64, INSEAD Euro-Asia Centre, 1999.

    4. "From the Ashes, a Global Force Emerges," *The Asset*, March 1999, 22.

    5. A. Ward, "Kim Tries to Mend His Damaged Reputation," *Financial Times*, 23 January 2003, 27.

    6. A. Ward, "Restructuring in the Reign of the 'Chaos-Maker,'" *Financial Times*, 13 March 2003, 8.

    7. T. Saywell, "Powering Asia's Growth," *Far Eastern Economic Review*, 2 August 2001, 40–43.

    8. C. Wood, "Decoupling Asian Economies," *Asian Wall Street Journal*, 14 October 2002, A13.

    9. See "A Panda Breaks the Formation," *The Economist*, 25 August 2001, 65.

    10. World Investment report 2001.

    11. A. Granitsas, "The Instant Noodle War," *Far Eastern Economic Review*, 8 January 2003, 42–43.

    12. Author interview, Thailand, November 1997.

    13. Author interview with Trade Minister, April 2000.

    14. The roots of these potential advantages of Asian heritage are discussed in detail in P. J. Williamson, "Asia's New Competitive Game," *Harvard Business Review* (September–October 1997): 55–67.

Chapter Two

    1. A. Granitsas, "In Evergreen's Wake," *Far Eastern Economic Review*, 24 October 2002, 20.

    2. M. Dickie and K. Hille, "Evergreen Magnate Is Setting His Sights on Distant Horizons," *Financial Times*, 5 March 2003, 31.

3. Granitsas, "In Evergreen's Wake," 20–22.

4. D. Ibison, "Business Links Make a Return in Japan," *Financial Times*, 21 January 2003, 24.

5. Author interview with stock analyst, Singapore, October 2001.

6. K. B. Chan and C. Chiang, *Stepping Out: The Making of the Chinese Entrepreneur* (Singapore: Simon & Schuster [Asia], 1994).

7. These informal networks are discussed in detail in M. Weidenbaum and S. Hughes, *The Bamboo Network* (New York: Free Press, 1996).

8. Chan and Chiang, *Stepping Out,* 273.

9. Author interview with CEO of Asian company, Hong Kong, May 1997.

10. Ibid., 275.

11. See "Asian Capitalism: The End of Tycoons," *The Economist*, 29 April 2000, 93–95.

12. For more detail on overseas Chinese business, see G. S. Redding, *The Spirit of Chinese Capitalism* (New York: Walter de Gruyter, 1990); Min Chen, *Asian Management Systems* (London: Routledge, 1995), chap. 5.

13. B. J. Lee, "How the Techies at Samsung Passed the Cowboys of Hyundai to Become Korea's Top Chaebol," *Asiaweek*, April 2002, 44–45.

14. See C. Rowley and J. Bae, eds., *Korean Business* (London: Frank Cass, 1998).

15. For more detail, see R. Whitley, *Business Systems in East Asia* (London: Sage, 1992).

16. For more on the increasing Asian and global role of competitors from China, see M. Zeng and P. J. Williamson, "The Hidden Dragons," *Harvard Business Review* (October 2003).

17. "Face Value: Legend in the Making," *The Economist,* 15 September 2001, 74.

18 C. De Trenck, with S. Cartledge, A. Daswami, C. A. Katz, and D. Sakmar, *Red Chips* (Hong Kong: Asia 2000 Ltd., 1998).

19. A. Ward, "Chinese Oil Group Plays Numbers Game," *Financial Times*, 9 July 2001, 28.

20. INSEAD Euro-Asia Centre, 2000, "China's Haier Group," case no. 08/2000-4898.

21. A. Hu and T. Sherborne, "The Little Red Book of Business in China," *Financial Times*, 2 July 2001, 8.

22. P. Marsh, "China Steelmakers Show Their Mettle," *Financial Times*, 15 April 2003, 30.

23. T. Ito, "Japan and the Asian Economies: A 'Miracle' in Transition," *Brookings Papers on Economic Activity*, no. 2 (1996): 205–273.

24. P. Williamson and S. Meegan, "Alliances as Innovation Accelerators: The Case of NTT DoCoMo's I-Mode and 3G Mobile Telecommunications," working paper no. 2002/127/ABA (Singapore: INSEAD, 2002).

25. Japanese executive, conversation with author, Osaka, May 1999.

26. Interview with author, Tokyo, May 1993.

27. C. H. Tan, *Venturing Overseas: Singapore's External Wing* (Singapore: McGraw-Hill, 1995).

28. E. T. Gomez, *Chinese Business in Malaysia* (Richmond, Surrey [UK]: Curzon, 1999).

29. M. Y. Yoshino, "Sime Darby Berhad," Case no. 9-797-017 (Boston: Harvard Business School, 1997).

30. J. Burton, "Halim Forced Out of Renong," *Financial Times*, 4 October 2001, 28.

31. J. Burton, "Malaysia Turns Away from Crony Capitalism," *Financial Times*, 7 August 2002, 8.

32. Z. Achi, C. Boulas, I. Buchanan, J. Forteza, and L. Zappel, "Conglomerates in Emerging Markets: Tigers or Dinosaurs?" *Strategy and Business* (second quarter, 1998): 1–4.

Chapter Three

1. A. St. George, C. Knoop, and M. Yoshino, "Li & Fung: Beyond 'Filling the Mosaic' 1995–1998," Case no. 9-398-092 (Boston: Harvard Business School, 1998).

2. Ibid.

3. "Link in the Global Chain," *The Economist*, 2 June 2001, 82.

4. S. M. Collins and B. P. Bosworth, "Economic Growth in East Asia: Accumulation versus Assimilation," *Brookings Papers on Economic Activity* 2 (1996): 135–203.

5. Ibid., 139.

6. See J. Felipe, "Total Factor Productivity Growth in East Asia: A Critical Survey," *Journal of Development Studies* 35, no. 4 (1999): 1–41; A. Young, "The Tyranny of Numbers: Confronting the Statistical Realities of the East Asian Growth Experience," *Quarterly Journal of Economics* (August 1995): 641–680; P. Krugman, "The Myth of Asia's Miracle," *Foreign Affairs* (November–December 1994): 62–78.

7. The U.S. and European samples consist of the top thirty companies by market capitalization ranked by the *Financial Times* 500 for 1999, after exclusion of financial institutions and companies involved in major merger activity during the year. The Asian sample is drawn from the largest companies in the *Asiaweek* 500 ranking. Data were drawn from the *Financial Times, Asiaweek,* and the annual reports of each company.

8. Includes fixed-line and mobile operators and telecommunications equipment makers.

9. The sample sizes among other countries in our sample were too small to give meaningful results.

10. Chi-Yuan Liang, "Total Factor Productivity Growth in the Republic of China Service Industry, 1962–96," in *Productivity Measurement in the Service Sector* (Tokyo: Asian Productivity Organization, 2001), 107–115.

11. T. Kondo, J. Lewis, J. Palmade, and T. Yokoyama, *Reviving Japan's Economy* (Tokyo: McKinsey Global Institute, 2000), 12–19.

12. R. Dhawan, R. Mangaleswaran, A. Padhi, S. Sankhe, K. Schween, and P. Vaish, "The Asian Difference in B2B," *McKinsey Quarterly,* no.4 (2000): 38–47.

13. N. Chowdhury, "Hapahazd Attempts to Diversify Wreck a Singapore Wholesaler," *Far Eastern Economic Review*, 24 January 2002, 50.

14. Y. Ghahremani, "Circling the Delivery Wagons," *Asiaweek*, July 2001, 26–27.

15. "Speeding Up Distribution on the Mainland," *Swire News*, no. 3 (2001): 11.

16. Ibid., 11.

17. M. Zain, N. Kassim, and E. Makhtar, "Use of Information Technology and Information Systems for Organisational Agility in Malaysian Firms," *Singapore Management Review* 25, no. 1 (2002): 69–83.

18. R. Dhawan et al., "The Asian Difference in B2B," 45.

19. These historical problems are discussed in C. A. Bartlett and S. Goshal, *Managing Across Borders* (Boston: Harvard Business School Press, 1989), 138–139.

20. J. Galbraith, D. Downey, and A. Kates, *Designing Dynamic Organizations* (New York: American Management Association, 2002).

21. A. Granitsas and D. Sheehan, "Manila's Strange Brew," *Far Eastern Economic Review*, 10 May 2001, 46–51.

22. M. Dole, "CRM Lands in Asia," *Ad Age Global* 1, no. 10 (2001): 19–21.

23. OgilvyOne, *Asian Business* 37, no. 12 (2001): 39.

24. "Speeding Up Distribution on the Mainland," *Swire News*, no. 3 (2001): 11.

25. Y. Ghahremani, "Circling the Delivery Wagons," 27.

26. "Japan Inc on the Treadmill," *The Economist*, June 9 2001, 91.

27. St. George, Knoop, and Yoshino, "Li & Fung," 8.

28. Ibid., 3.

29 N. Chowdhury, "New Rules of the Game," *Far Eastern Economic Review*, 24 January 2002, 47–50.

30. For more detail on how these networks might operate, see M. Borrus, D. Ernst, and S. Haggard, eds., *International Production Networks in Asia* (London: Routledge, 2000).

31. Economist Intelligence Unit, "Supply Chain Management in Thailand," *Business Asia*, 26 June 2000, 12.

Chapter Four

1. As Hong Kong venture capitalist Ilyas Khan put it: "A lot of industry leaders seem to accept, almost as an article of faith, that Asians copy—they don't create." In "Creative Asia," *Asiaweek*, July–August 2001, 69.

2. Wong Poh Kam, "Technology Acquisition Pattern of Manufacturing Firms in Singapore," *Singapore Management Review* 20 (January 1998): 149–161.

3. This problem is discussed in detail from different angles by contributors in W. W. Keller and R. J. Samuel, eds., *Crisis and Innovation in Asian Technology* (Cambridge: Cambridge University Press, 2003).

4. Koh Boon Hwee, interview with author, Singapore, July 2002.

5. This relationship is explored in detail in K. S. Jomo and G. Felker, eds., *Technology, Competitiveness, and the State* (London: Routledge, 1999).

6. See, e.g., L. Kim, *Imitation to Innovation: The Dynamics of Korea's Technological Learning* (Boston: Harvard Business School Press, 1997).

7. For a more detailed discussion, see L. Weiss, "Developmental States in Transition: Adapting, Dismantling, Innovating, Not Normalising," *Pacific Review* 14, no. 1 (2000): 21–56.

8. Quoted in C. Tan, "Sharing the Wealth," *Asian Business* (March 1999): 18.

9. A. Ward, "LG Chem's Bold Experiment Starts to Pay Off," *Financial Times*, 25 July 2002, 28.

10. D. Clyde-Smith and P. J. Williamson, "Whirlpool in China (A) Entering the World's Largest Market," Case no. 08/2001-4950 (Fontainebleau: INSEAD, 2001).

11. S. Donnan, "Indofood Wants Us to Say It with Noodles," *Financial Times*, 14 February, 2000, 24.

12. J. Teo, "Turning Waste into Money," *The Edge Singapore*, 8 July 2002, 12.

13. S. Crispin, "Fast Lane to Success," *Far Eastern Economic Review*, 12 September 2002, 38.

14. These dangers are analyzed in more detail in P. J. Williamson, "Strategy Innovation," in *The Oxford Handbook of Strategy*, ed. D. Faulkner and A. Campbell (Oxford: Oxford University Press, 2003), vol. 2, chap. 29.

15. These concepts are further explored in P. J. Williamson, "Strategy as Options on the Future," *Sloan Management Review*, vol. 40, no. 3 (spring 1999): 117–126.

16. The concept of orthodoxies as constraints on innovation was introduced by G. Hamel and C. K. Prahalad, *Competing for the Future* (Cambridge, MA: Harvard University Press, 1994).

17. S. London, "Gillette to Track Stock by Radio," *Financial Times*, 24 January 2003, 28.

18. Y. Ghahremani, "What's the Big Idea?" *Asiaweek*, July–August 2001, 75.

19. T. Saywell, "Asia's Magicians," *Far Eastern Economic Review*, 21 November 2002, 43–47.

20. C. S. Lee, "VIA's Gospel," *Asiaweek*, 18-25 May 2001, 37–44.

21. This question was suggested by G. Hamel, *Leading the Revolution* (Boston: Harvard Business School Press, 2000), 138.

22. See, e.g., L. Kim, "Crisis Construction and Organizational Learning: Dynamics of Capability Building in Catching-up at Hyundai Motor," *Organization Science* 9, no. 4 (July–August 1998): 506–521.

23. J. Probert and H. Schütte, "Shiseido in Europe (A) and (B)," Case no. 08/93-322 (Fontainebleau: INSEAD Euro-Asia Centre, 1994).

24. For more analysis of how to innovate successfully by learning from the world, see Y. Doz, J. Santos, and P. Williamson, *From Global to Metanational: How Companies Win in the Knowledge Economy* (Boston: Harvard Business School Press, 2001).

25. T. Saywell, "Customized Genes," *Far Eastern Economic Review*, 7 May 1998, 48–50.

26. F. Fukuyama, "The Clone Traders," *Financial Times*, 18/19, May 2002, sec. 2, 1.

27. See, e.g., I. M. Salleh, "Foreign Direct Investment and Technology Transfer in the Malaysia Electronics Industry," in *Foreign Direct Investment in Asia* (Singapore: Institute of Southeast Asian Studies, 1995), 133–159.

28. For further discussion of the role of new types of alliances in innovation, see P. Williamson and S. Meegan, "Alliances as Innovation Accelerators," working paper no. 2002/127/ABA (Fontainebleau: INSEAD, 2002).

29. Calculated from M & A Asia, Hong Kong, *M&A Asia Magazine* 14, no. 3 (2000).

30. "Lotus Starts to Blossom for Proton: Malaysian Car Maker Gains from British Firm's Technical Expertise," *Far Eastern Economic Review*, 26 July 2001, 18.

Chapter Five

1. Based on the methodology of the world-respected branding consultancy, Interbrand, which values a brand based on future earnings discounted to present value; in Interbrand, "Top 50 Global Brands League," *Brand News* (London: Interbrand, November 2001).

2. C. S. Lee, "The Region's Largest Companies 2002," *Asiaweek*, November 2001, 35.

3. C. H. Chua, P. J. Williamson, and A. DeMeyer, "Banyan Tree Resorts and Hotels: Building and International Brand from an Asian Base," Case no. 02/2003-5087 (Fontainebleau: INSEAD, 2003), 1.

4. Interbrand, "Top 50 Asian Brands League," *Asia Brand News* (Singapore: Interbrand, March 1999).

5. Chua, Williamson, and DeMeyer, "Banyan Tree," 6, and exhibit 6.

6. S. Ngan, "What's in a Name?" *The Bulletin* (Hong Kong), September 2002, 13.

7. R. Sim, "Branding the OSIM Way," *Customer Contact World*, April 2003, 29.

8. Chua, Williamson, and DeMeyer, "Banyan Tree," 7.

9. Survey of 1,283 respondents in ten Asian economies, reported in "Marques of Success," Special Report: Asian Lifestyles, *Far Eastern Economic Review*, 14 November 2002, 67.

10. See the "SuperBrands" survey available at <http: //www. superbrandsasia.com>.

11. K. Gotthelf, "Builidng a Brand and Losing Your Shirt," *Asian Business Strategy Ezine*, 3 March 2003.

12. A Ward, "Restructuring in the Reign of the 'Chaos-Maker,'" *Financial Times*, 13 March 2003, 8.

13. P. Temporal, *Branding in Asia* (Singapore: Wiley (Asia), 2000), 182.

14. M. A. Badri, D. L. Davis, and D. F. Davis, "Decision Support for Global Marketing Strategies: The Effect of Country of Origin on Product Evaluation," *Journal of Product and Brand Management* 4, no. 5 (1995): 49–64.

15. Douglas Wong, "Colonial Chic Sweeps Asia's Upmarket Malls," *Financial Times*, 2 August 2002, 29.

16. Temporal, *Branding in Asia*, 99.

17. A. Sauer, "Royal Selangor: Breaking the Mould," available at <http://www.brandchannel.com>.

18. D. Kruger and I. Fuyuno, "King of the Mall," *Far Eastern Economic Review*, 30 August 2001, 37.

19. Y. H. Kwan and G. Tocquer, "Shangri-la Hotels and Resorts—Achieving Service Leadership," Case no. 400-001-1 (Hong Kong: Centre for Asian Business Cases, School of Business, University of Hong Kong, 2000), 4.

20. Kwan and Tocquer, "Shangri-la Hotels and Resorts," 10.

21. A Smith, "Ashley Rights to Pay for Closures," *Financial Times*, 24 January 2003, 26.

22. Kruger and Fuyuno, "King of the Mall," 37.

23. Chua, Williamson, and DeMeyer, "Banyan Tree," 7.

24. "Fashion Model," *Far Eastern Economic Review*, 15 April 1999, 76; "Riding High," *Far Eastern Economic Review*, 7 May 1998, 58.

25. Chua, Williamson, and DeMeyer, "Banyan Tree," 6.

26. J. Gearing, "Trench Warfare," *Asiaweek*, July–August 2001, 28–31.

27. "Rolling Out the Red Carpet," *The Economist*, 7 September 2002, 76, and the author's direct experience.

28. H. Laurence, M. Yoshino, and P. Williamson, "STAR TV (A)," Harvard Case no. 9-394-212 (Boston: Harvard Business School, 1994).

29. J. Probert and H. Schütte, "*Asiaweek*: Positioning a Regional Magazine," Case no. 10/98-4785 (Fontainebleau: INSEAD Euro-Asia Centre, 1999), 6.

30. A. O. Thomas, "Transnational Satellite Television and Advertising in South East Asia," *Journal of Marketing Communications* 4 (1998): 231–236.

31. For a detailed examination of these factors, see L. T. Wright and C. Nancarrow, "Researching International 'Brand Equity': A Case Study," *International Marketing Review* 16, no. 45 (1999): 417–431.

32. Swire Pacific Ltd, "Taikoo Sugar Surprises," *Swire News*, no. 3 (2001): 13.

33. See, e.g., B. H. Schmitt and Y. Pan, "Managing Corporate Brand Identities in the Asia-Pacific Region," *California Management Review* 29 (Summer 1994): 32–41.

34. R. Kugler, "Marketing in East Asia: The Fallacies and Realities," in *Asian Business Wisdom*, ed. D. L. Dayao (Singapore: Wiley (Asia), 2000), 200.

35. P. J. Williamson, "Lever Brothers Thailand (C)," Case no. 9-396-088 (Boston: Harvard Business School, 1995).

Chapter Six

1. See K. Kojima, "Japanese-style Direct Foreign Investment, *Japanese Economic Studies*. 14, no. 3 (1986): 52–82; C. M. Dent and C. Randerson, "Korean Direct Investment in Europe: The Determining Forces," *Pacific Review* 9, no. 4 (1996): 531–552.

2. L. Lopez, "Petronas: A Well-Oiled Money Machine," *Far Eastern Economic Review*, 13 March 2003, 40–43.

3. H. W. C. Yeung, "Introduction: Competing in the Global Economy," in *The Globalization of Business Firms from Emerging Economies*, ed. H. W. C. Yeung (Cheltenham [UK]: Edward Elgar, 1999).

4. R. K. Zutshi and P. T. Gibbons, "The Internationalization of Singapore Government-Linked Companies: A Contextual View," *Asia Pacific Journal of Management* 15 (1998): 219–246.

5. C. S. Tseng, "The Process of Internationalization of PRC Firms," in *The Global Competitiveness of the Asian Firm*, ed. H. Schütte (New York: St. Martin's Press, 1994), 121–128.

6. A. De Meyer and P. J. Williamson, "Internationalisation of Asian Companies: A New Era?" working paper 2002/68/ABA, INSEAD, 2002.

7. See, e.g., R. Vernon, "International Investment and International Trade in the Product Life Cycle," *Quarterly Journal of Economics* 80 (1966): 190–207.

8. A. De Meyer and B. Pycke, "Samsung Berlin," Case no. 0297-4672 (Fontainebleau: INSEAD, 1997).

9. C. Bartlett, "Jollibee Foods Corporation (A)," Case no. 9-399-007 (Boston: Harvard Business School, 1999).

10. P. J. Williamson and K. Wilson, "DBS (A), (B), (C) & (D)," Case nos. 10/2000-4921 (Singapore: INSEAD, 2000).

11. See C. A. Bartlett and S. Ghoshal, *Managing Across Borders* (Boston: Harvard Business School Press, 1991); Y. Doz, J. Santos, and P. Williamson, *From Global to Metanational: How Companies Win in the Knowledge Economy* (Boston: Harvard Business School Press, 2001).

12. For a detailed analysis of Astra, see C. Butler, *Dare to Do* (London: Wiley, 2001).

13. P. J. Williamson and D. Clyde Smith, "Acer Group: Building an Asian Multinational," Case no. 01/98-4712 (Fontainebleau: INSEAD, 1997).

14. A. De Meyer and B. Pycke, "Samsung Berlin," Case no. 0297-4672 (Fontainebleau: INSEAD, 1997).

15. See J. A. Mathews, *Dragon Multinational: A New Model for Global Growth* (New York: Oxford University Press, 2001).

16. See A. Lo and C. K. Kao, "The Challengers: Uni-President," in *A Tiger's Leap: Asian Business Goes Global*, ed. A. De Meyer, C. M. Mar, F. Richter, and P. Williamson (Singapore: Wiley (Asia), forthcoming 2004).

17. C. J. Perng, "Singapore Post in the World's First Postal Tie-up," *The Straits Times*, 10 March 2000, 102.

18. S. Meagan and P. Williamson, "SingTel (B): Taking Control," Case no.02/2002-4998 (Singapore: INSEAD, 2002), 3.

19. Ibid., 6.

20. Yuzaburo Mogi, "The Pioneers: Kikkoman," in *A Tiger's Leap: The Globalisation of Asian Business*, ed. A. De Meyer, C. M. Mar, F. Richter, and P. Williamson (Singapore: Wiley (Asia), forthcoming 2004).

21. P. J. Williamson, "Lever Brothers Thailand (C)," Case no. 9-396-088 (Boston: Harvard Business School, 1995).

22. This change in thinking is more fully explored in Doz, Santos, and Williamson, *From Global to Metanational*.

23. These terms describing the role of different subsidiaries were introduced by Bartlett and Ghoshal, *Managing Across Borders*.

24. J. Ratner and R. Jacob, "Brief Rebuff Ended PCCW's Bold Plan," *Financial Times*, 11 February 2003, 31.

Chapter Seven

1. A. Mody and S. Negishi, "Cross-Border Mergers and Acquisitions in East Asia," *Finance and Development*, March 2001, 6–11.

2. T. Holland, "Mergers and Acquisitions," *Far Eastern Economic Review*, 24 February 2000, 46.

3. The term "strategic assembly" was introduced by P. Haspeslagh and D Jemi-

son, *Managing Acquisitions: Creating Value Through Corporate Renewal* (New York: Free Press, 1991).

4. J. Leahy, "M&A in Asia Falls 12.6% in Value," *Financial Times*, 6 January 2003, 23.

5. W. Van Honacker, "Kodak in China (A), (B) & (C)," Case no. 02/2000-4881 (Fontainebleau: INSEAD-CEIBS, 2000).

6. B. Gilley, "Overexposed," *Far Eastern Economic Review*, 28 June2001, 30–33.

7. J. Kynge, "Fuji Considers Chinese Deal to Rival Kodak," *Financial Times*, 27 February 2003, 24.

8. H. Laurence, P. Williamson, and M. Yoshino, "STAR TV (A)," Case no. 9-394-212 (Boston: Harvard Business School, 1994).

9. See P. C Skarzynski and P. J. Williamson, "Choke Points of Competition," *San Jose Mercury*, 15 November 1998, 2E.

10. S. Webb, "Asia's Race to Consolidate," *Far Eastern Economic Review*, 13 June 2002, 44–46.

11. A. Paul, "China's Haier Power," *Fortune*, 15 February 1999, 55–58.

12. R. Crawford, M. Zeng, and H. Schütte, "China's Haier Group: Growth Through Acquisitions," Case no. 08/2000-4898 (Fontainebleau: INSEAD, 2000), 5.

13. See Haspeslagh and Jemison, *Managing Acquisitions,* 258.

14. See ibid., chap. 3.

15. A Shameen, "Competition Makes Strange Bedfellows," *Asiaweek*, 13 July 2001, 48–49.

16. P. J. Williamson and K. Wilson, "DBS (A): Opportunistic Growth in Thailand," Case no. 10/2000-4921 (Fontainebleau: INSEAD, 2000), 3.

17. Crawford, Zeng, and Schütte, "China's Haier Group," 11.

18. Ibid.

19. P. J. Williamson and K. Wilson, "DBS (C): Embracing the Challenge of Integration," Case no. 10/2000-4921 (Fontainebleau: INSEAD, 2000), 3.

20. This process is extensively discussed in the international context in Doz, Santos, and Williamson, *From Global to Metanational: How Companies Win in the Knowledge Economy* (Boston: Harvard Business School Press, 2001).

21. S. Meagan and P. Williamson, "SingTel (A): Newfound Status" and "SingTel (B): Taking Control," Case nos. 02/2000-4998 and 02/2000-4999 (Fontainebleau: INSEAD, 2002).

22. Author's discussion with U.S. senate representatives, Washington, D.C., November 2000.

23. See Haspeslagh and Jemison, *Managing Acquisitions,* 258.

Chapter Eight

1. An interesting perspective on the tensions this creates for multinationals operating in Southeast Asia is provided by T. G Andrews, N. Chompusi, and B. J. Baldwin, *The Changing Face of Multinationals in Southeast Asia* (London: Routledge, 2003).

2. T. Saywell, "A Taste for Local Products," *Far Eastern Economic Review*, 19 December 2002, 52–56.

3. M. Zeng and P. J. Williamson, "The Hidden Dragons," *Harvard Business Review* (October 2003): 92–99.

Index

About the Author

PETER J. WILLIAMSON is Professor of International Management and Asian Business at INSEAD in Fontainebleau, France, and Singapore. Peter has worked with both Asian companies and multinationals throughout the region on strategy and capability development for more than twenty years. He has been actively involved in a number of joint ventures in China since 1983 and numerous mergers and acquisitions, and is an adviser to governments on trade and investment and also serves as a nonexecutive director of several listed companies.

Professor Williamson holds a Ph.D. in Business Economics from Harvard University. Formerly Dean of MBA Programmes at London Business School and Visiting Professor of Global Strategy and Management at Harvard Business School, Peter's research and publications span globalization, the internationalization of Asian companies, strategy innovation, competitive dynamics, and the use of alliances to accelerate growth. His other published books include *From Global to Metanational: How Companies Win in the Knowledge Economy* (2001) (with Yves L. Doz and Jose Santos) *The Economics of Financial Markets* (1995) (with Hendrik S. Houthakker); *Managing the Global Frontier* (1994) (with Qionghua Hu); and *The Strategy Handbook* (1992) (with Michael Hay).